Mothers and Food

Negotiating Foodways from Maternal Perspectives

Funded by the Government of Canada
Financé par la gouvernement du Canada | Canada

Demeter Press
140 Holland Street West
P. O. Box 13022
Bradford, ON L3Z 2Y5
Tel: (905) 775-9089
Email: info@demeterpress.org
Website: www.demeterpress.org

Demeter Press logo based on the sculpture "Demeter" by Maria-Luise Bodirsky <www.keramik-atelier.bodirsky.de>

Printed and Bound in Canada

Front cover artwork: Mindy Stricke and Jane Jones

Library and Archives Canada Cataloguing in Publication

Mothers and food : negotiating foodways from maternal perspectives / edited by Florence Pasche Guignard and Tanya M. Cassidy.

Includes bibliographical references.
ISBN 978-1-77258-002-0 (paperback)

1. Food--Social aspects. 2. Mothers. 3. Families. 4. Parenting. I. Pasche Guignard, Florence, 1981–, author, editor II. Cassidy, Tanya M., 1963–, author, editor

GT2850.M68 2016 394.1'20852 C2016-901279-4

Mothers and Food

Negotiating Foodways from Maternal Perspectives

EDITED BY

Florence Pasche Guignard and Tanya M. Cassidy

DEMETER

DEMETER PRESS

Table of Contents

Acknowledgements

This is the second book that we have published with Demeter Press, and we would like to reiterate our gratitude to Professor Andrea O'Reilly for supporting an initiative that has become two distinct (but related) projects: *What's Cooking Mom? Narratives about Food and Family* (2015) and the present volume, *Mothers and Food. Negotiating Foodways from Maternal Perspectives* (2016). We are indebted to the efficient and supportive Demeter Press staff for their invaluable help in bringing this book to life and their patience with us throughout this process.

We are grateful to the many scholars and authors who answered our initial call for contributions, encouraging us to explore the opportunity to edit not just one but two volumes with Demeter Press, extending our collaboration into international contexts. Our profound appreciation goes to the contributors to this volume who conduct research or work in Africa, Australia, and Europe as well as in North and South America. We also would like to thank participants to the Motherhood Initiative for Research and Community Involvement (MIRCI) conferences in Toronto and to the international Motherhood and Culture conference in Maynooth, Ireland, who showed interest in the topic of "mother and food." Their constructive feedback on our project from a motherhood studies perspective was a great encouragement for us.

Florence wishes to thank the Department for the Study of Religion at the University of Toronto for hosting her as a postdoctoral researcher and the participants of the 2013-2015 "Diasporic Foodways" working group at the Jackman Humanities Institute whose interdisciplinary approach and passionate discussions in food studies were directly relevant to her research and to this editorial project. Tanya wishes to thank her new colleagues in the Maternal and Infant Nutrition and Nurture (MAINN) unit at the University of Central Lancashire (UCLan) as well as her colleagues at both Maynooth University and the University of Windsor, in Canada, for their continuing support. We appreciate, in particular, the detailed comments from colleagues who agreed to have a pre-publication "taste" of the manuscript as anonymous peer-reviewers. Their critical advice has contributed into making the final "recipe" even better.

For both co-editors, this and our previous edited volume with Demeter Press were done as part of other broader research projects or in addition to them. During the process of editing this volume (2013-2016), we received funding supporting our academic engagements and our research projects from various sources, including the Swiss National Science Foundation, the EU Horizon 2020 Marie Skłodowska Curie Funding action as well as the kind and generous support from the private foundation of the late Joseph Vijuk and his partner, Drenda.

Finally, on behalf of the contributors, we thank all of those among our family, friends, and colleagues who supported us in various ways, both in academe, at home, and in the blurry zones in between, especially at times when we had "so much on our plate." Whether they commented on a draft, shared a bibliography, prepared us a packed lunch for a busy day, or washed the dishes after dinner, many helping hands were involved in sustaining us throughout the process. For such support networks, we are immensely grateful.

Introduction

FLORENCE PASCHE GUIGNARD AND TANYA M. CASSIDY

MOTHERS AND FOOD: NEGOTIATING FOODWAYS *from Maternal Perspectives* is our second volume published with Demeter Press on the topic of families and food. Along with our previous edited collection (*What's Cooking, Mom? Narratives about Food and Family*, 2015), this book results from a call for contributions that generated international interest across various disciplines which contribute to the now well-established field of motherhood studies. We chose to concentrate all of the absorbing personal narratives and autoethnographic pieces that we received, drawing from literary and social scientific perspectives, within our first book. Our second volume is also interdisciplinary, and although many of the contributors to this volume are also mothers, their contributions tend to focus their researchers' gaze on others as opposed to themselves. They examine, from multiple perspectives, the cultural representations and social interactions of the relationships between food and families, at the centre of which is the maternal role. These contributions discuss research that uncovers the social and cultural logic that governs how mothers take decisions about food, often within a range of constrained options, and how they account for them, both to themselves and others. The chapters in this book also look at how mothers are represented in their role as food providers, cooking and feeding their families, as well as at the social organization that underlies and supports all of these practices and processes. Combining historical, sociological, and anthropological perspectives, this volume adds substantially to an already rich scholarship on gender and food by replacing ignored, often silenced, maternal voices at the centre of inquiries regarding the work of "feeding the family" (DeVault). By calling attention to the "invisible labor that goes into planning, making, and coordinating family meals" (Bowen, Elliott, and Brenton 21), these chapters make important contributions to understanding in greater depth how this process affects mothers in their interactions with other important actors, such as their children, their partners, other relatives, caregivers, schools and daycares, the state, food companies, and larger communities. Looking at what mothers think and do—not only "through the kitchen window" but also in dining rooms, in their gardens, in supermarkets, in farmers' markets, or in restaurants—we expand our focus on the "intimate meanings of food and cooking" (Avakian) for women to consider some of the public ramifications. Our contributors, thus, explore how mothers are represented in meeting expectations in this vocation and how such culturally and historically determined social divisions of labour evolve in spatial and temporal terms.

Far from reinforcing the contentious association between "Food and Femininity" (recently and critically re-explored by Cairns and Johnston through a sociological lens) in general, the authors in this volume engage in collective debates about the respective locations of mother work and food work and about mothering and nurturing as unavoidable or natural relationships. Our contributors question stereotypical ideals of the selfless, even sacrificial at times, "nurturing mother." Although other scholars ask "why families eat the way they do" (Beagan et al.) and lay the focus on parenting and nurturing children, we actively focus on mothers and the many dimensions of food. Scholars have sought to complicate these imaginings over the last decades through studies about "intensive mothering" (Hays) or "total motherhood" (Wolf), in which some attention is paid to nutrition. Other works (DeVault; Counihan and van Esterik) have focused on the gendered dimensions of care work that involves feeding, in particular feeding infants (Bentley), and cooking in general (Crowther). At the same time, other recent discussions have looked at children's food cultures to uncover "what food means to children" (Ludvigsen and Scott) or at "kids' foods" (McDowell). Researchers more often consider the parents' roles in children's food preferences, but the children's roles and taste preferences as well as how these affect mothers' food "choices" rarely are investigated. This collection aims precisely at filling the gap between these two areas: one that looks at children's foodways and preferences, and one that looks at how gender is constructed through food practices, often with a focus on domestic cooking and the maternal role.

Many such studies show that nutrition and feeding are particular sites of what may make motherhood and mothering intensive. Our contributors question the identification of mothers as "natural" or "instinctive nurturers" of the family, despite the prevailing representations that picture them as such. Instead, their contributions show how social and cultural contexts framed by constraints limit maternal agency, which is culturally constructed rather than naturally given. Even if domestic food work and parenting tasks now tend to be shared more than in other times in history (at least in some Western or Euro-American contexts), it remains a statistical fact, whether we are talking about a "second" (Hochschild) or "third" shift (Gertsel), that most domestic food work, in particular that made for the benefit of children, is performed by mothers rather than by fathers. Even when other family members[1] take on the work of feeding the family, food and femininity remain closely associated (Cairns and Johnston) and still dominate the public imagination, evidenced by media discourses and marketing strategies. Among all other strands of the association between food and femininity, such as self-control, body shape and seduction through food (the cooking *wife* overlapping only partially with the cooking *mother*), we chose to focus on the maternal role rather than on the many pressures on women's bodies through food-related discipline, as well as on the gendered expectations and the inequitable division of household labour both in the domestic sphere and in other sites where mother work includes preparing food for children.

Some of our contributors explore the contradiction between (re)affirming the traditional gender role of the mother as a nurturer while withholding from them the power that goes along with the responsibility of feeding and the outcomes of feeding children. This volume features studies that highlight the political, social, and cultural tensions in which contemporary mothers get entangled. Mothers, more than other women, are subjected to increased social control and scrutiny because they are responsible not just for feeding themselves but their children as well. The health and body shape of the child is increasingly seen as the measure of the "good mother." Other criteria—such as access to quality food, which is often dependent on income and location and becomes a marker of social status—are forgotten or dismissed as less important than "individual choice" or "lifestyles choices" that focus on diets. Failure is attributed exclusively to mothers, although they often have little power over the results of feeding, and their agency depends on many other factors that are both socio-political and financial, as some of the chapters demonstrate.

The first section of our book examines the central topic of domestic food work and the family meal, and explores some of the ways in which mothers resist formulaic "ideals" that are imposed on them. Its four chapters pose the question why the frontline in reforming the food system has to be in someone's kitchen, while also recognizing that "[t]he emphasis on home cooking ignores the time pressures, financial constraints, and feeding challenges that shape the family meal" (Bowen, Elliott, and Brenton 25). Some of our contributions outline the dilemmas faced by mothers who have to juggle working part or full time for a necessary income and negotiate the demands of food practices that obey a variety of imperatives, in addition to just quality and quantity (i.e., food must be healthy, fresh, local, seasonal, organic, varied, creative ... desiderata that are sometimes incompatible with one another). Mothers have to care not only for themselves and their children but also for their social status, and sometimes their larger communities and the environment.

Some of the chapters in this first section have already set the stage for the theme developed in our second section: the confrontation between mothers and "the experts" (Nathanson and Tuley), in particular medical ones. The purpose of the chapters in the second section is to interrogate some of the assumptions and categories regarding maternal responsibility and ownership of problems as well as solutions. Evaluating the health impact of food practices is not the primary concern of our authors, who adopt sociological and anthropological perspectives. Rather, they show how mothers engage with a variety of contradictory discourses that promote "healthy eating" and norms of good mothering through food, sometimes pitting these discourses against one another. Starting with breastfeeding, mothers are held as primarily or exclusively responsible for the outcomes of their children's diets, although issues of race, class, income, and social status often prevent them from having full control and authority over how, what, when, and where they feed their family, especially in neoliberal capitalist economies.

In the third section of our volume, we move to what mothers do in the "insecure circumstances" that such neoliberal economies sometimes contribute to create. The topic of food security and insecurity in a variety of difficult circumstances or in preparation for such times is central to the five contributions in this section. War, poverty, climate change, sudden disasters and/or loss of income are just a few of the precarious circumstances that mothers prepare for or concretely deal with, sometimes for long periods of time. Often economic in origin, these tragedies affect the ability of mothers to feed themselves and their children, but mothers do improvise and deploy a remarkable range of coping strategies. These chapters explore the role played by mothers in partnership with, or as members of, public state agencies and governments programs, private initiatives, humanitarian associations, and charities. They also show how mothers often are left on their own to cope with food insecurity and negotiate their identities as providers of food for the family in adverse circumstances.

Following feminist scholarship that highlights "critical perspectives on women and food" (Avakian and Haber), some of the contributions also examine how food purchasing or producing, cooking, and feeding representations are stable or change over the years and how they come to include other people who mother (in Sara Ruddick's sense of *mother* as a verb rather than as a noun), such as fathers, grandparents, or other caregivers. This is the case, in particular, in the fourth section of this book, where representations of maternal food work are explored in a variety of media. Contributors look at materials such as marketing advertisements, public service advertisements that stress health prevention, advice books, and cookbooks that specifically target parents of young children, and picture books aimed at children themselves. Finally and decisively, some contributors focus on mothers' rich expressions in the "mamasphere," where food and feeding along with their attendant challenges are recurring topics of online conversations and debates.

Some chapters clearly demonstrate that choices made by mothers for themselves and their families are not just series of individual decisions governed by personal taste. A mother has to deal with expectations from many people, including partners, extended family, and others with whom she interacts. In line with the explorations of domestic food work, the contributions in the fifth section further explore the materiality of food and feeding, and highlight some of the constraints and incoherencies that frame this domestic food work. Looking at how material resources contribute to shaping food practice, not only in an economic sense but also in terms of spatiality and access, reveals a web of competing tensions. Accordingly, these contributions consider not only maternal agency but the agency attributed to food and to the spaces in which food work and feeding are carried out. Also, some chapters show how certain proponents of environmentally sustainable, socially fair, and healthy food systems tend, paradoxically, to reinforce elitist visions and promote apolitical disengagement through a return to an idealized home cooking. Mothers are pressured to perform this "privatization" of food ethics, yet no suggestions are offered as to how the more global food system could be changed positively and in a more inclusive way.

Despite the variety of the contexts, materials, and topics covered, we have identified recurring themes around which we offer these contributions, as they tackle the extremely diverse and sometimes visceral topic of mothers and food. At the same time, as this is an edited volume that brings together different perspectives and disciplinary approaches, we invite readers to pick and choose, to discover other themes that we did not highlight through the organizational structure of this book. Whether they live in the Global South or in the North, or whether their children are under or overweight, mothers deal with related sets of issues on a daily basis. At the global level, the same food system is dominated by big, for-profit corporations and agribusinesses that a growing number of voices, including maternal ones, protest against and challenge. At the same time, at the local level, as the chapters in this volume demonstrate, the effects produced by such systems often depend on socio-economic status and other criteria. They include the necessity to monitor children's diets because of food allergies, obesity, malnutrition or, sometimes, starvation not just at the family level but at the national one. At the heart of these global inequities, mothers are central actors in negotiating food systems, food politics, and culturally determined foodways. The contributors to *Mothers and Food* recognize this by going beyond the normative discourses of health and nutrition experts and beyond the idealistic images that are part of marketing strategies. We explore what really drives mothers to maintain or change their family's foodways, for better or for worse, paying particular attention to how this shapes their maternal identity.

NOTES

[1]See Szabo for a study of men's domestic cooking practices and Donohue for an edited collection that highlights voices of "fathers who cook for their families."

WORKS CITED

Avakian, Arlene Voski, and Barbara Haber, eds. *From Betty Crocker to Feminist Food Studies: Critical Perspectives on Women and Food.* Amherst: University of Massachusetts Press, 2005. Print.

Avakian, Arlene Voski, ed. *Through the Kitchen Window: Women Explore the Intimate Meanings of Food and Cooking.* Oxford-New York: Berg, 2005. Print.

Beagan, Brenda, Gwen Chapman, Josée Johnston, Deborah McPhail, Elaine M. Power, and Helen Vallianatos. *Acquired Tastes. Why Families Eat the Way They Do.* Toronto-Vancouver: University of British Columbia, 2014. E-book.

Bentley, Amy. *Inventing Baby Food: Taste, Health, and the Industrialization of the American Diet.* Oakland: University of California Press, 2014. Print.

Bowen, Sarah, Sinikka Elliott, and Joslyn Brenton. "The Joy of Cooking?" *Contexts* 13.3 (2014): 20-25. Web. 15 May 2015.

Cairns, Kate and Josée Johnston. *Food and Femininity.* New York: Bloomsbury, 2015. Print.

Cassidy, Tanya M. and Florence Pasche Guignard, eds. *What's Cooking, Mom? Narratives about Food and Family.* Bradford, Ontario: Demeter Press, 2015. Print.

Counihan, Carole and Penny van Esterik, eds. *Food and Culture: A Reader.* 3rd Edition. New York: Routledge, 2013. Print.

DeVault, Marjorie L. *Feeding the Family: The Social Organization of Caring as Gendered Work.* Chicago: University of Chicago Press, 1991. Print.

Donohue, John, ed. *Man with a Pan: Culinary Adventures of Fathers Who Cook for Their Families.* Chapel Hill: Algonquin Books, 2011. Print.

Gertsel, Naomi R. "The Third Shift: Gender and Care Work Outside the Home." *Qualitative Sociology.* 23.4 (2000): 467-483. Print.

Hochschild, Arlie, with Machung, Anne. *The Second Shift: Working Parents and the Revolution at Home.* New York: Viking. 1989. Print.

Ludvigsen, Anna, and Sara Scott. "Real Kids Don't Eat Quiche. What Food Means to Children." *Food, Culture and Society: An International Journal of Multidisciplinary Research* 12.4 (2009): 417-436. Web. 17 May 2015.

McDowell, Adam. "Death to the Chicken Finger. How We Created an Entire Generation of Unsophisticated, Picky Eaters—And Why We Must Stop the Tasteless Cycle." *thenationalpost.com.* National Post, Feb. 2015. Web. 2 May 2015.

Nathanson, Jessica, and Laura Camille Tuley, eds. *Mother Knows Best: Talking Back to the "Experts."* Toronto: Demeter Press, 2008. Print.

Ruddick, Sara. *Maternal Thinking: Toward a Politics of Peace.* Boston: Beacon Press, 1995. Print.

Szabo, Michelle. "Men Nurturing Through Food: Challenging Gender Dichotomies around Domestic Cooking." *Journal of Gender Studies* 23.1 (2014): 18-31. Print.

I.
DOMESTIC FOOD WORK AND THE FAMILY MEAL

1.
Feeding without Apology

Maternal Navigations of Distal Discourses in Family Meal Labour

AMBER E. KINSER AND KATHERINE J. DENKER

FAMILY MEALS SIT AT THE INTERSECTION of expert advice, child-centred philosophies, workforce demands, and "good" mother ideologies. As researchers and policymakers call for families to increase the frequency of shared family meals to solve a variety of problems related to children's well-being, we direct our focus toward mothers, who remain largely responsible for this labour. Borrowing from relational dialectics theory, we examine how mothers navigate distal discourses as they talk about the histories, processes, and problems associated with their feeding labour and family meal experiences. We draw from focus group data to discuss how mothers' food work and their family foodways function as contested terrain, centring women and their agency in our discussion. More specifically, we examine ways that mothers may reconstitute dominant discourses that shape their experiences of family meals, thus infusing those experiences with "agented action" (Horwitz 15). In particular, we focus on how mothers variously take up and push against discourses of individualism and "good" motherhood, centring and decentring different family meal images to meet their own personal and familial goals.

DISCOURSE AND RELATIONAL DIALECTICS THEORY

Baxter and Montgomery developed relational dialectics theory (RDT) as a way of exploring how relational partners manage opposing tensions in their relationship. Baxter extended the theory with the development of RDT 2.0, central to which is the understanding, as Norwood explains, that "the social world is a system of competing discourses" (qtd. in Baxter 28). RDT 2.0 calls for a deeper analysis of such discourses by exploring discursive struggle, discourse as situated in a larger conversation, and sites of interplay between competing discourses, among other variables. In the struggle between discourses, communicators empower and marginalize different narratives, thus imbibing certain ones with power and making them "normative, typical, and natural" (Baxter 123).

Comprising and giving rise to the larger social conversation are distal and proximal discourses. *Distal* discourses are shaped both by larger social narratives that are historical and/or currently in play—the ideology of the "good" mother (O'Reilly) or the master narrative of (heterosexual and child-bearing) marriage (Bergen), for example—and by the way that one expects others will respond to those narratives (Baxter 113). *Proximal* discourses, in contrast, are part of locally situated communication within relationships, from the narratives already shared between and influencing relational partners to the ways that each partner expects the other will respond (Baxter).

As we explore food work in the present study, RDT 2.0 offers insights into sites of identity collisions as individuals negotiate multiple constructions (Stephenson-Abetz and Holman). Examinations of distal discourses in family communication research are important, as often the impact of history and culture is lost in focusing on the proximal confines of the relationship (Sahlstein Parcell).

FEEDING THE FAMILY

For a decade and a half, researchers have argued that frequent family meals are a principal and indispensable component of optimally functioning families (Kinser, "At the Core"). Lamenting the ostensible decline of the family meal, researchers and the public discourse and policy campaigns that have emerged from their work have persistently urged "families" and "parents" to share family meals most days of the week (e.g., Berge et al.; CASAColumbia *I-VIII*). In these distal discourses, frequent family meals have been identified as a panacea for children that protects them from an array of adolescent struggles, including early sexual activity

(Fulkerson et al.), poor school performance, substance use (CASA-Columbia *I-VIII*), and cyber-bullying victimization (Elgar et al.), to name just a few of the problematic outcomes that family meals are said to remedy. Any quick online search reveals the affection that the media has for frequent family meal discourse, which has emerged, not coincidentally, at the same time as an "explosive rise of protectionism and ... narcissism around our kids" (Douglas and Michaels 307).

Given that mothers remain largely responsible for family feeding work (Bauer et al.; Bianchi et al.; Bowen, Elliott, and Brenton; Harnack et al.; Sobal 144) and despite impoverished attention to meal provision as gendered labour in the frequent family meal literature, family meal discourse is mother targeted. The outcomes of maternal labour are ultimately implicated when children's well-being outcomes fail to measure up.

Cultural assumptions about feeding the family are influenced by multiple factors—interactions among family members; contemporary food discourse; the interrelationship of the media, advertising, and market trends; and the willingness or failure of social policy to acknowledge social and structural inequity, among other factors. As these factors serve very different ends, their various messages are confounding for family food labour, resulting in mothers' anger, anxiety, guilt, and regret (Bowen, Elliot, and Brenton; Wood), and perceptions of risk in sharing information about their food labour practices (Ludlow et al.; Striley and Field-Springer). Conflicting notions about health and feeding are "fraught with notions of causality, morality, and responsibility with gendered nuances" (Paugh and Izquierdo 189).

As feeding derives from continuous, fragmented, and repetitious labour, those responsible are "always on call" (DeVault 5). Regardless of employment status, the number of hours spent on food preparation is higher for mothers than fathers (Bauer et al.; Bianchi et al.), even though maternal employment is blamed for perceived shortfalls of family feeding work (Boero; Herndon; McIntosh et al.). Gendered differences also are apparent in parents' responses to food matters as they are affected by spillover from work, with mothers still more focused on children's food intake than fathers (Devine et al., "Sacrifices"). Parents themselves have linked the labour of food work with a variety of positive outcomes, from increased family connection to providing healthy food (Quick et al.). However, barriers to achieving these outcomes by way of the family meal do exist, including child behavioural issues, scheduling issues, and insufficient participation of male partners (Mahlrota et al.; Quick et al.).

Dougherty argues that "food is material with material consequences" (209). As social expectations and class shape tastes, discourse about food shifts and functions to retain food's status as a class marker. Within these distinctions are associations with luxury- or necessity-based taste (Bourdieu) or the "right kind" of taste (Greene), as feeding work is conducted and experienced differently across classes (DeVault; Mink). For example, lower-income workers' limited access to healthy foods often results in less healthy eating patterns (Devine et al., "Sandwiching"). In addition, parents and families experience a continual growth of both work-family conflict and spillover, especially among parents (Devine et al., "Sandwiching"; Jabs et al.; Winslow). Increased work hours function as barriers, as higher work stress is associated with less frequent family meals, greater fast-food intake, and lower consumption of fruits and vegetables (Bauer et al.).

Despite the relentlessness of family meal responsibility and the fact that mothers remain the primary source for its labour in most families, little research has examined maternal points of view. This near void is especially problematic given the very focused, if conflicting, attention to both food and "good" motherhood assigned by contemporary distal discourses. In our study, we talked with mothers to gain insight into maternal experience of routine meal provision. Our work was guided by the following research questions: 1) how do mothers experience family meals in their current families? 2) what role do distal discourses play in shaping those experiences? and 3) how do mothers navigate various discourses relative to family meal provision?

METHODOLOGY

Thirty-one mothers across six focus groups discussed their experiences with and perspectives on family meals for this grant-funded project. We met with participants on campus and provided meals and financial compensation for them. To be inclusive, we offered various meeting times and provided child care and children's meals in a separate room of the same building during four of the focus groups. Mothers ranged from eighteen to fifty-five years old, with about half of them ranging between twenty-six and thirty-five years. They mothered a total of fifty-four children, whose ages ranged from one to twenty-one years, with about 60 percent of them ranging from one to five years. A majority of mothers had ties with one of the authors' university (current or former employees or their partners; current or former students or their partners; mothers of teen students at the on-campus K-12 school). The university and participants were located in south central Appalachia, where family is core to cultural identity and women are generally understood as equally core to the family and as having much authority in it. Just under half of the reported household incomes fell below USD 60,000, with half of these below USD 15,000. At the start of each focus group, participants ate the provided meal while completing a questionnaire. The questionnaire included questions about the participants and their families, the kind and amount of feeding work the mothers held responsibility for, and the degree to which certain elements of meal provision and consumption were useful or pleasant.

Focus group discussions were led by an evolving semi-structured moderator guide. Recognizing that one of the largest gaps in the literature is the dearth of input from mothers, we directed our attentions to finding out how our participants experienced family meals, what worked from their perspective and what did not, and what changes, if any, they would like to see. We used three open-ended discussion questions that asked about 1) their family dinners while growing up; 2) family dinners with their own children and families; and 3) whether they were interested in their meal experiences being different in any way and, if they did, what they would need in order for the changes to come about. The focus group discussions were audiotaped and transcribed verbatim; pseudonyms were used in the transcripts and in all writing. Guided by grounded theory techniques (Strauss and Corbin; Charmaz), we were led by the perspectives of our participants, observing and culling categories from the transcripts while relating what emerged to theory and findings in the literature.

FINDINGS

The mothers in our study were influenced by dominant distal discourses as they relate to motherhood and family meals, but they considered those discourses relative to other variables, including parenting goals; time constraints determined by work and school; financial constraints; family food allergies, restrictions, and preferences; and family member personalities and temperaments. Questionnaire responses revealed that these mothers held primary responsibility for an average of 70 percent of food work tasks including: planning; shopping; preparing; serving; knowing food preferences; management of family member conversation, food intake, and conflicts; and cleaning up after the meal, among other tasks. This finding supports previously cited research concluding that women remain primarily responsible for feeding work.

It is reasonable to assume, based on the amount of food work responsibility they report and given their interest in participating in the study, that most of our participants included food work as a component of maternal identity. Even so, they did not seem to ground maternal self-concept in their perceptions about how well they measured up to stereotypical images of family meal provision. Rather, these mothers exercised a great deal of agency and self-determination, pursued family meal provision largely in ways with which they were satisfied, given other demands, and rejected for the most part unrealistic expectations. That is, these mothers determined the extent to which, and the ways in which, they would go about meal provision, conducting their food labour, in many ways, without apology.

NAVIGATING DISTAL DISCOURSES THROUGH FAMILY MEAL MANAGEMENT

A primary emergent theme in the focus group data related to how women positioned themselves and their family food work relative to dominant, distal discourses. Mothers in our study were navigating multiple distal discourses that impinge on meal provision—dominant ideologies of motherhood, food and nutrition cultures, workforce norms, gendered divisions of family labour, and contemporary philosophies of the child-centred family and community, for example. Discourses are not deterministic; they can be employed, redirected, or embodied in ways that function as sites of resistance and can create space for alternative discourses. Additionally, not even dominant discourses necessarily operate wholesale; they can be dissevered, their various parts subject to rejection and/or creative modification (Butler; Foucault).

We found that the mothers in our study were not juggling these multiple discourses as much as they were strategically pitting them against one another, variously using one as a shield against the impact of another. By centring on one discourse and then later shifting focus to other discourses, participants both empowered norms and later marginalized them to serve their personal and maternal ends. Although the self-interest and utilitarian views of relational others that characterize "individualism" *per se* (Baxter; Bellah et al.) receive notable social critique, we were struck by the ways that they functioned as resourceful and effective defenses against maternal erasure. Mothers plucked and centred on a discourse of individualism from a host of discourses at varying times and in varying ways to use at their discretion as a way of reconciling the multiple conflicts inherent in the co-presence of equally, if differently, influential discourses that family meal rhetoric comprises.

CLAIMING AGENCY BY MARGINALIZING FAMILY MEAL DISCOURSE

As women explained their feeding work and how they felt about it, they communicated misgiving about their family foodways much less often and to a much lesser degree than we anticipated, given the force of good mother discourses that have been in play throughout much of U.S. history (Kinser, *Motherhood*). Although there were threads of maternal implication that ran throughout the data, they were significantly less prominent than the stronger threads of exoneration. Mothers frequently would avoid routine references to what they "should" or "should not" be doing. Often, they indicated that their options for a shared family meal were greatly restricted—by work, school, and financial constraints, for example—and that they were weary and spread thin. Still, they generally did not express an expectation, even if unmet, that they were responsible for making a conventional family meal happen regardless.

Several mothers alluded to stereotypical family meal images and their resistance to being dictated by such images. Sometimes, they opened up space for that resistance through their use of the term "fend." Gail, who is separated from her partner, said for example that her work schedule takes an enormous amount of her time and that dinnertime is

> *whenever I feel like it is. It might be eleven o'clock; it might be six o'clock; it might come whenever one fends for themselves and gets their food. That's not to say I never cook, but there's no schedule, rhyme, or reason to it. It's just about how much time I have, how much energy I have.*

Hazel, too, uses fending as a strategy for coping with work schedules. She and her partner each work full time but often are on different schedules, with her partner frequently at work. She said that she and her daughter

> *sort of fend for ourselves with our meals. And so, a lot of times we won't have a structured meal, and she really likes cantaloupe right now, so maybe I'll feed her a bowl of cantaloupe, and that's for dinner, and I'll have cereal.*

Hazel's mention of no structure reflects a larger theme for several of the mothers. In resisting the distal discourse of assumed "traditional" feeding practices of formal meals at the table, Hazel instead speaks to childrearing norms of devotional parenting and centres her discourse on adapting to the interests of her child. Other mothers likewise connect structure with location, using "the table" as the meal location, at times to facilitate structure and other times eating in one of the bedrooms or the living room to release the family from structure. Carla, for example, pushes against stereotypical images of the family sharing dinner by planning her evening meals around "where kids eat free" and eating out. By marginalizing the historic discourse of the family meal, Carla and others instead centre a discourse of individualism. The choice to do what is best for them at the time shields against guilt that might accompany the distal discourse of family feeding norms.

Lainey is a single parent who puts little stock in family meal discourse. She feeds her children what they will eat and counts on daycare food to contribute to nutritional content. She also serves dinner in a way that most helps *her* at the end of the workday. "I don't stress over the food," she said. During the week, her young daughters typically would eat in the living room with the television on while Lainey took her ten minutes of "break time": "It would be like ten minutes of where nobody's asking for 'Mommy can I do this? Mommy I need that. Mommy I want to go. Mommy, mommy.'" Again the discourse of individualism is highlighted, normalizing the mother's need for time alone and marginalizing a discourse of intensive mothering (Hays) that would require Lainey to sit with and attend to the children throughout the meal.

In each of the examples above, the competing discourses are evident. The mothers are speaking with resolve about their individualized approaches to food work. Yet their descriptions suggest that they do consider their practices *in relation to* the discourse of the "good" and sacrificial mother and her role in meal provision. That is, they often spoke in indirect reference to expectations about serving and sharing dinner at a prescribed time of day, eating at "the table," making a meal that has some preparatory complexity to it, and assuming all responsibility for getting children to eat the "right" foods.

CLAIMING AGENCY BY EMPOWERING FAMILY MEAL DISCOURSE

Although we found some participants resisting iconic images of meals orchestrated by mothers and served at the table, we conversely found other participants focusing intently on shared meals, often at the table, as a way of pushing against other discourses. Devoting time and energy to family meals represented efforts to reduce the power that work life (paid employment and college coursework) and a general U.S. cultural freneticism have in shaping the quality of family life. Some of the mothers who were working to execute regularly shared, sit-down meals still were not demanding the performance of family dinner roles residing in the popular imaginary. Becky, for example, who was unsure whether her approach emerged from her Asian upbringing or her experience living in the U.S. mountain south, was open to using whatever strategy would prevent her family's having to "sacrifice [their] value system," which included prioritizing family time. She was willing to accept that the best one could hope for might be "controlled chaos" and that one might need to employ the services of what some mothers referred to as an "iNanny"—iPads or iPhones given to very young children to occupy their attention and keep them at the table so that they can finish eating and be supervised and so that parents and older children can finish their meal. Becky's acceptance of fairly chaotic dinners and use of technology as a family meal facilitator oppose not only more widely invoked family meal images but also the dominant discourse of motherhood and its insistence that the mother herself must meet all of her child's needs (O'Reilly; Horwitz). This prescription has historically viewed with deep suspicion families, and especially mothers, using anyone or anything (e.g., daycare providers, television, iNannies) to help them attend to the children.

Mothers in same-sex couples may see particular advantage to shared family meals around the table. Lydia, who is a stay-at-home mother to her two teen children and to her and her partner's two young children, identifies as "one hundred percent the planner of the meals and the insister that it happens." Even though her older children find it challenging to connect to her younger two, and Lydia finds it complicated to create healthy dinners that satisfy her family's age ranges and eating preferences, Lydia uses family meals to position her family as at least equal to families of heterosexual couples. But this requires a great bit of orchestrating on her part. Because her teenagers "would rather eat, for sure, anywhere but home," she will "nag [her] kids to no end: '*When* are we gonna eat this week? Give me your day—give me your schedule,' like pushing, pushing." In explaining her resolve about sharing a family meal that she has prepared, despite the fact that she has to "fight for it," she said:

> *I think it separates [us] from families that aren't working ... it makes me feel like "We are gonna be better than that, we're not the masses, our family." Because we're a same sex couple, I feel like, I* always *feel this pressure that we have to do better, our kids* have *to be the ones that don't get in trouble, that get straight As, to prove that* you don't *need a mom and dad in the house to be a family. So, I have all these internal things that make me push for it. (emphases spoken by participant)*

Lydia works to normalize the family meal and same-sex mothering by marginalizing the individualist discourse invoked by her teen children and by empowering "good" mother and family meal discourses.

Eva tells a story of being spread very thin across work, church, children's activities, and meal provision. But she is adamant about sharing routine family dinners with her children and male partner. As her family is a football fan family, they eat many of their meals in front of the television during football season. In her insistence that all members of her family share a meal together nearly every night—a practice she proclaimed with the phrase "I don't do partials"—she is using some aspects of sacrificial motherhood in an attempt to work against the impact that discourses of individualism and child-centredness can have on family relationships. Rather than using technology as a family meal facilitator, Eva uses it as a parallel activity, adjoining two important family values for them—shared company and football fandom. Despite the position of the dominant discourse that TV viewing during family meals contributes to family member disconnection and/or obesity, families still include TV as a component of the meal. Eva seems aware that dinnertime television has its opponents, but makes exception in football season. She considers football to be a legitimate family meal participant and dinnertime interaction source. That television is involved in the meal and that during the week her children may be eating and going to bed later than their peers because dinner was delayed until the last family member arrived home are of notably lesser concern for her:

> *Yes, it may be in front of a football game or it may be when most kids are in bed—so sorry for my children's teachers—but that's the only time we can all be in one place and be still at the same time, just to be in each other's company, talking about whatever.*

Although the children and parents may be pursuing their own individual, instrumental goals and although church, school, and after school activities may revolve around the children, Eva marginalizes these discourses by empowering "good" mother and frequent family meal discourses.

SUMMARY

Distal discourses were centred for many of the mothers in our study in instances where they empowered the women and their choices. As the mothers focused their on the distal discourses of individualism or on language that reified maternal norms, they also marginalized other frames. In these instances, the centring discourses not only were given power to influence the mothers but also were underscored as having important influence on others who were *in situ*. Although our analysis does not account for the impact that the selection and centralization of a given discourse had on relational or familial others, it might be interesting to explore how attention to certain distal discourses affect later proximal discourses. In addition, it would be useful to explore how the reality of work and working mothers affects feeding in the family. Normative discourses about motherhood and family meals have shown in our study to be influential but far from deterministic in maternal food work. Through the strategic use of discourses, mothers created more complex identities as they pushed against prescriptive norms for feeding the family.

This project was funded by the Research Development Committee of East Tennessee State University. We wish to acknowledge the critical contributions of research assistants Meylin Mejia, Aimee Trawick, and Allison Smith.

WORKS CITED

Bauer, Katherine, Mary Hearst, Kamisha Escoto, Jerica Berge, and Dianne Neumark-Sztainer. "Parental Employment and Work-Family Stress: Associations with Family Food Environments." *Social Science & Medicine* 75.3 (2012): 496-504. Print.

Baxter, Leslie, and Barbara Montgomery. *Relating: Dialogues & Dialectics*. New York: Gilford, 1996. Print.

Baxter, Leslie. *Voicing Relationships: A Dialogic Perspective*. Los Angeles: Sage, 2011. Print.

Bellah, Robert, Richard Madsen, William Sullivan, Ann Swidler, and Stephen Tipton. *Habits of the Heart: Individualism and Commitment in American Life*. Thousand Oaks: Sage, 1985. Print.

Berge, Jerica M., Melanie Wall, Dianne Neumark-Sztainer, Nicole Larson, and Mary Story. "Parenting Style and Family Meals: Cross-Sectional and 5-Year Longitudinal Associations." *Journal of the American Dietetic Association* 110.7 (2010): 1036-1042. Print.

Bergen, Karla. "Accounting for Difference: Commuter Wives and the Master Narrative of Marriage." *Journal of Applied Communication Research* 38.1 (2010): 47-64. Print.

Bianchi, Suzanne, Melissa Milkie, Liana Sayer, and John Robinson. "Is Anyone Doing the Housework? Trends in the Gender Division of Household Labor." *Social Forces* 79.1 (2000): 191-228. Print.

Boero, Natalie. "Fat Kids, Working Moms, and the 'Epidemic of Obesity': Race, Class, and Mother Blame." *The Fat Studies Reader,* Eds. Esther D. Rothblum and Sondra Solovay. New York: NYU Press, 2009. 113-119. Print.

Bourdieu, Pierre. *Distinctions: A Social Critique of the Judgment of Taste*. Trans. Richard Nice. Cambridge: Harvard University, 1984. Print.

Bowen, Sarah, Elliott Sinikka, and Joslyn Brenton. "The Joy of Cooking?" *Contexts* 13.3 (2014): 13-20. Web. 19 Feb. 2015.

Butler, Judith. *Gender Trouble: Feminism and the Subversion of Identity.* New York: Routledge, 2006. Print.

Columbia University National Center on Addiction and Substance Abuse (CASAColumbia). *The Importance of Family Dinners*. Columbia University National Center on Addiction and Substance Abuse. 2003. Web. 5 April 2012

Columbia University National Center on Addiction and Substance Abuse (CASAColumbia). *The Importance of Family Dinners II*. Columbia University National Center on Addiction and Substance Abuse. 2005. Web. 5 April 2012

Columbia University National Center on Addiction and Substance Abuse (CASAColumbia). *The Importance of Family Dinners III*. Columbia University National Center on Addiction and Substance Abuse. 2006. Web. 5 April 2012

Columbia University National Center on Addiction and Substance Abuse (CASAColumbia). *The Importance of Family Dinners IV*. Columbia University National Center on Addiction and Substance Abuse. 2007. Web. 5 April 2012

Columbia University National Center on Addiction and Substance Abuse (CASAColumbia). *The Importance of Family Dinners V*. Columbia University National Center on Addiction and Substance Abuse. 2009. Web. 5 April 2012

Columbia University National Center on Addiction and Substance Abuse (CASAColumbia). *The Importance of Family Dinners VI* Columbia University National Center on Addiction and Substance Abuse. 2010. Web. 5 April 2012

Columbia University National Center on Addiction and Substance Abuse (CASAColumbia). *The Importance of Family Dinners VII*. Columbia University National Center on Addiction and Substance Abuse. 2011. Web. 17 Jan. 2012

Columbia University National Center on Addiction and Substance Abuse (CASAColumbia). *The Importance of Family Dinners VIII*. Columbia University National Center on Addiction and Substance Abuse. 2012. Web. 16 Sept. 2013

Charmaz, Kathy. *Constructing Grounded Theory: A Practical Guide through Qualitative Analysis*. London: Sage, 2006. Print.

DeVault, Marjorie L. *Feeding the Family: The Social Organization of Caring as Gendered Work*. Chicago: University of Chicago, 1991. Print.

Devine, Carol, Margaret Connors, Jeffery Sobal, and Carole Bisogni.

"Sandwiching It in: Spillover of Work Onto Food Choices and Family Roles in Low- and Moderate-Income Urban Household." *Social Science & Medicine* 56.3 (2003): 617-630. Print.

Devine, Carol, Margaret Jastran, Jennifer Jabs, Elaine Wethington, Tracy Farrell, and Carole Bisogni. "'A Lot of Sacrifices': Work–Family Spillover and the Food Choice Coping Strategies of Low Wage Employed Parents." *Social Science & Medicine* 63.10 (2006): 2591-2603. Print.

Dougherty, Debbie. *The Reluctant Farmer: An Exploration of Work, Social Class & the Production of Food.* Leics, UKK: Troubador, 2011. Print

Douglas, Susan, and Meredith Michaels. *The Mommy Myth: The Idealization of Motherhood and How It Has Undermined All Women.* New York: Free Press, 2004. Print.

Elgar, Frank J., Anthony Napoletano, Grace Saul, Melanie A. Dirks, Wendy Craig, V. Paul Poteat, Melissa Holt, and Brian W. Koenig. "Cyberbullying Victimization and Mental Health in Adolescents and the Moderating Role of Family Dinners." *JAMA Pediatrics* 168.11 (2014): 1015-1022. Print.

Foucault, Michel. *The History of Sexuality: An Introduction, Volume I.* New York: Vintage, 1978. Print.

Fulkerson, Jayne A., Mary Story, Allison Mellin, Nancy Leffert, Dianne Neumark-Sztainer, and Simone A. French. "Family Dinner Meal Frequency and Adolescent Development: Relationships with Developmental Assets and High-Risk Behaviors." *Journal of Adolescent Health* 39 (2006): 337-345. Print.

Greene, Carlnita. "Competing Identities at the Table: Slow Food, Consumption, and the Performance of Social Style." *Food as Communication: Communication as Food.* Eds. Janet Cramer, Carlnita Greene, and Lynn Walters. New York: Peter Lang, 2011. 75-94. Print.

Harnack, Lisa, Mary Story, Brian Martinson, Dianne Neumark-Sztainer, and Jamie Stang. "Guess Who's Cooking? The Role of Men in Meal Planning, Shopping, and Preparation in US Families." *Journal of the American Dietetic Association* 98.9 (1998): 995-1000. Web. 19 Feb. 2015.

Hays, Sharon. *The Cultural Contradictions of Motherhood.* New Haven, CT: Yale University, 1996. Print.

Herndon, April M. "Mommy Made Me Do It." *Food, Culture, and Society*. 13.3 (2010): 332-349. Print.

Horwitz, Erika. *Through the Maze of Motherhood: Empowered Mothers Speak*. Bradford, ON: Demeter, 2011. Print.

Jabs, Jennifer, Carol Devine, Carole Bisogni, Tracy Farrell, Margaret Jastran, and Elaine Wethington. "Trying to Find the Quickest Way: Employed Mothers' Construction of Time for Food." *Journal of Nutrition Education and Behavior* 39.1 (2007): 18-25. Print.

Kinser, Amber E. *Motherhood and Feminism*. Berkeley: Seal, 2010. Print.

Kinser, Amber E. "At the Core of the Work/Life Balance Myth: Motherhood and Family Dinners." *What Do Mothers Need?: Motherhood Activists and Scholars Speak Out on Maternal Empowerment for the 21st Century*. Ed. Andrea O'Reilly. Bradford, ON: Demeter, 2012. Print.

Ludlow, Valerie, Leigh Newhook, Julie Newhook, Kimberly Bonia, Janet Murphy-Goodridge, and Laurie Twells. "How Formula Feeding Mothers Balance Risks and Define Themselves as 'Good Mothers.'" *Health, Risk & Society* 14.3 (2012): 291-306. Print.

Mahlrota, Khushi, Allison N. Herman, Gretchen Wright, Yasmeen Bruton, Jennifer O. Fisher, and Robert C. Whitaker. "Perceived Benefits and Challenges for Low-Income Mothers of Having Family Meals with Preschool-Aged Children: Childhood Memories Matter." *Journal of the Academy of Nutrition and Dietetics* 113.11 (2012): 1484-1493. Web. 7 Jan. 2013.

McIntosh, William Alex, Karen S. Kubena, Glen Tolle, Wesley R. Dean, Jie-sheng Jan, and Jenna Anding. "Mothers and Meals. The Effects of Mother's Meal Planning and Shopping Motivations on Children's Participation in Family Meals." *Appetite* 55 (2010): 623-628. Print.

Mink, Gwendolyn. *The Wages of Motherhood: Inequality in the Welfare State, 1917-1942*. Ithaca: Cornell Univrsity, 1995. Print.

Norwood, Kristen. "Grieving Gender: Trans-Identities, Transition and Ambiguous Loss." *Communication Monographs* 80.1 (2013): 24-45. Print.

O'Reilly, Andrea. *Rocking the Cradle: Thoughts on Motherhood, Feminism, and the Possibility of Empowered Mothering*. Toronto: Demeter, 2006. Print.

Paugh, Amy, and Carolina Izquierdo. "Why Is This a Battle Every Night?: Negotiating Food and Eating in American Dinnertime Interaction." *Journal of Linguistic Anthropology* 19.2 (2009): 185-204. Print.

Quick, Brian, Barbara Fiese, Barbara Anderson, Brenda Koester, and Diane Marlin. "A Formative Evaluation of Shared Family Mealtime for Parents of Toddlers and Young Children." *Health Communication* 26.7 (2011): 656-666. Print.

Sahlstein Parcell, Erin. "Trajectories Research in Family Communication: Toward the Identification of Alternative Pathways for Inquiry." *Journal of Family Communication* 13.1 (2013):167-177. Print.

Sobal, Jeffery. "Men, Meat, and Marriage: Models of Masculinity." *Food & Foodways* 13 (2005): 135-158. Print.

Stephenson-Abetz, Jenna, and Holman, Amanda. "Home Is Where the Heart Is: Facebook and the Negotiation of "Old" and "New" during the Transition to College." *Western Journal of Communication* 76 (2012): 175-193. Print.

Strauss, Anselm, and Juliet Corbin. *Basics of Qualitative Research: Techniques and Procedures for Developing Grounded Theory*. 2nd ed. Thousand Oaks: Sage, 1998. Print.

Striley, Katie, and Kimberly Field-Springer. "The Bad Mother Police: Theorizing Risk Orders in the Discourses of Infant Feeding Practices." *Health Communication* 28.1 (2013): 1-11. Print.

Winslow, Sarah. "Work-Family Conflict, Gender, and Parenthood, 1977-1997." *Journal of Family Issues* 26.6 (2005): 727-755. Print.

Wood, Roy. *The Sociology of the Meal: Food and Social Theory*. Edinburgh: Edinburgh University, 1995. Print.

2.
Feeding the Squeezed Middle-Class Family

Maternal Stress, Dilemmas, Contradictions and the Third Shift

NERI DE KRAMER

MY STUDY OF THE FOOD PRACTICES of middle-class families in a neighbourhood in Philadelphia reveals that the biologically and socially reproductive work around food and feeding constitutes a considerable source of stress for mothers whose middle-class status is most precarious and is so time consuming and intensive that it amounts to a "third shift." In this chapter, I link the complication of the socially reproductive work of feeding children to the complication of the category "middle class" as economic pressures threaten the middle-class status of these families and the middle-class futures of their children.

The American middle class finds itself in a precarious economic situation. Since the abandonment of the social contract in the 1970s, middle-class hourly wages have failed to keep pace with the rate of inflation. As corporate as well as government redistribution policies have disintegrated, middle-class median income, as well as middle-class income growth and share of the national income, has declined. Although the U.S. Bureau of Economic Analysis reports recent economic growth in the United States, funds fail to trickle down to the bottom 90 percent of American wage earners whose wage is lower today than it was three decades ago (Reich, "The Middle Class Squeeze" 6; United States, Department of Commerce, U.S. Bureau of Economic Analysis). This rising income inequality, with an extreme concentration of wealth at the top, now statistically lumps together struggling working and middle classes (Piketty 580), raising interesting questions about class identity and processes of distinction. Seven years after the

2008 financial crisis, middle-class unemployment rates remain high, debts are soaring, and for the first time in a century, young Americans are not expected to surpass their parents' economic status (Lowrey MM12).

Faced with these economic realities, members of the American middle class have adopted a series of strategies to try and improve or preserve their structural position in society. Women have re-entered the workforce, especially in part-time, "flexible" positions (Susser 394). Families now rely on cheap, mass produced consumer products from the global marketplace, which frees up some funds for other expenses. And parents now raise their children in a more intense manner, which is aimed at giving them more of a competitive edge in the education and job markets (Davidson; Hays; Lareau). In addition, as the American middle class feels the economic ground under its feet shifting and traditional markers of class, such as a second car or a large house, fall out of reach, the process of symbolic distinction becomes more important for retaining middle-class identity and the search for a low-cost yet high-class means of distinction becomes more urgent.

In what follows, I argue that these strategies—undertaken by the middle class in their attempts to fend off downward mobility on both the structural and symbolic level—together create a set of almost untenable contradictions for middle-class mothers, particularly in the realm of food and feeding and particularly for those on the most limited budgets. The strategies for retaining class position are often directly at odds with one another as well as with previously established class norms and practices around food, body size, and parenting. Although fathers face contradictions of their own in their efforts to prepare the next generation for an increasingly insecure future, historical unequal gender expectations about the household division of labour tend to keep mothers primarily responsible for most socially reproductive work around food and feeding (Laslett and Brenner; Hochschild and Machung; Gerson), including the task of preserving their and their children's class-appropriate body size (Bordo).

The maternal practices and sentiments that I describe in this chapter are drawn from a broader ethnographic study on the food practices of a diverse group of middle-class families in Philadelphia.

Although social scientists have recognized the economic pressures on the American (and global) middle classes as a whole (Heiman, Freeman and Liechty; Katz; Davidson), the goal of my project is to map and understand the diversity *within* middle-class America, using food as a tool to illuminate diverse middle-class politics as well as the various processes by which middle-class status is negotiated, maintained, and communicated. Although all parents in my study have secondary degrees, live in the same well-regarded neighbourhood, and self-identify as middle class, their actual economic status varies widely. In my sample, I distinguish two principal groups: one is a financially struggling, "squeezed" group where one or both parents work in the public sector as teachers, in community organizations, or in Philadelphia city government. The other is a relatively wealthy group (though nowhere near Pikkety's "top decile" of income earners) that draws on modest funds of inherited wealth and/or has at least one of the parents working in the private sector, such as in corporate law, finance, real estate, or another for-profit corporation. Although on the surface, these two sets of families and their class aspirations are quite similar, the two groups live quite dramatically different daily lives, which is a function of the high variation in wealth and income among them. Here, I focus specifically on the contradictions that emerge for a group of mothers who are trying to run their households on the most limited budgets while, at the same time, fully subscribing to local, demanding, and expensive class norms around food, body size, and parenting.

The site of the study is the Mount Airy neighbourhood of Philadelphia, a quiet, desirable place to live and known for its progressive culture. It is one of only a handful of deliberately racially integrated neighborhoods in the country and also has many Jewish as well as same-sex households (Cashin 43-52; Perkiss). The local diversity is a great source of pride for Mount Airy's residents, including the generally liberal, leftist middle-class mothers in my study. Many specifically mention the diversity and "realness" of Mount Airy as great assets that compare favorably to the "bubble" that the Philadelphia suburbs constitute, even though the latter may, in some instances, be cheaper places to live and have better public school systems. Many Mount Airy residents have advanced degrees, earning the neighbourhood the nickname "PhD ghetto of Philadelphia" (Ferman, Singleton, and DeMarco 44).

In this "Berkeley of the East," as one mom called it, the food norms are local, organic, or otherwise alternative food. The mothers in my study are health conscious and environmentally and politically aware. They overwhelmingly prefer to buy local, organic food that is chemical free, not mass produced and that supports local food producers as directly as possible. Fast, processed, or convenience food from conventional supermarkets or chain restaurants is to be avoided. Although eating this way is beneficial to the environment and food producers, its primary benefit to the moms in my study is that it promotes health and, I would like to add, thinness, both of which have become embodied markers of higher-class status in contemporary America (Guthman).

Although much of the research on America's so-called obesity epidemic and its causes, effects, and distribution is currently being questioned (Campos; Campos et al.; Flegal et al. Guthman), it is clear that obesity and diet-related diseases have been markers of low-class status in the United States since the 1980s when obesity rates started rising dramatically, especially among Blacks, Hispanics, and low-income groups (Chang and Cristakis; Davison and Birch; Ogden et al.; United States, Office of the Surgeon General). For mothers held responsible for safeguarding the class status of their families and reproducing it for the next generation, this new embodiment of class has put the preservation of health and thinness at the centre of their parenting efforts. This has complicated the task of feeding the family because the easily accessible, cheap, low-quality, high-calorie, industrially processed food most implicated in obesity is often exactly the type of food that is aggressively marketed to children and that children want and ask for. In response to these dilemmas many mothers, including the mothers in my study, have adopted and internalized a doctrine of self-governance, what geographer Julie Guthman, following Robert Crawford, calls "healthism" (52-56). Healthism refers to the prioritization and moralization of health and the market-based practices to achieve it, including a switch to "alternative" or organic, unadulterated food, which is both symbolically distinctive and has the added benefit of promoting health and controlling weight.

For the middle-class mother, compounding the difficulty of maintaining her family's health and thinness are the dictates of the highly demanding local norm of parenting intensively. This intensive parenting norm can be characterized by an encouraging, empowering, and permissive attitude towards children, and is also expensive and time consuming. Sociologist Annette Lareau has called it "concerted cultivation": an approach to parenting that views a child as a "project" that needs to be "developed" and the role of parents to actively foster its talents, opinions, and skills (1-2). Although this parenting style has received a lot of attention and critique (Hays; Davidson; Katz), not many scholars have described the formidable contradictions that this method creates for mothers in the realm of food and feeding. For central to the empowerment of children are the notions of agency and choice, which means that mothers cannot simply say "no" to children who ask for certain foods. Children are considered agentive, choosing consumers in their own right, and their desires are to be taken seriously. Many mothers in my study consider a reliance on authoritative control to be harmful and disrespectful to their children.

Although there are some advantages to being raised this way, it makes it very hard for the middle-class mother to feed her children the alternative foods the doctrine of healthism prescribes precisely because she cannot just tell them what to eat. Instead, children must be influenced to *want* to eat this way so that they can be trusted to make their own consumption decisions without compromising their health or thinness. This stands in direct contrast to the more traditional parenting style commonly associated with American working-class mothers based on giving directives, enforcing discipline, and instilling a respect for authority (Lareau).[1] A mother who employs this parenting style could simply forbid her children to eat certain foods and manage their diet, health, and body size with a lot less time and effort.

The intensive parenting norm complicates the adoption of the local food norm for all middle-class mothers in my study because it is far from straightforward to get children to want to eat whole grains and organic vegetables. Yet mothers continue the struggle because alternative food clearly reflects and confirms middle- or upper-class status by signaling sophisticated and class specific taste preferences, highlighting an educated liberal politics, and strongly connecting to proper health and body size. Additional difficulties arise for the subset of middle-class mothers for whom this food is out of reach financially. Although all sorts of alternative food are easily accessible in Mount Airy's farmer's market, co-operative grocery store, restaurants, and cafes, several of the moms in my study could simply not afford to shop there. In fact, several families in my study confront the paradoxical situation in which their middle-class financial status (and with that their ability to afford to live in the neighborhood) is actually *dependent* on the cheap consumption goods that threaten this status symbolically. And of the many inexpensive goods available to the American consumer on a budget, none undermine middle-class status in quite the same way as does cheap, conventional, mass produced food, certainly in the Mount Airy context.

This situation then, of fully ascribing to certain norms but being unable to afford them, creates frustrating dilemmas and contradictions for the more cash-strapped mothers in my study and has complicated their tasks of shopping, cooking, feeding, and parenting considerably. Mothers of means are to an extent able to "opt out" of the conventional food system and the threats it represents by, for example, buying peace of mind by shopping exclusively at Whole Foods (and letting their children freely choose food in that environment), by having their CSA (Community-Supported Agriculture) share delivered, or by hiring a private chef. Mothers in the squeezed middle have to do it all themselves.

After a year of interviews and trailing mothers from their gardens to their kitchens to the store, I have concluded that the amount of work around food and feeding constitutes a "third shift"[2] of food care for mothers who self-identify as middle class but cannot actually afford a middle-class lifestyle. The term "second shift" was introduced by Hochschild and Machung in their study on the household division of labour in the late 1980s to refer to the labour women performed at home in addition to their paid work outside of the home. The "third shift" refers to the set of exclusively food-related tasks mothers in the squeezed middle carry out on top of their other two shifts. The third shift firmly ties less affluent middle-class mothers to their reproductive work, in some cases getting in the way of their professional progress and potentially even contributing to the economic stagnation of this group. At a minimum, the third shift of food care constitutes a new but hidden form of inequality between different members of middle-class America.

The third shift begins with research. Despite a strong preference for alternative food, mothers on a budget are dependent on lower-priced food from the conventional food system. In order to safely navigate it and find the most healthful foods within it, they report having to be "vigilant" and "armed" with research. Mothers in the squeezed middle spend more time doing research on food, the industrial food system, stores, and prices than the more affluent moms and are more thoroughly and accurately informed as result. This detailed knowledge about things, such as the chemicals used in the conventional food system, animal welfare, or labor issues, contributes to the feelings of guilt and anxiety mothers report experiencing around the food that they depend on. Moms conduct this research at night, after the children have gone to bed, and it is the number one topic of conversation in online communications between mothers. Complicating this already time consuming and sometimes disturbing information-gathering task is a deep mistrust of "the system," which makes mainstream publications and reports from well-established sources, such as *The New York Times* or the well-known Environmental Working Group, suspect. This means mothers spend additional time hunting for truly objective information from independent organizations in the nether reaches of the Internet.

Once the research is done, the activity of grocery shopping significantly adds to the third shift because mothers in this group often shop in multiple places to get the better deals that they researched. Some of their markets are far away and this makes it harder and more time consuming to shop. Shopping in conventional grocery stores with children in tow complicates things further for many of the foods mothers feel the need to avoid are foods that children notice and ask for. The intensive parenting norm prescribes that mothers listen to these requests, explain why they cannot get certain foods and, sometimes, enter into negotiations, which can draw out the shopping excursion. At the same time, political norms in this deliberately integrated neighbourhood make it impossible for mothers to be publically critical of certain foods. My interviews reveal that yet another reason mothers feel they cannot simply reject non-healthy foods is because children could perceive this as a judgment of those who eat them, and this elitism is to be avoided in the local context. This dilemma—of wanting to avoid certain foods without being able to explicitly reject them because of the delicacy of their association with low-income minorities—is, thus, another way in which the feeding and parenting tasks of mothers in the squeezed middle are more complicated than those of more affluent ones whose children are shielded from low-income people with different consumption habits.

Another way in which the mothers in my study address the disconnect between ascribed-to food norms and financial reality is by adopting a DIY approach to food and feeding. All cook most of their food from scratch, and many grow or pick much of their own produce in the spring, summer, and fall, much of which they then pickle, can, or preserve. Many women also bake their own bread, cakes, and other goods; some roast their own green coffee beans, and a few keep chickens for eggs and bees for honey. This approach is a logical response to the financial precarity of this subgroup of middle-class families in this context because it allows mothers to feed their families the healthy, local, organically grown, humanely produced food that they value so highly but at a fraction of the price this food costs at the farmer's market, co-op, or premium grocery store. In addition, the DIY approach to feeding the family has the added benefits of tasting great and of being high status and distinctive. To be knowledgeable about where one's food comes from and skilled in how to grow, preserve, and prepare it all contribute to these families' cultural capital and form a clear example of how middle-class status can be performed and achieved through food practices (Naccarato and Lebesco 8), usually carried out by women.[3]

Homesteading, which is what this work essentially amounts to, thus promotes class-appropriate health and body size, helps to save money and is symbolically distinctive, contributing in multiple ways to the preservation of the otherwise quite precarious class status of these families. Yet, needless to say, this way of feeding the family is extremely time consuming because of the amount of time it requires women to spend in the garden and kitchen as well as the amount of research and planning that it involves. The DIY activities the mothers in my study are immersed in, thus, add most work to their third shift and, sometimes, have the self-defeating effect of interfering with the pursuit of more lucrative work that could help solidify their middle-class status in a more structural way. As one informant confided: "I technically should be looking for work, we need more money, but I can't see how I could work full time and still do all the gardening, cooking and baking." Other moms have expressed similar sentiments. To understand their unwillingness to give up these intensive food activities, one needs to look at the community it has helped create. Many mothers closely co-operate with one another around gardening and cooking, exchange information, and receive a lot of recognition and support from the other mothers in the group. Going back to work or taking up full-time work could potentially threaten this support network and sense of community, which is risky in the context of structural insecurity.

In addition to keeping mothers from pursuing more lucrative work, with potentially real financial consequences, the third shift also limits the time that they are able to spend with their children, which can have structural effects in the next generation. This constitutes another difficult dilemma for the tenuously situated mothers in my study because spending extensive amounts of time in conversations and activities with one's children is what the local parenting norm prescribes and is what moms want to do. Yet simultaneously trying to comply with the local food norm makes long and meaningful engagement with their children much harder. This situation creates strong feelings of insecurity, inadequacy, and guilt in many mothers for they are well aware that children need to be intensively instructed, prepared, and coached to do well in school and life later on; they consider this socially reproductive work their job. This is especially true for the educated mother who is financially dependent on the local public schools but painfully aware of the subpar education her children are receiving there. Concurrently, mothers are also aware that they are still the primary parent held responsible for the health and physical well-being of their children, which makes the prioritization of healthy food and instilling class-appropriate eating habits seem prudent, too (and perhaps a more attainable and concrete parenting goal in the face of their children's insecure and unclear futures).

In conclusion, my study of the food practices of a diverse set of middle-class families in Philadelphia reveals that the socially reproductive work around food, feeding, and parenting creates contradictions and a considerable source of stress for mothers in the "squeezed middle" and is so time consuming and intensive that they amount to a "third shift." I have showed that the third shift can be understood as both a response to and a reproduction of the tenuous situation of these middle-class families, as they try to cling to specific and demanding local class norms around food, body size, and parenting in their attempt to ward off downward mobility. The extra work of the third shift and the difficult dilemmas these often conflicting class norms pose for moms on a budget reproduce and exacerbate gender inequality within the tenuously situated middle-class home. By contrast, more affluent mothers are better situated to buy themselves out of some of the tasks that are keeping women of lesser means continuously busy in and around the home, and are better able to cultivate themselves and their children and to adapt to an insecure future. This means that the challenges in the lives of this group of middle-class mothers described here constitute a new but hidden form of inequality among seemingly very similar members of the middle class, living in the same neighborhood and ascribing to the same norms and values.

NOTES

[1]This also constitutes the "French parenting" approach, well characterized by popular writer Pamela Druckerman in *Bringing up Bébé*.

[2]I thank Jeff Maskovsky for suggesting this term.

[3]Fathers, too, are involved in vegetable gardening, although mothers are the driving force behind these activities. Many of the fathers in my study are avid home beer brewers however, which is another

example of a money-saving yet highly distinctive DIY approach to food. The big difference is that home-brewed beer only benefits the class status of the adults in the family and does not benefit the children, as mothers' food activities do.

WORKS CITED

Bordo, Susan. *Unbearable Weight: Feminism, Western Culture, and the Body*. Berkeley: University of California Press, 1993. Print.

Campos, Paul. "Our Imaginary Weight Problem." *The New York Times*, 2 Jan. 2013. Web. 7 Jan. 2013.

Campos, Paul, Abigail Saguy, Paul Ernsberger,Eric Oliver and Glenn Gaesser. "The Epidemiology of Overweight and Obesity: Public Health Crisis or Moral Panic?" *International Journal of Epidemiology* 35.1 (2006): 55-60. Web. 7 Jan. 2013.

Cashin, Sheryll. *The Failures Of Integration: How Race and Class Are Undermining the American Dream*. New York: PublicAffairs, 2005. Print.

Chang, Virginia W., and Nicholas A. Christakis. "Income Inequality and Weight Status in US Metropolitan Areas." *Social Science & Medicine* 61.1 (2005): 83–96. *ScienceDirect*. Web. 8 Jan. 2013.

Crawford, Robert. "Health as a Meaningful Social Practice." *Health* 10.4 (2006): 401-420. Web. 18 Jan. 2013.

Davidson, Elsa. *The Burdens of Aspiration: Schools, Youth, and Success in the Divided Social Worlds of Silicon Valley*. New York: New York University Press, 2011. Print.

Davison, K. K., and L. L. Birch. "Childhood Overweight: A Contextual Model and Recommendations for Future Research." *Obesity Reviews: An Official Journal of the International Association for the Study of Obesity* 2.3 (2001): 159-171. Print.

Ferman, Barbara, Theresa Singleton, and Don DeMarco. "West Mount Airy, Philadelphia." *Cityscape: A Journal of Policy Development and Research* 4.2 (1998): 29-59. Print.

Flegal, Katherine, Brian Kit, Heather Orpana, and Barry Graubard. "Association of All-Cause Mortality with Overweight and Obesity Using Standard Body Mass Index Categories: A Systematic Review and Meta-Analysis." *JAMA* 309.1 (2013): 71–82. Web. 7 Jan. 2013.

Gerson, Kathleen. *Hard Choices: How Women Decide About Work, Career and Motherhood.* Berkeley: University of California Press, 1986. Print.

Guthman, Julie. *Weighing In: Obesity, Food Justice, and the Limits of Capitalism.* 1st ed. Berkeley: University of California Press, 2011. Print.

Hays, Sharon. *The Cultural Contradictions of Motherhood.* New Haven: Yale University Press, 1998. Print.

Heiman, Rachel, Carla Freeman, and Mark Liechty, eds. *The Global Middle Classes: Theorizing Through Ethnography.* Santa Fe: School for Advanced Research Press, 2012. Print.

Hochschild, Arlie, and Anne Machung. *The Second Shift: Working Families and the Revolution at Home.* Revised. Penguin Books, 2012. Print.

Katz, Cindi. "Just Managing: American Middle-Class Parenthood in Insecure Times." *The Global Middle Classes: Theorizing Through Ethnography.* Eds. Rachel Heiman, Carla Freeman, and Mark Liechty. Santa Fe: School for Advanced Research Press, 2012. 169-189. Print.

Lareau, Annette. *Unequal Childhoods: Class, Race, and Family Life.* 1st ed. Berkeley: University of California Press, 2003. Print.

Lowrey, Annie. "Do Millennials Stand a Chance in the Real World?" *The New York Times,* 26 Mar. 2013. Web. 6 Apr. 2015.

Laslett, Barbara, and Johanna Brenner. "Gender and Social Reproduction: Historical Perspectives." *Annual Review of Sociology* 15 (1989): 381-404. Print.

Naccarato, Peter, and Kathleen Lebesco. *Culinary Capital.* 1st ed. Oxford: Berg Publishers, 2012. Print.

Perkiss, Abigail. *Making Good Neighbors: Civil Rights, Liberalism, and Integration in Postwar Philadelphia.* 1st edition. Ithaca, NY: Cornell University Press, 2014. Print.

Piketty, Thomas. *Capital in the Twenty-First Century.* Cambridge, Massachusetts: Harvard University Press, 2014. Print.

Reich, Robert. "The Middle-Class Squeeze." *The New York Times,* 22 Jan. 2014. Web. 31 Aug. 2014.

Susser, Ida. "The Flexible Woman Regendering Labor in the Informational Society." *Critique of Anthropology* 17.4 (1997): 389-402. Web. 30 Jan. 2013.

United States. Office of the Surgeon General. "The Surgeon General's Call To Action To Prevent and Decrease Overweight and Obesity (U.S.)." *National Center for Biotechnology Information*. Government of the United States, 2001. Web. 8 Sept. 2015.

United States. U.S. Department of Commerce. U.S. Bureau of Economic Analysis. "National Income and Product Accounts." *National Accounts*. U.S. Department of Commerce, 2014. Web. 28 Aug 2014.

3.
The Critical Kitchen

Public Kitchen Discourses and Private New Zealand Families

RACHEL LAMDIN HUNTER AND KAHURANGI DEY

MOTHERS IN NEW ZEALAND INHABIT a gendered world in which they are commonly (and often solely) responsible for the sourcing, preparation and disposal of family food in their own private homes. This individualized setting for family life appears in "the language and logic of impersonal, competitive, contractual, commoditized, efficient, profit-maximising, self-interested relations" (Hays qtd. in Kinser 316-317). The dynamics described are those we as authors associate with the increasingly dominant influence of neoliberal ideas. David Harvey expresses the practical manifestation of these ideas in the proposition "that human wellbeing can best be advanced by liberating individual entrepreneurial freedoms and skills within an institutional framework characterized by strong private property rights, free markets, and free trade" (3). "The New Zealand Experiment," as outlined by law professor Jane Kelsey, turned a previously social democratic nation into a world model for neoliberalism. The economic and social policy changes initiated in 1984 by a Labour government included a structural adjustment agenda, now usually associated with programs imposed by agencies such as the World Bank and the International Monetary Fund on nations seeking financial assistance. The continuation of the neoliberal agenda in New Zealand beginning in the 1980s and continued by successive governments of differing political orientations has resulted in a unique neoliberal environment that has been in existence for nearly three decades. Our paper reflects on the New Zealand kitchen as an interesting case to highlight the extent to which neoliberal ideas now pervade social spaces.

WORLDS OF WORK AND HOME

In 1988, New Zealander Marilyn Waring's ideas in *Counting for Nothing: What Men Value and What Women Are Worth* about the inclusion, and gendered nature, of the work done by women in systems of national accounts began a journey of ongoing global influence in feminist economics, resulting in change in many countries (Langeland) as well as in alternative measures, such as the United Nation's Human Development Index. In this chapter, we contend that neoliberal and competitive individualistic values, even when shaped to highlight women's contribution as Waring did, are ultimately limiting and, perhaps, even disadvantageous to the well-being of mothers. We support the noticing of politics and policy influencing women's lives that Waring initiated and that has borne results in some nations, as highlighted in Margunn Bjørnholt and Alisa McKay's 2014 edited collection *Counting on Marilyn Waring: New Advances in Feminist Economics*. However, a critical appraisal of the effects (some unintended) of such an approach to the valuing of work done by women cautions us against the wholesale support of a solution that, in the case of national accounts for example, includes more of women's work—the unpaid but productive economy. In this chapter, we argue that the system which has attempted to capture and reflect actual productive human effort has simultaneously introduced a new set of constraining factors to be corralled by women. Dyer, Humphries, Fitzgibbons and Hurd argue that liberal approaches of inclusion (where currently excluded elements are to be assimilated into existing systems) do not transform current neoliberal capitalist oriented systems but, instead, monetize or commodify work that has enduring value over and above economic interests. Similarly, we notice that the work women do is undervalued both economically and socio-politically, which results in women continuing to experience disproportionate disadvantage and financial oppression in the worlds of work and home (Waring).

We take and critique, as our examples, the range of discourses around food and provision of food in families, which are presented to mothers (and other "consumers") in New Zealand.

DISCOURSE AND THE CRITICAL KITCHEN

Our interest in discourse stems from the work of Norman Fairclough, who in *Discourse and Social Change*, suggests researchers appreciate the layering and context of discourses that are inclusive of three features: the textual elements (text dimension); the production and interpretation of texts (referring to discursive practice); and the situational and institutional context (that is, social practices) (4). We understand discourse as the result of a way of thinking or societal background voice that, over time, becomes taken for granted and naturalized, commonly going unnoticed and unquestioned, with effects unintended and uncontested by those whose lives are shaped by the discourse.

Our use of the term "critical kitchen" is in keeping with our approach to the analysis of texts, discourses, and social practices underpinned by neoliberal ideas that shape mothering food practices in New Zealand, a small Pacific country of 4.5 million people. As mothers and critical thinkers, we (the authors) are daily confronted with the nutritional and social needs of our families and children, but we also grapple with our concern for worldwide issues of food, poverty, and the environment, and we know we are not alone. We believe many homes are potential "critical kitchens." Recent research in the field of women's work and family lives indicates that the vast majority of unpaid work at home, including the provision and preparation of food, continues to be undertaken by women (Kan and Gershuny 153; Harkness 253; Lewis 218). In families where there are children, mothers continue to do a disproportionate majority of household work (Crompton and Lyonette 602). And despite increasing numbers of mothers in paid work (Harkness 243), no appreciable uptake of household work or caregiving by other family members has offset this (Esping-Anderson 168). For this reason, it is little wonder that critical thinking with regards to food provision is undertaken by women. Although ways of thinking and societal background voices celebrate neoliberal individualism, the corollary for mothers is a set of circumstances in which they participate in society as employees and workers as well as continuing to be planners, providers, and preparers in their households.

In this chapter, we draw attention to the following two themes that are readily noticeable to us: first, the "frequent family dinners" discourse highlighted and critiqued by Amber Kinser and, second, the "consumer choice" ethos featuring the theme of family (maternal) choice regarding the purchase and preparation of food. We argue that such movements serve to individuate and privatize societal and institutional (or even global) food issues that feature in the work of mothering feminists and eco-feminists such, as Kinser and Vandana Shiva in "Women and the Gendered Politics of Food."

FAMILY MEALTIMES AND FREQUENT FAMILY DINNERS

A dominant part of mothering includes overseeing or assuming responsibility for family nutrition and mealtimes (Kinser), both of which are commonly used by researchers and policymakers as markers or determinants of well-being. Such social research easily becomes prominent media headlines, offering glib, simplistic, and beguiling statements about the importance of family mealtimes, often without any background, qualification, or context to the research. UNICEF, in a 2007 Report Card on child well-being in wealthy nations (of which New Zealand is deemed one), survey the number of times per week that parents and children eat the main meal of the day together at a table (24), in their assessment of children's subjective well-being. UNICEF also reports on the percentage of children in OECD countries who eat breakfast every school day, eat fruit every day, or who are overweight (*Child Poverty in Perspective)*. Hamilton and Hamilton Wilson are among those researchers who also recommend family mealtimes as a protective factor against child and adolescent health problems, including addictions (346). What few researchers point out is the complexity of buying, carrying, storing, planning, cooking, serving and cleaning up from food provision in busy families (Bowen, Elliott, and Brenton 22). Referring to the works of others in this area, Kinser affirms that "those responsible for family meal provision find it a highly complex undertaking even in its most basic forms" (322). Food provision is strongly gendered, and in this, mothers' labour is unnoticed and invisible, believed to be unproblematic, and poorly understood, let alone acknowledged (Kinser). Instead, the external societal gaze on what meals and foods we eat, how often we eat them together, and their possible health effects, have become outward measures of a mother's individual achievement of well-being in her family, and her success as a mother.

Individualized family mealtime discourse individuates social issues, such as child behavioural problems, addictions, and family conflict, leaving each mother to navigate these with the belief that family mealtimes help to secure her children's long-term well-being and life chances (Utter et al., *Eating Together at Mealtimes* 24; Utter et al. "At-Home Breakfast Consumption" 571). Kinser not only critiques the nostalgic emphasis on family mealtimes, behind which the hard work of mothers goes unnoticed, but she also draws attention to societal and institutional factors, rather than individual (family or maternal) choices that drive food selection. She suggests mothers have become "culpable for outcomes that are rooted far outside of them.... These problems sit at the societal, not the individual, level but dominant discourses privatize and individualize them nevertheless" (317). We argue that a persistent privatization of the problem of mealtimes into individual families, with responsibility on individual mothers rather than acceptance of and provision for sustenance in the wider community, is an example of the influence of neoliberal ideas and ideals in this construction of family life.

MULTIPLE DISCOURSES OF CONSUMER CHOICE

In this section, we outline several of many multiple competing discourses that are all about "choice." Textual elements, their production and interpretation, and social practices all reinforce and bolster the notion that mothers (and families) could, or, rather, should, choose these great life-giving options, which are good for the environment, purse, and health, but sometimes struggle with one another. We wonder whether such food discourses resonate with and inspire well-being in families or to what extent they complicate the individualized and disconnected maze that is modern mothering.

In New Zealand, we observe the phenomenon of "The Destitute Gourmet." This is a phenomenon consisting of a blog, website,

Facebook page, series of books, and cooking class events created by New Zealand chef Sophie Gray in her effort to promote "fashionable food that doesn't cost a fortune". Gray includes ideas for judicious supermarket shopping and savvy cost cutting. The message is that with some "clever" thinking and planning, gourmet food is within the financial reach and tight schedule (and hence responsibility) of all families (i.e., mothers) if they choose.

The "quick and easy to prepare" discourse is prevalent in television advertising and programming and is aimed at those who typically shop and cook for their families. British chef Jamie Oliver demonstrates this with the production of a healthy family meal with a mere fifteen minutes of preparation time ("Jamie's 15 Minute Meals"). Supermarket marketers have adopted this challenge also, such as the New World supermarket's "Quick & Easy Dinner Recipes" that take thirty minutes or less to prepare. The same supermarket features a "Meal Maker" section, where all the ingredients for advertised recipes are located in one place. The accompanying message is that mothers who work full time and arrive home tired can now quickly and easily prepare a meal that is nutritious *and* delicious for the whole family.

Mothers are led to believe that quick, cheap, healthy, and delicious food is available if they adopt particular individual tactics of shopping wise, cooking smart, and prioritizing. The "good mother" tries to do it all—make sure food is healthy and nutritious, pay for it, get it home, cook it, and serve it—despite the pressures of business, household budgets, and the intangible, impersonal effects of "the economy." On top of this, she is urged to recognize and choose food that is local, free range, organic, ethical choice, and fair trade. And even with such a critique of the multiple and competing discourses becoming more available in public discourse, the bottom line is still that "if only you mothers would get it right, then feeding your family could be cheap, healthy, and quick."

We notice New Zealand families are presented with the discourses of family mealtimes and consumer choice based on the premise of a seamless and happy family mealtime of quick, cheap, healthy, and delicious food. Although we have used our New Zealand situation to illustrate our argument, we think mothers globally will notice the promises being sold along with food. The discourses are reinforced through national and international policy and practice as a societal must, yet the underlying message is that food and health matters are essentially private individual problems to be solved within families. Our argument is that these messages are problematic for mothers, as they are at odds with the reality of the complexity of managing mealtimes.

FOOD, CHILDREN AND MARKET SOLUTIONS

The curious conflation of food availability with recipe availability or structural factors that affect food availability is noted with concern by Kinser. Recipes are not always within the means of all families. For many low-income households, time- and labour-saving devices are of limited value (despite upbeat media and advertising to the contrary) because multiple and complex pressures remain due to challenges of income and other determinants of capacity and well-being (Kinser).

In New Zealand, we note—along with Max Rashbrooke, in his 2013 edited collection *Inequality: A New Zealand Crisis* contributed to by New Zealand researchers—the phenomenon of widening social inequalities, including household income as well as other social determinants of health (education, employment, housing, access to services, material poverty) and their connection to inequalities in access to and availability of food (Obesity Action Coalition (OAC)/Quigley and Watts Ltd 5-7; St. John and Craig 12-25; Expert Advisory Group on Solutions to Child Poverty 15-16). Bryan Bruce, in his documentary *Inside Child Poverty*, notes that rising inequalities in income levels (as a determinant of health and well-being) have been experienced in New Zealand since neoliberal social and economic reforms began thirty years ago, in a society where a desire for egalitarianism was formerly part of the moral and economic fabric. Growing discontent toward the dominant position of market-led principles in the form of "big business" (e.g., the dairy giant Fonterra) now causes some individuals to question the expense and marketing of particular foods, which over time have become less affordable for many families, in part due to food production and transport costs (Bruce; Edmunds). Since the 1980s, food in New Zealand (the most notable example of which is dairy produce, in particular milk) has become less affordable due to income inequality (St. John and Wynd) and rising prices (Bruce). Also, over this time, the impact of this increasing foodlessness has been felt by the some of the most vulnerable, such that in the second decade of the twenty-first century, one in four New Zealand children live in poverty (Expert Advisory Group on Solutions to Child Poverty).

We read with interest Kinser's statement that

> instability and work environments of low status jobs, as well as the work demands and stress of those jobs, affect food and meal decisions; and that school and work locations impact healthful food access during the day and thus impact health and hunger needs at dinner. (324)

This is of particular importance in New Zealand, where little is collectively provided for children or adults to eat at low cost and convenience during the day; school meals are not universally provided by legislation, thus "family food, wherever it is consumed, is the mainstay of nutrition for NZ School children" (Rockell et al. 203). However, the inequalities now evident in modern neoliberal economies portray a picture of increasing numbers of families who are unable to afford sufficient nutritious food. Growing concern from local agencies focused on child well-being and from recent media attention has resulted in several government and private sector partnerships aimed at ameliorating the effects of poor access to healthy food. Since 2013, KickStart Breakfast (involving the government and large businesses Fonterra and Sanitarium) has provided breakfast in certain (low-income community) schools each weekday morning, and Fonterra is funding a separate Fonterra Milk for Schools program to provide all primary-aged school children with a small carton of milk daily. Such programs might be seen as market-provided solutions to the problems of poor nutrition or availability posed by inequalities characteristic of a neoliberal economy. Prior to 2013, the Red Cross ran a similar program to the Fonterra and Sanitarium KickStart Breakfast. However, the Red Cross program was terminated when the major sponsor withdrew its support. The concern with privatizing and individualizing food issues is that corporate provision of solutions is dependent on the goodwill and continuing financial and managerial commitment of the private organizations. To us, these unintended and uncontested effects of the dominant privatized discourses in a neoliberal market-led economy shape the lives of all in New Zealand.

PRIVATIZATION OF GLOBAL FOOD ISSUES AND GLOBALIZATION OF PRIVATE FOOD ISSUES

Anti-globalization and eco-feminist Vandana Shiva explores the consequences of neoliberal market-led economies on food and women in "Women and the Gendered Politics of Food," and postulates that the work of billions of women has been replaced by "Gene Giant" and "Food Giant" corporations that adopt control of food production and processing worldwide. Power and control shift from women's hands to faceless global corporations, and in the process "[women's] knowledge and work, skills, productivity, and creativity related to food are destroyed" (Shiva, "Women" 27). When the control leaves women's hands, they end up responding to external expectations rather than being self-determining.

In recognizing the specifically gendered (and we would say, power-laden) characteristics of food systems of production, processing, and provision, Shiva in *Soil Not Oil: Climate Change, Peak Oil, and Food Insecurity* argues that power and control of food and food systems should be locally and regionally held rather than globally centralized. At the individual level and in our houses and homes, Shiva urges us to "reclaim the kitchen ... [and reject] frozen dinners and false foods" with a personal connected food consciousness and awareness and an intimacy with food production, preparation, and provision (Shiva qtd. in Shoot 6). As highlighted in many of her works, Shiva's food resistance is based on women's rights to save seeds and be resilient food producers for themselves, their families, and their communities ("Say No," "Women," and *Soil Not Oil*). Arguing against the commodification of food, Shiva, draws links between the subjugated position of women within global food systems and women's different approaches to food as sustenance ("Women" and *Soil Not Oil*). Although our critical imagination cautions us that Shiva's urging risks guilt or shame for mothers in their quest to be good enough or the perfect mother in their role as food provider in their family, we welcome Shiva's contributions and see them as a future direction for research about mothers and food. We believe such thought has potential for mothers in the critical kitchen to begin to reimagine their relationships with food producers, processors, packagers, and presenters.

Shiva notices the problem as well ("Women," *Soil Not Oil*). Yet rather than looking to market provision, she proposes solutions that are local and regional and that give rise to community networks, which provides support to mothers who are otherwise doing it individually and who believe the problem is theirs alone to solve.

Similar to other countries where neoliberal ideas prevail, power and control has become concentrated in New Zealand food industries. Food giants in New Zealand include Fonterra, a major presence in the dairy industry (nationally and globally) and Zespri, the sole seller of New Zealand kiwifruit outside Australasia. Foodstuffs and Progressive Enterprises are the two organizations that dominate the supermarket trade. The comparatively scant population of New Zealand, in relation to its geographical area, creates challenges of logistics in terms of easy food provision (proximity of supermarkets) and transport, particularly in rural areas. We see our geographic location, rural population needs, small population, and schooling context as constraining factors, which means access to shops and supermarkets is limited for many, both rural and urban, and little food is provided outside of private homes. In accordance with our rural location and small population, few choices are available for families to "eat out" other than take-away bars or fast food chains, mostly in towns and cities. Supermarket convenience food includes prepackaged meals or "TV dinners," but these are not widely used. Such a lack of access and social provision augments pressure on mothers, even as they are asked to believe that they are faced with "choice" regarding family food.

CONCLUSION

With the recognized moral load placed on the importance of food—not just nutritional value and calories consumed but also a measure of social well-being—we the authors note with concern the influences of these diverse and varying discourses on the work that mothers do in providing food for their families in an era of intensifying neoliberalism. Our thinking has moved us to critically appreciate the possibilities for women in New Zealand by understanding some of the discourses that pervade popular media. We critique these discourses that we believe stem from a neoliberal food rhetoric. We believe that even though such discourses may be intended to make life easier, overall they stem from a market-dominated system that makes life harder by individuating many of the global issues, such as cheap and quick food. The problems of food provision for mothers in New Zealand are corporatized world problems; problems of a world where nutrition, family time, and sustenance are increasingly commercialized and commodified. These problems are not specific to New Zealand, we know that they are being experienced the world over. We consider that the contrast between New Zealand before the neoliberal policies and New Zealand today is stark and conclude that so-called progress for women in neoliberal economies has come at a price that is demonstrated in family mealtimes and nutrition.

WORKS CITED

Bjørnholt, Margunn, and Alisa McKay. *Counting on Marilyn Waring: New Advances in Feminist Economics*. Bradford, Ontario: Demeter, 2014. Print.

Bowen, Sarah, Sinikka Elliott, and Joslyn Brenton. "The Joy of Cooking." *Contexts* 13.3 (2014): 20-25. Web. 17 Feb. 2015.

Bruce, Bryan, dir. "Inside Child Poverty—A Special Report [Motion Picture]." *TV 3*. MediaWorks TV 2011. Web. 8 Sept. 2015.

Crompton, Rosemary, and Clare Lyonette. "The New Gender Essentialism—Domestic and Family "Choices" and Their Relation to Attitudes." *The British Journal of Sociology* 56 (4) (2005): 601-620. Print.

Dyer, Suzette, Maria Humphries, Dale Fitzgibbons, and Fiona Hurd. *Understanding Management Critically: A Student Text*. London, UK: Sage, 2013. Print.

Edmunds, Susan. "Food Glorious Food—But What a Price." *New Zealand Herald*, 29 Jan. 2012. Web. 08 Sept. 2015.

Esping-Andersen, Gosta. *The Incomplete Revolution: Adapting Welfare States to Women's New Roles*. Cambridge UK: Polity Press. 2009. Print.

Expert Advisory Group on Solutions to Child Poverty. *Solutions to Child Poverty in New Zealand: Evidence for Action. Office of the Children's Commissioner*. N.p., 2012. Web. 08 Sept. 2015.

Fairclough, Norman. *Discourse and Social Change*. Cambridge, Mass: Polity Press. 1992. Print.

Gray, Sophie. *Destitute Gourmet*. N.p. n.d. Web. 22 August 2014

Hamilton, Susan, and Jane Hamilton Wilson. "Family Mealtimes: Worth the Effort?" *ICAN: Infant, Child, and Adolescent Nutrition* 1.6 (2009): 346-350. Print.

Harkness, Susan. "The Household Division of Labour: Changes in Families' Allocation of Paid and Unpaid Work." *Women and Employment*. Eds. J. Scott and H. Joshi. Cheltenam, UK: Edward Elgar Publishing, 2008. 234-267. Print.

Kan, Man Yee, and Jonathan Gershuny. "Gender Segregation and Bargaining in Domestic Labour: Evidence from Longitudinal Time Use Data." *Gender Inequalities in the 21st Century*. Eds. R. Crompton and J. Scott. Cheltenham, UK: Edward Elgar Publishing, 2009. 153-173. Print.

Kelsey, Jane. *The New Zealand Experiment: A World Model for Structural Adjustment*. Auckland, NZ: Auckland University Press, 1995. Print.

Kinser, Amber E. "At the Core of the Work/Life Balance Myth: Motherhood and Family Dinners." *What Do Mothers Need? Motherhood Activists and Scholars Speak out on Maternal Empowerment for the 21st Century*. Ed. A. O'Reilly. Bradford, Ontario: Demeter Press, 2012: 316-330. Print.

Langeland, Terje. "Women Unaccounted for in Global Economy Proves Waring Influence." *bloomberg.com*. Bloomberg, 19 June 2013. Web. 5 July 2013.

Lewis, Jand. "Gender Equality and Work-Family Balance in a Cross-National Perspective." *Gendered Lives: Gender Inequalities in Production and Reproduction*. Eds. J. Scott, S. Dex, and A.C Plagnol. Cheltenham, UK: Edward Elgar Publishing, 2012. 206-224. Print.

Obesity Action Coalition (OAC)/Quigley and Watts Ltd. *A Rapid*

Review of the Literature on the Association Between Nutrition and School Pupil Performance. Agencies for Nutrition Action. Agencies for Nutrition Action, 2005. Web. 8 Sept. 2015.

Oliver, Jamie. *Jamie's 15-Minute Meals.* London: Michael Joseph. 2012. Print.

Rashbrooke, Max. *Inequality: A New Zealand Crisis.* Wellington, NZ: Bridget Williams Books. 2013. Print.

Rockell, Jennifer. E., Winsome R. Parnell, Noela C. Wilson, Paula M. Skidmore, and Asher Regan. "Nutrients and Foods Consumed by New Zealand Children on Schooldays and Non-Schooldays." *Public Health Nutrition* 14.2 (2010): 203-208. Web. 8 Sept. 2015.

Shiva, Vandana. "Say No to Western Rejects: Neoliberal Policies Have Taken a Toll on Our Ecosystem. But More and More Indians Are Rising to Defend Nature's Gifts." *indiatoday.intoday.in*. India Today, 26 Dec. 2011. Web. 8 Sept. 2015.

Shiva, Vandana. "Women and the Gendered Politics of Food." *Philosophical Topics* 37 (2) (2009): 17-32. Print.

Shiva, Vandana. *Soil Not Oil: Climate Change, Peak Oil, and Food Insecurity.* London, UK: Zed Books. 2008. Print.

Shoot, Brittany. "Why Organic Farming Will Save the World." *Herizons* 16 (2010): 16-19. Web. 08 Sept. 2015.

St. John, Susan, and David Craig. *Cut Price Kids: Does the 2004 "Working for Families" Budget Work for Children? Child Poverty Action Group*. N.p, 2004. Web 8 Sept. 2015.

St. John, Susan, and Donna Wynd. *Left Behind: How Social and Income Inequalities Damage New Zealand Children. Child Poverty Action Group*. N.p, 2008. Web. 8 Sept. 2015.

United Nations International Children's Fund (UNICEF). *Child Poverty in Perspective: An Overview of Child Well-being in Rich Countries.* Florence, Italy: Innocenti Research Centre. 2007. Print.

Utter, Jennifer, Simon Denny, Sue Grant, Elizabeth Robinson, Shanthi Ameratunga, and Terry Fleming. *Eating Together at Mealtimes: The Role of Family Meals in the Health and Wellbeing of Young People in New Zealand. Families Commission—Social Policy Research and Evaluation Unit (SUPERU)*. SUPERU, 2011. Web. 8 Sept. 2015.

Utter, Jennifer., Robert Scragg, Cliona Ni Mhurchu, and David Schaaf. "At-Home Breakfast Consumption among New Zealand

Children: Associations with Body Mass Index and Related Nutrition Behaviours." *Journal of the American Dietetic Association* 107.4 (2007): 570-576. Print.

Waring, Marilyn. *Counting for Nothing: What Men Value and What Women Are Worth*. Wellington, New Zealand: Allen & Unwin/Port Nicholson Press. 1988. Print.

4.

Nurturing the Sustainable Family

Natural Parenting and Environmentalist Foodways in Francophone Contexts

FLORENCE PASCHE GUIGNARD

MOTHERS WHO, TO VARIOUS EXTENTS, include "eco-friendly" ideals and practices in their everyday mother work are known in Anglo-American contexts as "sustainable mothers" (Takeshita), "green moms," "eco-moms," or, simply, "natural moms." In a variety of Francophone media, mothers who engage in natural family living are often referred to as *les mamans nature* (the "nature moms"), a label that some of them reclaim, at least within their online communities, while others reject it. This contribution examines only a few of the many research areas raised by the issues of food and feeding within natural parenting. For the Francophone mothers whom I interviewed[1] as part of a larger research project[2] and whose publicly accessible conversations I followed online, commitments inspired by environmentalist discourses are particularly clear in their consumption choices and diets that differ from prevailing norms (e.g., decreasing or avoiding meat consumption, preferring organic food, buying local, etc.). Two important notions are recurring in their discursive strategies of accountability: that of "nurturing the sustainable family" and that of a "sustainable environmentalism." Although both are implemented mostly by mothers in these European Francophone contexts, they may, nevertheless, be read as a form of resistance against the child-centredness of the ideology of intensive mothering (Hays).

Natural parenting can be defined as a cluster of representations, discourses, and practices that borrow most of the basic tenets of attachment parenting and add to them a specific environmentalist agenda. Natural parenting is often in line with lifestyles of health and sustainability (as studied by Emerich) and voluntary simplicity, also known as "frugal" or "simple living" (Bobel 49). I examined discourses about foodways that are found more frequently though not exclusively among these families where mothers (and often fathers as well) pay particular attention to issues of health and sustainability. That "natural" processes are valued over "artificial" or "technological" ones does not imply an indiscriminate rejection of *all* forms of technology. Rather, natural mothers engage in a careful examination of the benefits and risks of late twentieth and early twenty-first-century technology, especially in the domains of medicine, nutrition, and communication. "High-tech" means are used to communicate and promote lifestyles and techniques of parenting that are perceived as rather "low-tech" and that tend to go against the grain of mainstream parenting in their particular contexts. Generally supportive online communities articulated around shared beliefs and practices give natural parenting an important presence and visibility in the online "mamasphere."

Although natural parenting constitutes a mediated and international phenomenon, my research focused mostly on Francophone contexts in Europe. There, mothers from various socio-economic statuses and levels of education[3] espouse the principles of natural parenting to various extents. Only a few of them would readily self-identify as "green angel[s] in the house" (Redela 195) or as "radical homemakers reclaiming domesticity from a consumer culture" (as in the title of Hayes's book). More than half of the twenty-five mothers whom I interviewed so far (along with a few fathers), work outside of the home for a wage (at least part-time) or expected to shortly return to paid work. Staying at home was not necessarily a "choice" for the mothers who did so: many stayed home because their partners were paid significantly more or because they could not find work, were on extended sick leave, or were temporarily benefitting from financially generous, extended parental leaves (in France and in Canada, but not in Switzerland or Belgium). Many of the at home mothers whom I interviewed nevertheless embraced this situation and insisted on its positive aspects for both themselves and their children.

In the contexts surveyed for this research, both the "attachment parenting" and the environmentalist components of "natural parenting" are subject to criticism coming from (1) conventional Western biomedicine healthcare providers (particularly opposed to practices such as home birth, vaccine hesitancy, or co-sleeping), (2) some feminists (see Badinter), (3) older generations of (grand)parents, (4) parents of the same generation who follow conventional norms, and (5) mainstream media. The latter tend to caricature the *mamans nature* and their practices in a negative light. Among others, natural parenting is perceived as too demanding for mothers who have to be at the service of their children constantly, available on demand (in the case of breastfeeding, for instance), or who have to perform the "extra work" required by some environmentally friendly practices or objects (like using washable diapers)[4]. In France, over 80 percent of the care and domestic work at home is still performed by women, and having a child accentuates the imbalance between men and women (Régnier-Loilier). This, however, is not a new phenomenon and is the case also for parents who follow conventional styles of childrearing. Environmentalist imperatives alone cannot be blamed for patriarchal domination, gender inequality in the domestic sphere, and all the pressures exercised on mothers regarding children's nutrition. Whether potatoes are organic or conventionally grown does not itself determine whether the mother, the father, or someone else will have to purchase or grow them, prepare and supervise the meal, and clean up the kitchen afterwards.

The food practices of the mothers whom I interviewed combine the ethical, health, and environmental imperatives of natural parenting with a typical "French parenting" approach to food and feeding. As described for instance by Druckerman and Le Billon, such an approach emphasizes the fact that adults are in charge of decisions regarding food. My informants take nutritional benefits into consideration, but they are also concerned about the environmental and social impact of their consumption on local and global economies. Their conversations frequently include the topic of the potential damages to what they refer to as "nature," "the environment," "the planet," or "the Earth." As ethical or "engaged consumers" (Dubuisson-Quellier), natural mothers also seek and spread information about the production, packaging, and transportation of food as well as issues such as industrial and domestic food waste.

Seeing themselves as the first in line to implement privatized solutions to what they see as global issues, my informants seek to bring "local solutions to global disorders," as in the title of Coline Serreau's influential documentary referred to by several of them. Because they feel helpless about "changing the world" or "society as a whole," they turn to a form of "inward change." Their motivation is not only an individual and consumerist response to dealing with risk, called "inverted quarantine" (Szasz), but also a small step towards global improvement, which includes "nurturing" children through attempting to convey to them specific values and a desire for social justice and environmental sustainability. These mothers actively reclaim the agency that they have as engaged consumers, in their domestic food practices and through their mothering.

NURTURING THE SUSTAINABLE FAMILY VERSUS FEEDING THE ORGANIC CHILD

Fabienne, one of my informants and a French mother in her early thirties, lives with her three-year-old and her Swiss husband in their newly built eco-house near Geneva. She gave birth at home with a midwife, used washable diapers, and now resorts to homeopathic medicine to treat her not yet vaccinated but rarely ill daughter, whom she breastfed for fourteen months. Fabienne describes her lifestyle as one of "voluntary simplicity." She prefers buying organic and fair trade products "though not exclusively." Her style of parenting and many of her choices are rather uncommon among her circle of friends and relatives, some of whom have nicknamed her daughter "*le bébé bio*" (the organic baby). This designation resonates with that of the "organic child," coined by Cairns, Johnston, and MacKendrick in their study on "mothering through ethical consumption" in a North American context.

According to Cairns and her colleagues, the figure of the organic child "reflects the intersecting ideals of motherhood and alternative consumption, which work together to define good mothers as those who preserve their children's purity and protect the environment through conscientious food purchases" (101). In the following, I contrast their concept of "feeding the organic child" with that of "nurturing the sustainable family." Using the plural figure of the "sustainable family" as a metaphor for this Francophone European approach to the intersection of food and parenting informed by environmentalist imperatives, I underline its characteristics and the emphasis it places on maternal or familial convenience. Real or alleged benefits *to the child* are not the primary focus of such discourses.

The European "sustainable family" and the North American "organic child" should not be understood as radically opposed, however, as both certainly can be found on both sides of the Atlantic and in other contexts as well. Like Fabienne, several of my informants have heard this label of "organic baby" applied to their children, sometimes as a derogatory statement over the present or anticipated results of their unconventional mothering. My intention in contrasting the two figures is rather to point out how discourses by Francophone mothers themselves take into account wider perspectives in defining an alternative norm of "good motherhood." Elements of these definitions might bear similarity, but mothers emphasize and prioritize them differently.

Although practices such as buying certified organic food or cooking from scratch are found in both contexts, the discursive strategies that account for them are different in scope and focus. The mother of the sustainable family does not define her mothering primarily or exclusively through food purchases and alternative consumption, but through a range of other practices and preferences for options that she constructs not only as "healthy" but also as "sustainable." Examples of this holistic and extended definition of sustainability include using or making herbal remedies and homemade cosmetics or refusing to buy certain items, even "healthy" ones, because of the excessive plastic packaging. More importantly, the notion of sustainability extends to the practices themselves and not only to their results: it must be sustainable *for the mother herself* to include environmentally friendly practices, especially those that involve food work, into her parenting style.

In the discourses of most *mamans nature*, the focus shifts away from the child and his or her health as the measure of "good motherhood" to be replaced on the family as a whole, with attention also paid to its adult members (including themselves and the father). Holistic notions of local sustainability, fairness in international trade, social justice, convenience, pleasure in taste, and feeding children often take precedence over notions of risk, health, and purity that appear to be central to the motivations of the Canadian mothers studied by Cairns, Johnston and MacKendrick. I asked mothers from France why they breastfed and often did so for a time longer than average in a context where the breastfeeding initiation rate is only sixty-nine percent (according to a 2012 study conducted in France, see Salanave et al.) and weaning of most babies occurs within the first few months. Their answers were varied. These are some of the common reasons they mentioned: "Because it is convenient" or "Because I am too lazy to prepare and wash bottles or get up at night" or "Because I enjoy breastfeeding and it is easier than bottle-feeding." One mother who was trying to live a more radical form of frugal living even expressed the idea that refusing to give her money to industrial agribusiness corporations was an act of "resistance against an unfair system" (*un système injuste*). She saw her breastfeeding as a form of boycott and as a personal empowerment: her lactation placed her into the active role of food producer rather than in that of dependent consumer.

A few mothers also pointed out the environmental dimension of breastfeeding and that of "proximity," echoing both the notion of "*maternage proximal*" (a term used to describe a range of attachment parenting practices emphasizing bodily closeness) and that of locavore ideals. Just as the groceries that these mothers purchase come from trusted local producers or retailers (such as farmers markets or cooperatives), their own human milk, too, comes from a trusted and local source and needs no packaging and transportation. One vegan mother also explained to me that human milk does not derive from animal exploitation (of dairy cows), which she opposed on ethical grounds through anti-specist argumentation.

The mothers whom I interviewed never denied that breastfeeding benefits babies, but this was not always central in their discourse.

Rather than reciting the "breast is best" motto,[5] which would also work to qualify them as good mothers (at least for the first few months) in this context, they emphasized that this type of infant nutrition was their "choice," a convenient one for them, and a "natural" one at that, despite the paradox (see Bobel).

Health is not the only criteria in the principles guiding the feeding practices and consumption of the *mamans nature*. Most of them are well aware that "organic" does not always equal "sustainable." Each one of the mothers I talked to has particular demands (on herself and other family members, as well as on retailers or producers). Their criteria for food choices range widely: most have expectations that are idealistic but not always enforced, and some, more rarely, implement a strict ethos that binds the mother as the family's principal shopper or producer, in the case she gardens or is an active participant in a food co-op.

Most of my informants adhered to the idea that a mother is responsible not only for the health of all family members, including herself, but also for the consequences of their consumption on the family and on the planet. Moreover, many also insisted that the practices involving some supplementary planning and domestic work should be a voluntary *choice* that they engage in out of conviction and not a burden. Johanne, a Swiss mother of two children aged one and three, repeatedly underlined that whichever choices she made in her parenting and lifestyle were *hers* and taken in complete agreement with her husband, though never imposed by him. For instance, she chose to no longer resort to hormonal contraceptives, to avoid vaccinating her children, and to use cloth diapers for her children and washable menstrual hygiene products for herself. She insisted that she was completely in control, coherent, and not influenced by any group or doctrine while making these choices. Johanne defined herself as "apolitical" and as a "non-practising Christian," not as an active member of any religious or cultural association. When I asked Johanne about decisions regarding food in her household, she answered the following, using the French indefinite pronoun "*on*" (here translated as "we"), thus speaking in her and her partner's voice:

We favour what is local, organic, and biodynamic[6] within

> *the limits of our budget* [dans les limites de nos finances].... *Now we [rent] a house with a garden, so we can have a vegetable garden* [jardin potager], *but we are not rigid about it.... [For instance, if we want] strawberries, we do our best to wait until they are in season. [We normally] try to [eat] fruits only when they are in season. We are lucky to live beside a [farm] centre that has a self-service biodynamic garden* [potager]. *So, automatically, we tap into it. But it is true that, for instance, if I feel like having an avocado, I will buy an organic avocado, even if it comes from Peru. So, we are not going to restrain ourselves because the fruit has been transported for thousands of kilometres. We are not completely rigid about this. We practice an environmentalism that is ... I want to say "smart" but this is not the [appropriate] term. We are not aggressive, sectarian, or whatever. We practice an environmentalism that we can sustain and that allows us to live. We are careful with electricity and water. We tend to be into "degrowth"* [on est plutôt en décroissance]. *We buy almost exclusively second-hand items. But if we need a new computer, even if the old one still works, but is too slow, then we will buy a new computer.... We try to do a conscious environmentalism* [une écologie consciente], *but, sometimes, we go further than other [people go], also out of economical reasons* [aussi par économie] ... *For instance up to three quarters of our cupboards are filled with clothes from Caritas or the Red Cross [thrift stores] because this participates in such an effort, but [it is] also an economical one.*

For Johanne, buying an imported (but organic) avocado is the exception that confirms the rule. She characterizes the choices that she and her family engage in as an "effort." Nevertheless, Johanne does not let a strict environmentalist agenda dictate all of her choices, and she used this example to illustrate her flexibility. At the time of our interview, Johanne and her husband both worked in education and research, but she held a part-time position. Their minimal income did not prevent the lifestyle sought by Johanne. That such practices are valued in lifestyles of voluntary simplicity and that they also participate in an environmentalist effort allow mothers to rebrand them as "good practices," that they embrace with awareness rather than under constraint.

Just like the Canadian mothers "feeding the organic child" studied by Cairns, Johnston, and MacKendrick, the Francophone mothers I talked to mentioned health issues and the fear of pesticide residues and other chemicals as a motivation for buying (or growing) organic food, along with a general distrust of conventional agriculture and of processed industrialized foods. In addition, many of them also mentioned their desire to support local economies through purchasing their food directly from small local producers and farmers. This was the case for Gwenaëlle, a French mother in her forties living in Britanny. For health reasons, and after many experiments, she had adopted a paleo diet that required her to consume considerable amounts of high-quality meat. Her husband and their eight-year-old son also were following this diet, though less strictly. After mentioning that her spouse was doing most of the cooking at home, she added that he bought their meat from local producers whom they "trusted" ("*on leur fait confiance*"). Well aware that she lives in an area of France famous for its meat production, Gwenaëlle also emphasized her desire to support the local economy. Other informants mentioned the absence of long-distance transportation, freshness, taste, and a generally superior quality of the produce as incentives for buying from local producers or farmers markets. For many of them, the preference for locally sourced food frequently trumps the criteria of *official* organic certification.

FOOD, FEEDING, AND NATURAL PARENTING IN FRANCOPHONE CONTEXTS

Prevailing discourses *about* natural parenting or *by* mothers who engage in natural family living in Anglo-American contexts tend to focus on the expected benefits to the child of following certain principles and practices, such as those of attachment parenting (Faircloth, *Militant Lactivism;* "Attachment Mothering"). Other factors in their food choices, such as promoting sustainable local economies or fair trade, add to common concerns centred around the contested topics of appropriate nutrition, risk (of contamination and deficiency), children's health (illness, obesity), growth, and acceptable body shape. In keeping with dominant discourses about food and parenting in France and the wider Francophone area, mothers rarely place their children's taste preferences at the centre of their choices. The motivations of the mothers who "nurture the sustainable family" tend to shift the focus away from feeding the individual "organic child" and place it on themselves or on their family as a whole, while they acknowledge their insertion into wider and complex networks of social and economic interactions at local and global levels. Even though they engage in individual efforts, mostly in the domestic sphere through ethical or minimized consumption, the *mamans nature* refuse to endorse the full responsibility for preventing pollution and environmental degradation. They also challenge the notion that "we each can protect the earth by changing our day-to-day practices" (Takeshita 129). In the short term, what they really seek to change (or maintain) is their family's lifestyle and an increase in the quality of their living standards (*qualité de vie*) that include tasty meals cooked with fresh, quality ingredients. Although their rhetoric partially corresponds to that of individualized and privatized strategies of North American "sustainable motherhood," Francophone mothers also are critical about "green washing" marketing and about the enforcement of a form of green *total motherhood* (Wolf) on them. Instead, their discourses do not spare criticism against exploitative and unsustainable agribusiness and unfair governmental policies on health and agriculture, even if they concentrate their efforts on individual, privatized, and domestic efforts, where they feel that they have the most effective and immediate agency.

Taste and pleasure in meals taken in (good) company are central to the French acceptation of "commensality" or eating together (in the sense of sitting together at the table to eat the same meal at the same time). Giving children a food education that includes not just knowledge about nutrition but also proper table manners and a sensorial taste literacy (*une éducation au goût*) is a duty attributed chiefly, though not exclusively,[7] to mothers. In addition to such norms about food and feeding children, the mothers in my study also emphasized their engagement with "sustainable environmentalism" (*une écologie durable*). Sustainability is given as one of the principal reasons for following organic diets, whenever this made sense to them ethically, financially, and practically. Choosing their food with care and paying attention to their consumption habits were perceived as central to an everyday practice imbued with a sense of morality and responsibility towards the environment, their own children and future generations as well. The idea of "nurturing the sustainable family," thus, conveys the idea that such choices are explained to children and communicated to them as representative of a certain ethic (based on values such as compassion, responsibility, and coherence). Although the notion of preserving ecosystems, near or far, is important to them, my informants rarely claim to engage in environmentally friendly practices for the sake of "saving the planet" or of nature[8] itself. Rather, they emphasized a better quality of their present life as their immediate goal. The ecofeminist and often spiritualized notion of "Mother Earth" or "Mother Nature" is almost absent from their discourses. The only mother that matters is the one who does the actual job of nurturing the sustainable family.

Despite some extra labour involved, which their discursive strategies tended to minimize, the mothers whom I interviewed stress the pleasure they derive from practices that they frame as environmentally friendly, such as breastfeeding, cooking from scratch, or gardening. They repeatedly refute the idea that such choices are enforced on them (whether by an individualistic neoliberal environmentalist ethos, by their male partners, by their alternative healthcare providers, by specific religious groups, etc.). Although they recognize the necessity of someone engaging in practical care work that includes providing, preparing, and serving food, they generally emphasize that they, as mothers, are not the only ones who can do it. Far from completely embracing (as described in Paltineau 122-134) the ideal of "intensive mothering" (Hays), these Francophone mothers resist it to some extent by shifting the focus away from the child and back onto themselves. When this was the case, they insisted that their (male) partners were as much involved (or more) than they were in domestic, food and childcare work and were willing to allocate sufficient resources to support such choices.

"Feeding the organic child" (Cairns, Johnston, and MacKendrick) is not seen as an ultimate ideal to be reached but rather as a potential result from a larger perspective that consists in "nurturing the sustainable family." This includes a desire for "green living" through ethical consumption and ideals of voluntary simplicity or even, for a few among the mothers most radically engaged in frugal living, that of *décroissance*, with all its political implications (Latouche).[9] Their notion of sustainability usually is far reaching: this lifestyle must be sustainable for all, including mothers themselves. This means that compromise is acceptable. Mitigation of certain demands sometimes is recognized as a necessity and not as a failure, neither in mothering nor in the commitment towards environmentally friendly diets and lifestyles. In addition, other criteria, such as proximity or seasonality, are privileged over the consumerist imperative of "*buying* organic." More importantly, ideological agendas, including environmentalist ones, should not render a mother tired and unhappy. As it is understood and implemented in the European Francophone contexts I surveyed, natural parenting requires awareness, extended planning skills, some supplementary work, but no sacrificial attitude. The potential constraints or restrictions arising from extending the principles of lifestyles of health and sustainability to parenting and food work are not seen as oppressive by my informants but as necessary, and sometimes even pleasant, efforts. For most of them, the goal is not to reach an ideal but to tend to it. These mothers emphasize the quality of life that their environmentally minded mothering immediately affords them and not just their children. They acknowledge their own incoherencies and imperfections while deriving satisfaction from the practices that they engage in.

NOTES

[1]Research interviews were conducted in French. All translations in this chapter are my own. I use pseudonyms to name all of my informants in this contribution.

[2]I acknowledge funding from the Swiss National Science Foundation for two postdoctoral mobility fellowships granted for the completion of the research project entitled *Natural Parenting*

in the Digital Age. At the Confluence of Mothering, Religion, Environmentalism, and Technology. I thank the Department for the Study of Religion at the University of Toronto for hosting me during this project.

[3]The socio-economic status of my informants has a wider range than that of Bobel's American informants (most of whom were middle-class wives and mothers). Her study on the "paradox of natural mothering" is based on fieldwork conducted in the U.S. in the late 1990s.

[4]Lalanne and Lapeyre have discussed the specific case of washable diapers. For a more general criticism, see Badinter.

[5]There is no widespread equivalent in French to the catchy expression in English "breast is best."

[6]Biodynamic agriculture is a holistic and sustainable method of organic farming that often goes beyond the demands of regular organic certification. It is inspired by the philosophy of Rudolf Steiner (1861-1925), and it is popular among proponents of anthroposophy.

[7]In France, this responsibility is partially shared with schools that offer hot school lunch programs to all students (*la cantine*) and that include in their curriculum activities in "taste education," such as the "week of taste" (*la semaine du goût*).

[8]For a mostly secular context (especially in France) and in contrast with specific North American discourses that derive meaning from spiritual or religious traditions, my Francophone informants rarely draw from ecofeminist positions. Concepts such as "Mother Earth" or "Mother Nature" are more popular in certain North American discourses on sustainable motherhood but are not characteristic in similar Francophone discourses.

[9]There are several definitions for the economic, political, and social concept of *décroissance* that I translate here with the English word degrowth. One of the main ideas it conveys is that unlimited economic growth is not necessarily beneficial to society and individuals. Although this is technically imprecise, several of my informants used the term "*décroissance*" to refer to their own practices of ethical consumption, minimized consumption, lifestyles of voluntary simplicity, frugal living, or participation in collaborative economies.

WORKS CITED

Badinter, Elisabeth. *Le Conflit: La femme et la mère*. Paris: Flammarion, 2010. Print.

Bobel, Chris. *The Paradox of Natural Mothering*. Philadelphia: Temple University Press, 2002. Print.

Cairns, Kate, Josée Johnston, and Norah MacKendrick. "Feeding the 'Organic Child': Mothering through Ethical Consumption." *Journal of Consumer Culture* 13.2 (2013): 97–118. Print.

Druckerman, Pamela. *Bébé Day by Day. 100 Keys to French Parenting*. New York: The Penguin Press, 2013. Print.

Druckerman, Pamela. *Bringing Up Bébé. One American Mother Discovers the Wisdom of French Parenting*. New York: The Penguin Press, 2012. Print.

Dubuisson-Quellier, Sophie. *La consommation engagée*. Paris: Presses de Sciences Po, 2009. Print.

Emerich, Monica. *The Gospel of Sustainability: Media, Market and LOHAS*. Urbana: University of Illinois Press. 2011. Print.

Faircloth, Charlotte. *Militant Lactivism? Attachment Parenting and Intensive Motherhood in the UK and France*. Oxford: Berghahn Books, 2013. Print.

Faircloth, Charlotte. "Is Attachment Mothering Intensive Mothering?" *Intensive Mothering: The Cultural Contradictions of Modern Motherhood*. Ed. Linda Rose Ennis. Bradford, Ontario: Demeter Press, 2015. 180-193. Print.

Hayes, Shannon. *Radical Homemakers: Reclaiming Domesticity from a Consumer Culture*. Richmondville: Left to Write Press, 2010. Print.

Hays, Sharon. *The Cultural Contradictions of Motherhood*. New Haven: Yale University Press, 1996. Print.

Lalanne, Michèle, and Nathalie Lapeyre. "L'engagement écologique au quotidien a-t-il un genre?" *Recherches Féministes* 22.1 (2009): 47-68. Web. 16 Oct. 2013.

Latouche, Serge. *Petit traité de la décroissance sereine*. Paris: Mille et une Nuits, 2007. Print.

Le Billon, Karen. *French Kids Eat Everything {And Yours Can Too}: How Our Family Moved to France, Cured Picky Eating,*

Banned Snacking, and Discovered 10 Simple Rules for Raising Happy, Healthy Eaters. Toronto: HarperCollins, 2012. Print.

Paltineau, Maya-Merida. "From Intensive Mothering to Identity Parenting." *Intensive Mothering: The Cultural Contradictions of Modern Motherhood.* Ed. Linda Rose Ennis. Bradford, Ontario: Demeter Press, 2015. 120-141. Print.

Redela, Pamela Morgan. "Eco-Momma: The Green Angel in the House." *Stay-at-Home Mothers. Dialogues and Debates.* Eds. Elizabeth Reid Boyd and Gayle Letherby. Bradford, Ontario: Demeter Press, 2014. 195-201. Print.

Régnier-Loilier, Arnaud. "L'arrivée d'un enfant modifie-t-elle la répartition des tâches domestiques au sein du couple?" *Population & Société Bulletin mensuel d'information de l'Institut national d'études démographiques* 461 (2009): 1-4. Print.

Salanave, Benoît, Catherine de Launay, Caroline Guerrisi, and Katia Castetbon. "Taux d'allaitement maternel à la maternité et au premier mois de l'enfant. Résultats de l'étude Épifane, France, 2012." *Bulletin épidémiologique hebdomadaire* 34 (2012): 383-387. Web. 14 May 2015.

Serreau, Coline, dir. *Solutions locales pour un désordre global.* Memento Films Distribution, 2010. Film.

Szasz, Andrew. *Shopping Our Way to Safety: How We Changed from Protecting the Environment to Protecting Ourselves.* Minneapolis: University of Minnesota Press, 2007. Print.

Takeshita, Chikako. "Eco-Diapers: The American Discourse on Sustainable Motherhood." *Mothering in the Age of Neoliberalism.* Ed. Melinda Vandenbeld Giles. Bradford, Ontario: Demeter Press, 2014. 117-131. Print.

Wolf, Joan B. *Is Breast Best? Taking on the Breastfeeding Experts and the New High Stakes of Motherhood.* New York: New York University Press, 2010. Print.

II.
HEALTH, MEDICINE, AND NUTRITION

5.
Mothering Discourse and the Marketing of Dairy as a Cancer-Fighting Food

ALISSA OVEREND

DESCRIBED AS THE MOST FEARED of modern diseases (Lupton), cancer is the leading cause of death in Canada (Canada, Statistics Canada), the second leading cause of death in the United States (United States, the U.S. Department of Health and Human Services, Centers for Disease Control and Prevention), and the seventh leading cause of death worldwide (World Health Organization). Cancer is linked in the Western cultural imaginary with premature and slow death, merciless treatments, contagion and a lack of control over the illness, and with a lurking, unpredictable, and elusive presence (Sontag). With much uncertainty and fear surrounding what has been euphemistically dubbed the "big C" (Clarke), it is not surprising that food is increasingly marketed as an individualized way to reduce one's risk of illness. As Halkier points out, "media discourses and communication campaigns ascribe responsibility to individual ordinary food consumers for helping to solve such societal problems by changing their daily routines" (89).

Although early links between cancer and diet were largely dismissed (Johnson and Fenwick), widespread acceptance, along with new evidence, of the role of diet in cancer prevention and treatment is growing. According to the American and Canadian Cancer Societies, diet affects as much as one third of all cancers. If the more acknowledged role of dietary risk factors is combined with cancer's epidemic status, alongside aggressive advertising campaigns, it is easy to see why consumer consciousness concerning cancer and food has piqued. One need not look far for books, websites, television talk shows, commercials, movies, and government documents laden with advice, opinions, recipes, and testimonials regarding "cancer-fighting" foods. Diets high in fruits and vegetables have consistently been associated with the risk reduction—and in some cases disease reversal—of cancer (Johnson and Fenwick; Weldon). The role of other food items in the fight against cancer, however, remains both ambiguous and contentious. With many potential food heroes and villains at the table, arguably none is as controversial, at least in Western contexts, as dairy. Inundated between the supposed benefits of "got milk," and the presumed controversies of "not milk," it is increasingly consumers who are left to siphon through the "babble of voices" that speak to cancer and dairy options (Tulloch and Lupton 365) in an attempt to decipher "who [or what] can we trust" (Tulloch and Lupton 364).

Depending on which consumer-available information, dairy consumption, on the one hand, reduces one's risk of cancer and, on the other hand, increases it. This contradictory message is complicated by the fact that both dairy and cancer take many forms and that cancer has many other environmental triggers (Moorman and Terry). Yet despite the ongoing confusion, milk's paradoxical health message persists. Smith-Howard details that "from the turn of the twentieth century, milk and dairy foods have simultaneously been presented to consumers as pure products of nature *and* as products remade by human intervention and modern technologies" (3, emphasis in original). Although there are many facets of dairy's ambiguity that I find both intellectually compelling and troubling, what I focus on in this discussion is how its construction as a functional[1] and cancer-fighting food comes to be produced and consumed in and through the discourses of "good" (often white, middle-class) motherhood. Specifically, I examine the ways in which the structural epidemic of cancer gets framed as an individualistic problem of nutrition, wherein mothers are chiefly responsible for care and protection. My aim, to be clear, is not to expose the supposed truth of the cancer and dairy debate—I cannot say with certainty that dairy either increases or decreases one's risk of cancer. Instead, what I do here is question *how* the seeming truths about dairy and cancer come to be produced and consumed through dominant mothering discourses—discourses that posit food as a symbolic extension of mothering. Concerned with what an analysis of mothering can tell us about the marketing of dairy as a cancer-fighting food (and vice versa), I analyze the visual, symbolic, and discursive representations of motherhood at work in the Dairy Farmers of Canada's (DFC) recent *Get Enough* milk campaign.

GET ENOUGH MILK

Moving from the rhetoric of "Got Milk"[2] to "Get Enough" milk, the DFC's 2012 advertising campaign includes a still-airing thirty-four second television commercial, that has also been uploaded to YouTube (Dairy Farmers of Canada, "Why Milk Products?") and a corresponding website (*Get Enough*) with added information on the benefits of milk products, goal setting strategies, serving sizes, and advice and recipes from (non-registered) dieticians. The overall message of the campaign encourages viewers to consume the recommended daily servings of milk and alternatives, as outlined by Canada's Food Guide.[3] Conspicuously, at a time when North Americans are consuming more dairy than at any point in recorded history (Wiley), the DFC's central campaign claim is that "the majority of Canadians do not consume the minimum recommended servings for their age group." The ad does not inform viewers that the recommended daily intakes of milk and alternatives have nearly *doubled* since the inauguration of Canada's Food Rules in 1942 (Falbe and Nestle). Encouraging consumers to "get enough" dairy (i.e., as much dairy as they can) as well as addressing those skeptical of dairy consumption—including here the proponents of recent health-oriented diets that preclude *any* cow's milk products (Kristensen, Boye, and Askegaard)—the Get Enough television commercial begins with a question

Figure 1: Dairy Farmers of Canada, "Why Milk Products?"

Figure 2: Dairy Farmers of Canada, "Why Milk Products?"

Figure 3: Dairy Farmers of Canada, "Why Milk Products?"

increasingly posed of the dairy industry: "why milk products" (see Figure 1)?

The industry-driven response in the commercial is established along a blue lifeline, mirroring the shape of an electrocardiogram and functioning as a metaphor for the pulse of life itself—a pulse sustained throughout the commercial by the requisite consumption of dairy. Along dairy's lifeline, the audience first encounters a self-assured, thin, middle-aged, middle-class white woman who *is* getting her requisite daily consumption of dairy, marked moralistically with the dairy industry's white check of approval (see Figure 2).

The two men next to her (who appear to be her son and husband because of their age and proximity) are not so fortunate, their failure made obvious by a disapproving "X," reaffirming that the lack of *enough* dairy consumption is categorically incorrect (see Figure 3).

Although the woman's health behaviours are lauded on an individual level—as the one mainly responsible for the health of her family, and here, symbolically, as the "giver of milk"—she fails. Reinforcing the links between milk, motherhood, and the social work of care, discourses of good mothering are normatively tied to representations of thin, able-bodied, white, middle-class femininity (subjectivities who have structural advantages that their disabled, working-class and/or racialized counterparts do not) and are maintained in traditional ways as a woman's responsibility.

Instilling the threat of bad mothering as well as the fear of the lack of milk consumption among children and men, the female announc-

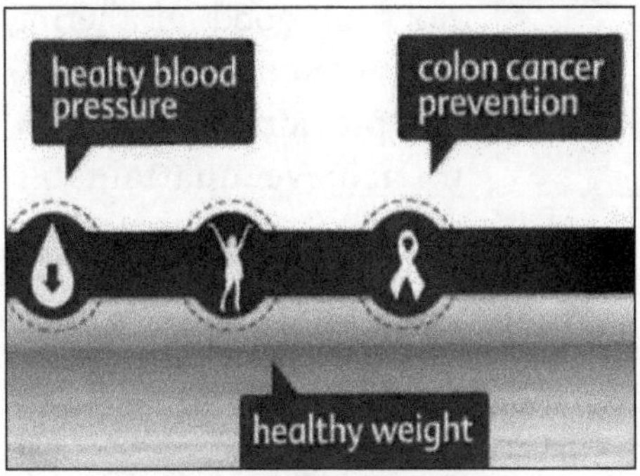

Figure 4: Dairy Farmers of Canada, "Why Milk Products?"

er (and the ongoing voice of health reasoning) states that "most of us are missing out on the many health benefits of milk products." These health benefits are quickly and simplistically tied to contemporary health concerns—heart attacks, obesity,[4] and cancer—and pitted alongside easily recognizable, consumable images—the philanthropic symbol of blood donation, a thin female, and one of the most branded symbols of the twenty-first century: the breast cancer ribbon (see Figure 4).

According to King, "the ribbon ... pink and round, feminine and innocent, [is] a national emblem of 'awareness' and good, sensible, consumption-based citizenship" and has become a staple of cause-related marketing (43). Despite the ads claim for the prevention of colon cancer, the strategic use of the ribbon not only effectively conflates the consumption of dairy with the prevention of all cancers, including the hyper-feminized case of breast cancer, but also, in doing so, functions to further interpolate female consumers (and notably those still chiefly responsible for food care in the family) into the virtues of dairy consumption.

By using discourses of good mothering, the Get Enough campaign reinforces white, middle-class femininity as the image of "responsible" and "intensive" mothering and as those equipped to be the keepers of family health. As Held and Rutherford aptly note, "expectations and ideas about what it is to be a good mother, or even a 'good enough' mother, have been subjected to constant cultural negotiation and scrutiny, particularly since the mid-19th century when motherhood itself came under the purview of a number of scientific and medical experts" (1). Significant here is that motherhood and mothering discourse are not static—they change in relation to social and cultural categories, of which many of these in contemporary contexts are heavily mediated (Halkier). With the aggressive, industry-produced links between normative construc-

Figure 5: Dairy Farmers of Canada, "Why Milk Products?"

tions of good mothering and cancer-prevention, the pressure and anxiety to achieve unattainable standards makes mothers lucrative targets for marketing and renders the charge of bad mothering (notably to those who are structurally disadvantaged) a particularly potent discursive technique. With a growing cacophony of "expert voices weighing in on what it [takes] to be a good mother, coupled with the heavy practical demands of the job itself, motherhood [has become] increasingly anxiety-provoking for many women" (Held and Rutherford). Helping to produce this constructed fear, the lifeline sustained in the ad ends abruptly with the purposefully provoking question: "what are you missing out on?" with a link to more information on their website (see Figure 5).

Once on their website, the once-simplistic fact that dairy consumption "prevents colon cancer," becomes much less equivocal. Allowances that "milk products *could* lower the *risk* of colon cancer", and that "there is enough data to conclude that milk *probably* helps prevent colorectal cancer" (*Get Enough*, emphasis added) are an obvious refraction of their commercial claim and hardly a ringing endorsement for the cancer-fighting properties of milk. Also apparent on their website are the continued efforts to link good mothering with dairy consumption. In a patronizing reversal of roles, it is moms who are encouraged to drink their milk (see Figure 6).

Whereas kids are told to drink their milk if they want to grow up big and strong, moms are being told to drink their milk to "help prevent certain diseases"—diseases that we already know from the ad and from their website include heart attacks, obesity, and the "big C." The implication of the image in question is that by drinking the recommended number of daily milk servings, moms can effectively stave off life-threatening illnesses and spare their

Figure 6: *Get Enough*

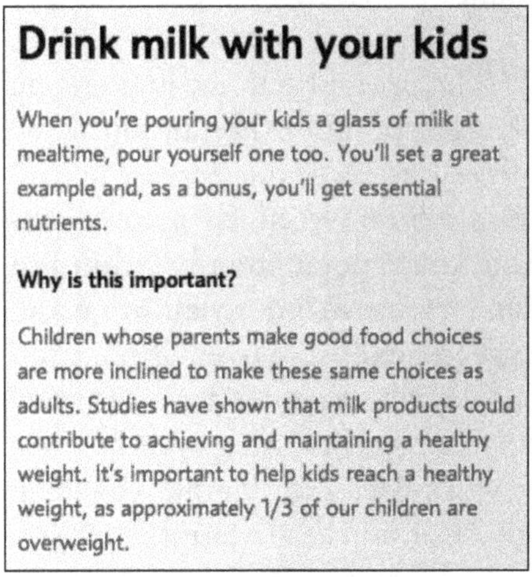

Drink milk with your kids

When you're pouring your kids a glass of milk at mealtime, pour yourself one too. You'll set a great example and, as a bonus, you'll get essential nutrients.

Why is this important?

Children whose parents make good food choices are more inclined to make these same choices as adults. Studies have shown that milk products could contribute to achieving and maintaining a healthy weight. It's important to help kids reach a healthy weight, as approximately 1/3 of our children are overweight.

Figure 7: *Get Enough*

children, like the young girl holding up the glass in the image, from needless loss and sorrow. The avoidance of cancer is squarely positioned as an individual's responsibility and places mothers at the helm of that responsibility, this time for their children's emotional well-being.

At stake in a related image on the DFC's website (see Figure 7) is not the mother's own health, but her[5] role-modelling behaviours. As the image details, setting "a great example" for her kids is centralized over any "essential nutrients" that she might also receive by drinking daily recommended servings of milk. Encouraging mothers not to pass their "unhealthy" food habits on to their presumably innocent offspring, "the combinations of science and moral conduct," as Coveney notes, "are never so apparent as they are in nutrition" (*Food, Morals and Meaning* 28). Part science, part salvation, the often-unquestioned rhetoric of the Get Enough campaign is outwardly moral: if a person is disciplined today, they will be rewarded with good health (and the good health of their children) tomorrow. As McNaughton sums up, mothers are held responsible for the health of their offspring "from the womb to the tomb" (164). Although the idea of good food was once about "tasty, rich dishes, it now connotes something much different" (Coveney, *Food, Morals and Meaning* 2). "Good" food has come to signify self-control and a concern for one's health, whereas "bad" food has become indicative of moral weakness and a lack of concern for one's health. The assumption that mothers can prevent childhood obesity (and other contemporary illnesses) by simply modelling positive, consumptive milk-drinking behaviour is absurd. However, this discourse functions, nonetheless, as an exercise in power, discipline, and governance, consumed through normalized images of responsible mothering and effected by the social regulation of mothering bodies through dominant discourse.

THE BIOPOLITICS OF MOTHERING RESPONSIBILITY

Unacknowledged across contemporary strategies of disease prevention, including the examples provided by the DFC, is any discussion of the systemic or structural causes of illness—causes that go beyond individual health choices and actions. In targeting mothers as individuals in the consumption of their product, the systemic and structural inequalities leading to the increase in cancer incident and mortality rates are both effectively ignored and symbolically erased. Nowhere in these population-based health strategies are references to the an increase in industrialization and urbanization (where there is a greater exposure to environmental toxins), changes in diet and lifestyle (where people are consuming more prepackaged and pre-prepared foods), higher levels of stress because of greater economic and workplace uncertainties, changing family forms, and an increasingly uncertain health terrain. Instead, exerting pressure that mothers have the time and knowledge to prevent such wide-reaching illness catastrophes, the Get Enough website further individualizes illness prevention by including a link to the "free Get Enough Helper App" (see Figure 6). Marketed as empowering, the Get Enough Helper App is a prime example of what Crawshaw calls "the use of social marketing as a strategy to improve the health of populations from a distance" (200). In the example in question, increasingly tired and busy moms need not read labels or consult their doctors, they need only consult their smartphones to take responsibility for their own well-being and the well-being of their children. As O'Donohoe, Hogg, Maclaran, Martens, and Stevens assert, "marketing and consumer culture construct particular images of what mothers are, what they should care about and how they should behave" (1).

Mothering in late modernity is understood as "both the private responsibility of individual mothers, and also a matter of public scrutiny and intervention, with mothering practices defined as 'good' or 'bad' in expert and policy discourses" (Lee quoted in McNaughton 165). Of course, ideals about what constitutes a good or bad mother are both fluid and deeply cultural, shaped by larger structural forces and underwritten by a range of classist, racist, sexist, and heterosexist assumptions. Such ideas are also intricately linked to discourses of risk, where the good mother resists or avoids any action or activity that might be potentially unhealthy for her child. As white, middle-class women have historically had greater amounts of freedom and capital (both social and material) to devote to the job of intensive mothering, they have been the most targeted by advertisers who sell good motherhood along with (and through) their products. Given that invocations of good motherhood are always already ideological, they become easily affixed to cultural norms, and specifically here, to those of healthism "where a preoccupation with self-help, personal responsibility and individual accountability for health and wellbeing ... create a market economy ripe for private and corporate investment" (Coveney, "In Praise of Hunger" 147).

Food-related health marketing is a relatively recent addition to the public health arsenal. Its aim is to encourage health-seeking behaviours in individuals through the *consumption* of industry product. This aim is fundamentally different than being concerned with the health of the population. If the latter were true, the government would be equally concerned with the *avoidance* of food products with known links to illness and would issue warning labels similar to those that were added to tobacco products (Lawrence and Germov). Warning labels might entail something like the following: "this is a food high in salt, and salty foods eaten frequently increase your risk for hypertension." Despite the fact that milk and dairy products are high in salts and saturated fats (food facts the dairy industry is not too keen to share), this is far from the message of dairy-related advertising (Wiley), including the Get Enough campaign analyzed here. At a time when the vast majority of Canadian mothers are in the paid labour force; when fast food and vending machines are ubiquitous; when GMOs, pesticides, and preservatives routinely pass federal food inspections and make their way into everyday food items; when fast-food advertisements regularly target children as young as two years old; and when health-related food labels are purposefully obfuscated to overwhelm and misguide consumers, it is increasingly clear that as critical consumers of mediated culture, we need to look past the individualization of responsibility. It is also clear that targeting mothers through the use of the all-too-familiar discourses of good and bad motherhood only serves to further individualize the problem, while simultaneously reinforcing sexist, classist, and racist ideologies of maternal responsibility.

CONCLUSIONS

The overriding purposes of the dairy industry's claims to health—and specifically here to cancer prevention—are commercial. In other words, any collateral health benefits (or detriments) that occur through the consumption of dairy are tertiary. Given that all but the poorest countries in the world produce more food on average than is needed by their populations, the food industry in North America is especially competitive (Falbe and Nestle). The impetus to sell a food product in a largely oversaturated market explains why food producers so aggressively defend the health claims of their products (Falbe and Nestle) especially at a time when many of these health claims are under scrutiny.

Although food continues to be at the heart of discussions concerning health and illness, what is changing, and significantly so, is the social, political, and cultural context in and through which health-based food claims are being actively repackaged and remarketed. Foundational in these strategies, as I have argued here, are familiar discourses of white, middle-class "good" mothering. By centralizing individual-based strategies, diet is presented as "the appropriate and benign solution[s] to the problem of cancer", despite the fact that cancer is highly correlated with systemic and environmental inequalities (Clarke and Everest 2598). Gendered discourses of family nutrition are further presented as a solution that creates "potent possibilities for discrimination and stigma towards mothers who do not follow the [industry] prescribed practices" (Ristovsky-Slijepcevic 178). With dairy presented as a symbolic extension of mothering care and protection practices, dairy-related marketing discourses create the assumption that with the right "guidance" and appropriate "nudges" mothers are solely responsible for their own well-being, the well-being of their families, and, to a certain extent, the well-being of the nation. Nutrition strategies that centralize motherhood, typified in the Get Enough campaign, reify an endless inculcation of self-management, self-improvement, and individualized responsibility at the expense of any macro-level, industry, or government obligation. Marketing tactics, such as the ones analyzed here, further "exacerbate the moralization of mothering in relation to food" (Halkier 100)—a facet not new to motherhood but one aggressively repackaged in late-modern, media-saturated contexts.

Health-based food claims, as Lawrence and Germov point out, present one of the most complex and political public health policy debates confronting governments today. Rife with ambiguity and contradiction, health-based food claims engage competing and conflicting values, interests, and beliefs. In an ongoing age of neoliberal governing practices, government deregulation, the medicalization of the food supply, and the broadening net of the medical-industrial complex, we are in the auspices of a new public health—one where the stakes have been radically transformed. As Kristensen, Boye, and Askegaard contend, "it is essential to analyze who makes moral arguments, how these arguments are deployed, and the kinds of effects they have" (198). The need to critically reframe, renegotiate, and ultimately repackage the current terms of food (and dairy) related health claims is admittedly a challenging one. I believe it is also a necessary one in order to move beyond static, deterministic accounts of motherhood; strictly biological and seemingly agentic individual health choices; and to shift the frame away from individualized (often privileged) mothering responsibility. By questioning the terms of dairy-related advertising, I have argued that what we find are deeply embedded (often unquestioned) links between mothering and consumptive practices—links that contribute to myths and stereotypes of good and bad mothers as being bound up in consumer "choice." What we also find is that contemporary possibilities of mothering as well as contemporary possibilities of illness prevention lie less with recommended daily servings of milk (or any other singular, individualized health behaviours) than they do with the social, political, and economic conditions in which we find ourselves.

NOTES

[1]Detailed by Lawrence and Germov, a functional food affirms a direct influence over a consumer's health by claiming to deliver a health benefit beyond general sustenance (148).

[2]The U.S. dairy industry's successful Got Milk campaign ran between 1993 and 2014 and aggressively linked dairy consumption with health, strong bones, disease prevention, and overall vitality through the use of high-priced spokespersons and corporate sponsorship.

[3]Last changed in 2007, the daily recommended servings of dairy are as follows: two to three servings for adults, three to four servings for children, two to four servings for youth, and three to four servings for nursing, pregnant, and aging women (Health Canada).

[4]The dominant framing of obesity as a public health threat has not gone without well-founded critiques. LeBesco argues that the fat body has become a moral symbol of failed and unproductive citizenship, and as Gard and Wright contend, "any correlating obesity prevalence with disease incidence is, at best, an indication of a possible link between size and health for a population, rather than an undeniable truth (qtd. in McNaughton 165).

[5]Although the image does not specify gender, given that mothers have been the central target in both the DFC's commercial and their related website content, I am interpolating the subject of the message as female. As McNaughton asserts, "although fathers and more rarely same-sex partners are implicated … gender ste-

reotypes about responsibility for feeding children ... are cast as mothers" (164).

WORKS CITED

"Cancer Facts and Statistics." *American Cancer Society*. American Cancer Society, 2013. Web. 19 June 2013.

Clarke, Juanne Nancarrow. "Cancer, Heat Disease and AIDS: What Do the Media Tell Us about These Diseases?" *Health Communication* 4.2 (1992): 105–20. Print.

Clarke, Juanne Nancarrow, and Michelle Everest. "Cancer in the Mass Print Media: Fear, Uncertainty and the Medical Model." *Social Science & Medicine* 62.10 (2006): 2591-2606. Print.

Coveney, John. *Food, Morals and Meaning: The Pleasure and Anxiety of Eating*. New York: Routledge, 2000. Print.

Coveney, John. "In Praise of Hunger: Public Health and the Problem of Excess." *Alcohol, Tobacco, and Obesity: Morality, Mortality, and the New Public Health*. Eds. Kirsten Bell, Darlene McNaughton and Amy Salmon. New York: Routledge, 2011. 146-160. Print.

Crawshaw, Paul. "Governing at a Distance: Social Marketing and the (Bio)Politics of Responsibility." *Social Science and Medicine* 75.1 (2012): 200- 207. Print.

Dairy Farmers of Canada. "Why Milk Products? *YouTube*. YouTube. 12 Mar. 2012. Web. 3 Oct. 2014.

Falbe, Jennifer, and Marion Nestle. "The Politics of Government Dietary Advice." *A Sociology of Food and Nutrition: The Social Appetite*. Eds. John Germov and Lauren Williams. New York: Oxford University Press, 2008. 127-146. Print.

Get Enough. Dairy of Farmers of Canada, 2014. Web. 3 Oct. 2014.

Halkier, Bente. "Contesting Food—Contesting Motherhood?" *Motherhoods, Markets and Consumption: The Making of Mothers in Contemporary Western Culture*. Eds. Stephanie O'Donohoe, Lydia Martens, Lorna Stevens, Margaret Hogg, and Pauline Maclaran. New York: Routledge, 2013. 89-103. Print.

Held, Lisa and Alexandra Rutherford. "Can't a Mother Sing the Blues? Postpartum Depression and the Construction of Motherhood in Late 20th-Century America." *History of Psychology*

5.12 (2012): 107-123. Print.

Johnson, Ian T. and G. Roger Fenwick. *Dietary Anti-Carcinogens and Anti-Mutagens: Chemical and Biological Aspects*. Norwich, UK: The Royal Society of Chemistry, 2000. Print.

King, Samantha. *Pink Ribbons, Inc.: Breast Cancer and the Politics of Philanthropy.* Minneapolis: University of Minnesota Press, 2006. Print.

Kristensen, Dorthe Brogård, Heidi Boye, and Søren Askegaard. "Leaving the Milky Way! The Formation of a Consumer Counter Mythology." *Journal of Consumer Culture* 11.2 (2011): 195-214. Print.

Lawrence, Michael, and John Germov. "Functional Foods and Public and Health Nutrition Policy." *A Sociology of Food and Nutrition: The Social Appetite*. Eds. John Germov and Lauren Williams. New York: Oxford University Press, 2008. 147-175. Print.

LeBesco, Kathleen. *Revolting Bodies: The Struggle to Redefine Fat Identity*. Amherst: University of Massachusetts Press, 2004. Print.

Lupton, Deborah. *Food, The Body and The Self*. Thousand Oaks: Sage Publications, 1996. Print.

McNaughton, Darlene. "From the Womb to the Tomb: Obesity and Maternal Responsibility." *Alcohol, Tobacco, and Obesity: Morality, Mortality, and the New Public Health*. Eds. Kirsten Bell, Darlene McNaughton, and Amy Salmon. New York: Routledge, 2006. 163-176. Print.

Moorman, Patricia G., and Paul D. Terry. "Consumption of Dairy Products and the Risk of Breast Cancer: A Review of the Literature." *The American Journal of Clinical Nutrition* 80.1 (2004): 5-14. Print.

"Nutrition and Fitness." *Canadian Cancer Society*. Canadian Cancer Society, 2013. Web. 19 June 2013.

O'Donohoe, Stephanie, Margaret Hogg, Pauline Maclaran, Lydia Martens, and Laura Stevens. "The Making of Mothers." *Motherhoods, Markets and Consumption: The Making of Mothers in Contemporary Western Culture*. Eds. Stephanie O'Donohoe, Margaret Hogg, Pauline Maclaran, Lydia Martens, and Lorna Stevens. New York: Routledge, 2013. 1-13. Print.

Ristovski-Slijepcevic, Svetlana. "Responsibility for Family's Health:

How Nutritional Discourses Construct the Role of Mothers." *Alcohol, Tobacco, and Obesity: Morality, Mortality, and the New Public Health*. Eds. Kirsten Bell, Darlene McNaughton, and Amy Salmon. New York: Routledge, 2006. 177-190. Print.

Sontag, Susan. *Illness as Metaphor and AIDS and Its Metaphors*. New York: Picador, 2001. Print.

Smith-Howard, Kendra. *Pure and Modern Milk: An Environmental History Since 1900*. New York: Oxford University Press, 2014. Print.

Statistics Canada. "Leading Causes of Death, by Sex (Both Sexes)." Statistics Canada. Government of Canada, 2011. Web. 10 Sept. 2015.

Tulloch, John, and Deborah Lupton. "Consuming Risk, Consuming Science: The Case of GM Foods." *Journal of Consumer Culture* 2.3 (2002): 363-383. Print.

United States. The U.S. Department of Health and Human Services. Centers for Disease Control and Prevention. "Leading Causes of Death." *Centers for Disease Control and Prevention*. Government of the United States, 2014. Web. 10 Mar. 2014.

Weldon, Glen. *Dietary Options for Cancer Survivors: A Guide to Research on Foods, Food Substances, Herbals and Dietary Regimens That May Influence Cancer.* Washington, DC: American Institute for Cancer Research, 2002. Print.

World Health Organization (WHO). "Top 10 Causes of Death." WHO, 2014. Web. 10 March 2014.

Wiley, Andrea. *Re-Imagining Milk: Cultural and Biological Perspectives*. New York: Routledge, 2011. Print.

6.
Vigilance and Valour in the Kitchen

Feeding, Eating, and the Intellectual Work of Motherhood in Food-Allergic Families

HEATHER HEWETT

IN EARLY 2005, JUDITH WARNER published the best-selling book *Perfect Madness: Motherhood in the Age of Anxiety*, in which she argues that a kind of "mommy mystique" had descended on contemporary U.S. parenting. Warner levied a perceptive feminist critique of the increasingly unattainable ideals attached to mothering in middle- and upper-income families, describing how many women felt anxious in their pursuit of increasingly intensive, perfect parenting. I was a first-time mother when her book came out, trying to figure out my new role within all the cultural noise surrounding motherhood. Although her analysis helped me understand a great deal, it fell short in one significant way: its portrayal of parental anxiety surrounding food and food allergies. I was attuned to this omission because my husband and I were in the process of figuring out that our daughter, a toddler, had several allergic diseases, including multiple, life-threatening food allergies.

Warner's understanding of food allergies are folded into her analysis of the "madness" of parenting in the culture at large and her observation that many parents seemed far more fearful about perceived dangers to their children (such as sexual abuse or neglect in daycare, violent crimes, and kidnapping by strangers) than in the past. This increased anxiety, she and others have contended, resulted from an increase of stories in the media and not actual statistics.[1] She further argues that

> The deluge of stories on fatal food allergies has made its mark on the American parental psyche as well: by the late

> 1990s, fully one-third of American households believed that at least one of their family members had a food allergy. This despite the fact that the most generous expert estimate of the incidence of food allergies among children under three (the most vulnerable group) is not more than 8 percent. (196)

Although Warner correctly asserts that increasing awareness of the existence of food allergies may well be a significant contributing factor to overdiagnosis, she suggests a larger doubt about the rising percentage of children identified as having food allergies in the U.S. This disbelief echoes the larger medical debate about the precise number of children who have food allergies and the accompanying media stories about whether or not industrialized nations, such as the U.S., have really been experiencing a true food allergy "epidemic." In *Perfect Madness*, however, the author's dismissiveness shifts into parental blame when she explains the "leading theory" for food allergies, the hygiene hypothesis: "parents today may, ironically, have made their kids more prone to life-threatening allergic attacks by keeping them *too* well protected and, in particular, too clean" (234). Although Warner is correct that this was (and still is) a leading medical theory, her explanation makes no reference to the cultural and historical dimensions of this hypothesis—that allergic diseases may partly result from collective lifestyle changes in post-industrialized societies—instead reducing it to a matter of individual parenting choices and neuroses.

I do not wish to single Warner out unfairly, particularly because food allergies are not the focus of her book, and her larger points about parental anxiety and the amplified ideals surrounding motherhood (what scholars variously term intensive mothering, concerted cultivation, or overparenting) make important contributions to public conversations about parenting, gender, and social expectations.[2] Indeed, it is entirely possible (and even likely) that heightened worries in U.S. culture more broadly may contribute to the ways that some individual parents perceive and manage allergic diseases. However, Warner's comments primarily seem to repeat problematic narratives about food allergies, in particular the tendency to blame individual families for their occurrence.

Despite the success of her book overall, she fails to acknowledge how vigilance around food in the context of a food allergy diagnosis may also stem from causes unrelated to overparenting. In particular, the medical diagnosis of anaphylactic food allergy can result in particular worries that the general population, including many feminists, have been slow to understand fully. If feminists wish to empower parents to be aware of, and resistant to, escalating cultural ideals of motherhood and parenting, we need to understand the complex realities and challenges that can accompany a food allergy diagnosis.[3]

In this essay, I explore the presence and potential effects of parental blame on primary caregivers, often (though not always) mothers, of food-allergic children.[4] How is this blame gendered, and how might it affect the way that mothers in particular think about food, family meals, and the work of feeding their children? I focus on the 2012 memoir by Susan Weissman, *Feeding Eden: The Trials and Triumphs of a Food Allergy Family*, which provides one mother's reflections on the challenges of preparing food and eating together after her son is diagnosed with food allergies. Drawing from feminist scholarship on motherhood, blame, food, and invisible disabilities, I explore how this memoir reveals the complex feelings, particularly anxiety and self-blame, experienced by Weissman. Ultimately, this author undertakes certain kinds of food work, both in and out of the kitchen, in order to redefine family meals and dismantle stigma and guilt. By bringing a feminist lens to the text, I hope to further the understanding of the particular challenges food allergies present to the larger project of "unbending gender" as well as to open up the gendered dimensions of food work and caregiving (Williams).

MOTHER BLAME AND FOOD ALLERGIES

For much of the previous century, mothers have been blamed for their children's illnesses, for medical diagnoses, such as schizophrenia and autism, as well as for a range of other behaviours and personality traits (Ladd-Taylor and Umansky). In a similar fashion, the history of allergic disease has been suffused with maternal blame. As historian Mark Jackson writes, in the 1930s and 1940s, asthma was seen to be caused by insufficient motherly love or, on the other hand, "smother love" (87). As doctors began to understand the role of the modern indoor environment in environmental allergies, they placed "the burden of maintaining domestic health ... with mothers" (172). This emphasis on the "pivotal role of mothers" in "fashioning the pre-natal and early childhood environment that might precipitate allergies" also suffused later twentieth-century studies of parental smoking (175). During the same time period, a "considerable volume of international research was aimed at determining whether substantial changes in the Western diet were responsible for the increasing prevalence of asthma, hay fever and eczema," which included studies looking at specific foods as well as the impact of breastfeeding and formula (174). More recently, Jackson observes, the hygiene hypothesis and ensuing debates (e.g., maybe dirt *helps* stop infants from developing allergies) have reversed the perspective on cleanliness entirely (175-178). On most of these questions, medical knowledge remains inconclusive—yet the focus on maternal responsibility constantly threatens to shapeshift into maternal blame.

As psychologist Paula J. Caplan argues more broadly, Western culture has created unreasonable, simplified representations of motherhood: the "Angel/Witch, Perfect Mother/Bad Mother myths" that leave little to no room for "Reasonably Good Mother myths" (3, 69). She observes that "A mother is not allowed to make many good efforts but be humanly flawed; she has to be perfect, because so much is at stake—the physical and mental health of her children, for which she is assumed to be totally responsible" (69). To fail at attaining the perfect "physical and mental health" of one's children is to risk falling into the category of "bad" mother. These unreasonable expectations surrounding "good" motherhood are even more out of reach for some mothers because of the ways in which mothering ideals are raced and classed. Some mothers are placed under greater scrutiny than others; for example, racist stereotypes place black motherhood into the "bad" mother category (Collins; Charlton). Either way, these cultural myths encourage finger pointing at mothers for the many different things that can go "wrong" with their children. And if society still equates mothering with nurturing and nurturing with food, few things are worse—indeed, even "unnatural"—than a child unable to ingest the food provided by its mother.

Although it's possible for individuals to reject these mothering ideals, they are easily internalized. My own interviews with primary caregivers of food-allergic kids suggest that many mothers struggle with self-blame and guilt.[5] I have spoken with mothers who blame themselves for what they ate when pregnant or breastfeeding; for feeding their children formula; for breastfeeding; for signing their children up for experimental treatments, such as oral immunotherapy trials; for *not* signing their children up for experimental treatments; for accidentally causing an allergic reaction by feeding their children the wrong foods. (I have experienced many of these moments of self-blame myself.) Despite the fact that medical research is ongoing about how to prevent food allergies, self-blame seeps into many of the stories mothers tell about their children.[6] As one allergist and food-allergy mom observed in her blog, *The Allergist Mom*:

> During my pediatric residency I saw guilt literally destroy parents in front of my eyes ... And it didn't matter how many, "It's not your fault", that I poured over them, they didn't believe me. They couldn't let themselves believe me. What their child was about to endure had to be someone's fault and it made complete sense to them that they had to own the blame. After all, we are completely responsible for the well-being of our children and so, of course, we feel equally responsible for their disease. (Boudreau-Romano)

Although Boudreau-Romano does not specify "mothers" in these reflections, it is quite likely that many of these parents were, in fact, mothers. As with household labour more generally, women disproportionately shoulder the work of family health care; according to a 2013 survey undertaken by the Kaiser Family Foundation, nearly three-quarters of mothers in the U.S. "are the ones who take charge of health care responsibilities such as choosing their children's provider, taking them to appointments, and following through with recommended care, compared to approximately a fifth of fathers" (Ranji 1). Thus the tendency of mothers to assume blame for their children's condition may have to do with their frequent status as "primary caregiver" as well as the shifting nature of current medical recommendations regarding the prevention of food allergies. As scientific understanding evolves and the guidelines change, mothers frequently discover that what they thought was "right" turns out to be "wrong."[7] It's understandable that some mothers internalize self-blame for these decisions.

Caplan's observations have been extended by sociologists who have looked at the impact of blame on mothers of disabled children, particularly those with invisible, mental disabilities. In her study of mothers of children with ADHD, mood and conduct disorders, and autism spectrum disorders—diagnoses that, like food allergies, receive far more attention now than in the past—sociologist Linda M. Blum argues that maternal blame persists in new forms. One the one hand, the pathologizing of mothers so common under Freud has ceded to frameworks of "biological psychiatry" (what Blum terms "brain blame") so that mothers are not blamed directly for causing mental disabilities. On the other hand, the women in Blum's study "expressed a sense of relentless responsibility in the face of medical uncertainty, an imperative to concertedly search for solutions" as well as "proximate blame for falling short of relentless, concerted action" (209). Many of her subjects experienced "stigma" if they failed with to act with "valour" (205). In a neoliberal context, she argues, the bar for individual valour is raised even higher, as mothers became "vigilantes" expected to take matters in their own hands when advocating for their children (212).

Blum's research provides many parallels for understanding the experiences of mothers of food-allergic children. Much like a child with mental disabilities, a child with life-threatening food allergies is not immediately recognizable by sight—allergic diseases are also an invisible disability. In addition, both mental illnesses and allergic diseases are surrounded by medical uncertainty. Although scientists have far more understanding of the complex interaction of cells, the immune system, and the environment that results in allergen sensitization—allergies are not caused by either a lack or an excess of a mother's love—they still do not fully understand allergic disease. In my interviews with mothers of food-allergic children and my participant observation of online communities, I have found that many mothers undertake similar "relentless, concerted action" on behalf of their kids and often express a feeling that they are not doing enough. Although this valour can take many forms, in this article I focus on how it unfolds around food and what sociologist Marjorie L. DeVault calls "feeding work" (118).

FOOD WORK IN *FEEDING EDEN*

The memoir *Feeding Eden* provides one window into the emotional and psychological experiences that can follow a child's food allergy diagnosis. Although this memoir represents only one family's story, and thus cannot shed light on the vast range of possible experiences, it presents a reflective narrative that expands the understanding of shame as well as the kinds of ideological and emotional "feeding work" undertaken by its author, Susan Weissman.

The author describes the feelings she and her husband felt when their young son was diagnosed with extensive, anaphylactic food allergies in New York City in the early 2000s:

> We understood that Eden's allergies weren't our fault, but nonetheless, it felt like we had failed: we had made a child who could die from eating food—our food. It was such a poisonous emotion that we didn't know where to look—backward or forward. Backward was sorrow, and forward was the understanding that surely we would continue to screw up—to take unworthy risks or unnecessary precautions—despite all our efforts. We were starting a brand-new learning process but at Eden's expense. And now we had to learn how to eat again. (55-56)

Even though Weissman knows better, she cannot stop feeling responsible for her son's allergies. Her sense of guilt encompasses much more than causing her child's illness; it centres on making "a child who could die from eating food—our food." Weissman's guilt at her "failure" as a parent gets at one of the most confusing characteristics of food allergies: healthy and nutritious food becomes something that can harm a child. Food literally turns into a poison, which is perhaps why she describes her guilt as a "poisonous emotion." As a result, she has to relearn everything that she once knew about food and cooking.

Although Weissman does not consider how gender might (or might not) inflect her feelings, feeding work remains gendered. Statistically, according to the 2013 American Time Use Survey, women spend more than twice as much time on food preparation and clean up than men (Bureau of Labor Statistics). In the case of the increased labour involved in the wake of a food allergy diagnosis—essentially, relearning how to cook and eat—it can be assumed that women disproportionately shoulder this additional work as well. (Even a cursory examination of the number of food allergy blogs and cookbooks authored by women supports this assumption.) Feminists have pinpointed multiple reasons underlying the gendering of food work. Like other kinds of reproductive labour, food work has long been viewed as "women's work"—and in the U.S., caregiving remains socially devalued, unpaid, and unsupported (Crittenden). DeVault further argues that an ideological component informs the unpaid work of food preparation and clean-up: "feeding work" is "one of the primary ways that women 'do' gender" (118). In other words, certain routines and activities, such as cooking, become a way of "doing" femininity, and the "commitment" to this work becomes "an apparently 'natural' part of the gendered self" (119).

If, in fact, preparing food can play a role in producing a sense of one's gendered identity, then the challenges of feeding a food-allergic child might encompass more than relearning how to cook food (difficult enough as this is). If the inability to feed one's child can threaten one's sense of self, it may jeopardize the very root of how some mothers understand and feel about themselves as women. Alternatively, for some mothers, gender may not matter; not everyone who undertakes the work of mothering may identify as female. If "mother" is defined in the way that Sara Ruddick suggests—as someone who takes on "the responsibility of child care, making its work a regular and substantial part of one's working life" regardless of gender identity (17)—the activities and practices of mothering still include food work. In the context of food allergies, buying "safe" foods and preparing them become even more aligned with what Ruddick defines as the "central constitutive, invariant aim of maternal practice": preserving the life of one's child (19). For all parents, feeding their children is a central activity for keeping them alive—but with food allergies, feeding their children the wrong foods can be dangerous. In this context, it would be difficult for food work *not* to become a central focus for mothering food-allergic children. Food emerges as the focal point for both nourishing and protecting one's child. For some mothers, it may also become one more way to enact their valour as "good" mothers.

As DeVault argues, a great deal of food work remains invisible (56). Whereas DeVault focuses on the mental labour of planning meals, Weissman's memoir explores the additional emotional and intellectual labour that precedes this stage when food allergies enter the kitchen. This labour takes many forms, and it shifts over time. Initially it manifests as an internal conflict: after her son is diagnosed, her own feelings about food become complicated. She and her husband find that their own eating becomes disordered, as they begin to "cheat" on each other by sneaking taboo foods in secret (51):

> Drew and I drifted into erratic, nearly erotic eating behaviors (think bread crusts dipped straight into the butter container and a few honey-roasted nuts tossed down our throats late at night before we tossed that "gift" in the garbage, rinsed our mouths, and washed our hands). Our stolen moments ruined any appetite we might have had left for family meals. (53)

The language of eroticism suggests that they are engaging in illicit activities by partaking of "forbidden" foods. By definition, eating the foods to which their son is allergic excludes him, and Weissman catches herself experiencing "impure thoughts" of cheese biscuits and Snickers bars (52). Both she and her husband engage in "transgressions" of sneaking Chinese food and corn chips, and these "closeted" binges occur in secret from each other (51). This infidelity, as in a marital affair, threatens their appetite for shared family meals and puts them in "danger of becoming uninterested in each other's appetites" (54). Having lost the "feeling of mutual pleasure" that they once shared together during meals, Weissman fears that lives fuelled by "separate sustenance" might lead to an un-coupled existence in other ways as well (54). Although she does not say it, she fears losing their identity as a married couple and a family. As anthropologist Richard Wilk puts it, "the meal is both a powerful symbol of the family and an event that makes the family, so a great deal is at stake" when conflict arises (434). For Weissman, this conflict is symbolized by the EpiPen, which represents "all that we could not experience as a family" (55). How can they eat together when so many foods are off-limits for Eden?

Weissman eventually comes to understand that the problem with all this "nibbling, binging, and obsessing" eating behaviour lies in "shame," which she describes as "stuck like a fish bone in our throats" (55). She feels ashamed for "causing" her son's allergies, for eating food he cannot, and for not enjoying the food that they eat together as a family. She also feels shame about the additional time that they now spend thinking about, planning, and discussing food (such as constantly having to ask their hosts about food preparation when they are invited to someone's home for dinner). She is surprised by the "intensity" that characterizes their endless food talk: "an intensity reserved for people who were *starving*" (53). With this comment, she reveals one of the marks of her own class privilege—not having to worry about food—and its partial disappearance with her son's diagnosis. They may live in Manhattan, surrounded by some of the world's "best" food, but they can no longer partake of it (50).

Weissman realizes that they need to reclaim the "mutual pleasure" that they had once experienced when eating (54); they must find new ways of preparing food and eating together that will nourish them all. Thus begins her journey to find or make "food that tasted as good as our love" (56). Although she understands that food should not be "mistaken" for love, she also comes to see that everyone sitting at their dining room table must "believe they deserve to eat" (59). The absence of certain foods does not have to mean the end of shared meals. In response to the stigma and guilt that she was feeling, Weissman reclaims and redefines how and what her family eats, making peace with her son's diagnosis and embracing new ways of cooking and eating.

In addition to time spent in the kitchen, this requires a kind of ideological food work based on an understanding of the value of this labour for her and her family. In this respect, her efforts to redefine the meaning of food parallel the tactics of some within the food movement. Consider Michael Pollan's call to strike back at the tendency to reduce food to its nutritional components with a more holistic approach:

> Scientists operating with the best of intentions, using the best tools at their disposal, have taught us to look at food in a way that has diminished our pleasure in eating it while doing little or nothing to improve our health. Perhaps what we need now is a broader, less reductive view of what food is, one that is at once more ecological and cultural. What would happen, for example, if we were to start thinking about food as less of a thing and more of a relationship?

As with Pollan, Weissman proposes that food is about relationships. In the wake of a food allergy diagnosis, her entire family must renegotiate food and their relationships with one another.

RETHINKING FOOD

Weissman's successful reimagining of food and shared eating—a new vision that arguably occurs, at least partly, through the process of writing a memoir—enables her not only to deconstruct anxiety and shame but also to approach food with a greater clarity of vision. Food allergies lose their stigma and at least some of their power, instead becoming a condition to be managed. Granted, the transformation borne of this labour depends on both class and educational privilege; the cost of food is never presented as an issue for Weissman's family, nor does access to health care seem impeded by cost (although their medical journey is full of obstacles and frustrations). Furthermore, although gender tends to remain obscured under the label "parent" in the memoir, it seems that Weissman does most of the caregiving and food work (and in this, she is hardly alone). The work of rethinking and rewriting food appears to remain Weissman's responsibility (as well as her opportunity), and one can argue that this additional time and labour merely reinforces family life and eating in the U.S. as private and gendered endeavours, without much institutional or governmental support.

Yet these structural concerns lie outside the frame of Weissman's story. Instead, her memoir deftly illuminates some of the hardest challenges faced by food-allergic families; if anything, it suggests that the riddle of how to redress the gendered inequities that persist in caregiving and food work becomes even more complex in the presence of food allergies. It is easy to offer the feminist advice that "everyone" should get back into the kitchen (Flammang)—but how, exactly, can this happen when specialized knowledge is necessary, and when mistakes could be deadly? Although Weissman does not address the difficulties of delegating care and feeding work, this issue has come up in many of the interviews that I have conducted; it has also presented itself in the life of my own family. Here, there are no easy answers. From experience, I can say that my husband and I have tread carefully when it comes to food prepared by anyone else. We've both done the extra work of educating and communicating with anyone who prepares food for our daughter, and we've realized that helping her learn to self-advocate (and cook) for herself is perhaps one of the most important tasks we have as parents. The challenge of feeding our family has been lessened considerably by the support of friends (both hers and ours) who understand exactly what she can and can't eat.

But no one can ask for help without better public education about food allergies, something that Weissman strives for and achieves with her memoir. Although food allergies can lead to fear, anxiety, guilt, and unhealthy obsessions with food, they can also engender creativity, powerful insights, and new ways of coming together. The challenges of this work—its intellectual complexity, its high stakes, its demand for both time and resources—suggest that we, as individuals and as a society, need to find ways to value, support, and share the feeding and nurturing of food-allergic children and the parents who undertake this work. In the absence of a cure for food allergies, it is perhaps the only thing that we can do.

NOTES

[1]See, for example, Susan Douglas and Meredith Michaels's *The Mommy Myth*.

[2]See Sharon Hays's discussion of intensive mothering, Annette Lareau's discussion of concerted cultivation, and Margaret Nelson's discussion of overparenting.

[3]These challenges vary with the severity of the allergies and the socio-economic location of the family. In this article, I focus on allergies that cause the immune system to overreact by producing a particular kind of antibody, Immunoglobulin E, or IgE. However, a list of other conditions can also affect the relationship of individuals and their families to food (these include different kinds of allergic reactions, food intolerances or sensitivities, and other autoimmune disorders and conditions).

[4]I understand "mother" as anyone doing the work of mothering, as defined by Sara Ruddick, regardless of gender identity; however, most statistics that track mothers' household labour define "mother" as a cisgender woman.

[5]At the date of this writing, I have conducted twenty-two qualitative interviews with a range of mothers.

[6]As of this writing, the newly published LEAP study (Du Toit et al.) suggests that the "early oral introduction of peanuts could prevent allergy in high-risk, sensitized infants and in nonsensitized infants" (811). These findings run counter to previous recommendations, notably those of the American Academy of Pediatrics (AAP) between 2000 and 2008, that recommended a delay in the introduction of peanuts and other allergenic foods to infants at a high risk of developing allergies; see Du Toit et al. and the American Academy of Allergy, Asthma & Immunology (AAAAI) recommendations (qtd. in Fleischer et al.). Also see de Silva et al.

[7]At the time of this writing, medical guidelines include exclusive breastfeeding until at least four months (and/or the use of non-dairy, hydrolyzed formula for high-risk infants); eating a "normal, healthy" diet without restrictions; and introducing foods at the proper time. See the EAACI Food Allergy and Anaphylaxis Guidelines (Muraro et al.). As mentioned above, however, recommendations of when to introduce allergenic foods continue to change.

WORKS CITED

Blum, Linda M. "Mother-Blame in the Prozac Nation: Raising Kids with Invisible Disabilities." *Gender and Society* 21.2 (2007): 202-226. Web. 27 Aug. 2012.

Boudreau-Romano, Sarah M. "Child, Heal Thy Mother." *The Allergist Mom*. N.p., 8 Feb. 2012. Web. 28 Mar. 2015.

Bureau of Labor Statistics. U.S. Department of Labor, United States. *American Time Use Survey: 2013 Results*. 2014. Web. 9 Dec. 2014.

Caplan, Paula J. *The New Don't Blame Mother: Mending the Mother-Daughter Relationship*. New York: Routledge, 2000. Print.

Charlton, T. F. "The Impossibility of the Good Black Mother." *The Good Mother Myth: Redefining Motherhood to Fit Reality*. Ed. Avital Norman Nathman. Berkeley, CA: Seal Press, 2014. 177–183. Print.

Collins, Patricia Hill. *Black Feminist Thought: Knowledge, Consciousness, and the Politics of Empowerment*. 2nd Ed. New York: Routledge, 2009. Print.

Crittenden, Ann. *The Price of Motherhood: Why the Most Important Job in the World Is Still the Least Valued*. New York: Metropolitan Books/Henry Holt & Co., 2001. Print.

De Silva, D. et al. "Primary Prevention of Food Allergy in Children and Adults: Systematic Review." *Allergy* 69.5 (2014): 581–589. Wiley Online Library. Web. 22 Feb. 2015.

DeVault, Marjorie L. *Feeding the Family: The Social Organization of Caring as Gendered Work*. Chicago, IL: University of Chicago Press, 1994. Print.

Douglas, Susan J, and Meredith W. Michaels. *The Mommy Myth: The Idealization of Motherhood and How It Has Undermined Women*. New York: Free Press, 2004. Print.

Du Toit, George et al. "Randomized Trial of Peanut Consumption in Infants at Risk for Peanut Allergy." *New England Journal of Medicine* 372.9 (2015): 803-813. Web. 29 Mar. 2015.

Flammang, Janet A. *The Taste for Civilization: Food, Politics, and Civil Society*. Champaign, IL: University of Illinois Press, 2009. Print.

Fleischer, David M. et al. "Primary Prevention of Allergic Disease

Through Nutritional Interventions." *The Journal of Allergy and Clinical Immunology: In Practice* 1.1 (2013): 29-36. Web. 29 Mar. 2015.

Hays, Sharon. *The Cultural Contradictions of Motherhood*. New Haven: Yale University Press, 1996. Print.

Jackson, Mark. *Allergy: The History of a Modern Malady*. London: Reaktion Books, 2007. Print.

Ladd-Taylor, Molly, and Lauri Umansky, eds. *Bad Mothers: The Politics of Blame in Twentieth-Century America*. New York: NYU Press, 1997. Print.

Lareau, Annette. *Unequal Childhoods: Class, Race, and Family Life*. Berkeley, CA: University of California Press, 2003. Print.

Muraro et al., On Behalf of EAACI Food Allergy and Anaphylaxis Guidelines Group. "EAACI Food Allergy and Anaphylaxis Guidelines. Primary Prevention of Food Allergy." *Allergy* 69 (2014): 590–601. Wiley Online Library. Web. 22 Feb. 2015.

Nelson, Margaret K. *Parenting Out of Control: Anxious Parents in Uncertain Times*. New York: NYU Press, 2010. Print.

Pollan, Michael. "Unhappy Meals." *The New York Times Magazine*, 28 Jan. 2007. Web. 9 Dec. 2014.

Ranji, Usha, and Alina Salganicoff. "Data Note: Balancing on Shaky Ground: Women, Work and Family Health." *The Henry J. Kaiser Family Foundation*. Kaiser Family Foundation, 20 Oct. 2014. Web. 31 Mar. 2015.

Ruddick, Sara. *Maternal Thinking: Toward a Politics of Peace*. Boston: Beacon Press, 1995. Print.

Warner, Judith. *Perfect Madness: Motherhood in the Age of Anxiety*. New York: Riverhead Books, 2005. Print.

Weissman, Susan. *Feeding Eden: The Trials and Triumphs of a Food Allergy Family*. New York: Sterling, 2012. Print.

Wilk, Richard. "Power at the Table: Food Fights and Happy Meals." *Cultural Studies — Critical Methodologies* 10.6 (2010): 428-436. SAGE Journals. Web. 23 Mar. 2014.

Williams, Joan C. *Unbending Gender: Why Family and Work Conflict and What To Do About It*. Oxford: Oxford University Press, 2001. Print.

7.
Feeding the Family When the Mother Is Sick

CATHERINE MORLEY

THIS PAPER DESCRIBES SOME OF THE findings from a study on how women who have the primary household feeding role—most of them were mothers and were experiencing an illness or a disability—managed to feed themselves and their families. The study was influenced by DeVault's writing on feeding the family—the social organization of feeding as gendered work; Lupton's ideas on food, the body, and the self; and Fischler's works on food and identity. As DeVault writes:

> Households are quite varied, homes for motley groups of actual individuals with their particular quirks and idiosyncracies. Both inclination and necessity produce variation in daily activities within and among households. But the work of "feeding the family" tends to collect these unruly individuals and tame their centrifugal moves, cajoling them into some version of the activity that constitutes family. Because this work of social construction is largely invisible, such efforts simultaneously produce the illusion that this form of life is a "natural" one. (91)

I was intrigued by the idea that if feeding the family is as complex as DeVault describes, what happens when the person responsible for feeding the family is sick or has experienced disability. I used the phrase "changed health status" to include women in the study who had experienced a variety of health conditions rather than studying women with a similar medical diagnosis (e.g., diabetes or cancer). I did this because focusing only on a diagnosis would have given precedence to it rather than to the women's experiences and because I was interested in how, if at all, the type of health condition affected eating and feeding experiences.

My interest in this topic originated in my work in cancer care as a registered dietitian. Biomedical approaches to practice dominated my university and internship training. Thus, I became puzzled by conversations that arose during nutrition counselling sessions about meanings associated with eating and feeding, about how relationships with or through food changed when someone in a household experienced serious illness, and about why people cried so often in my office when talking about eating and food issues. I had been trained to assess nutrient needs and to provide advice to people on what to eat to meet these needs. The longer that I worked (and having experienced the illness and death of one of my brothers), the less I thought that this approach was helping. Giving precedence to nutrient needs to achieve physiologic ends seemed to minimize and trivialize the eating challenges that people experienced when living with changed health status. For my doctoral research, I wanted to learn more about this phenomenon to better be able to offer what Wilber describes as "the kind of help that helps" (255). Women who had feeding responsibilities for children and partners were of particular interest. As a mother, I thought that trying to juggle feeding oneself and one's family while negotiating treatments, managing symptoms or injury, and running a household was about as complex an eating or feeding situation as I could imagine. I chose to study women who were experiencing or who had experienced this set of circumstance to be better prepared to actually "help" in my work in nutrition counselling. At the time of the study, I could find no published accounts of feeding the family in households in which the person who had the primary feeding responsibility had experienced changed health status.

RESEARCH APPROACH

In-depth interviews were conducted with eleven women (nine of whom were mothers) who had the primary feeding responsibility in their households. They were referred to the study by dietitian colleagues or self-referred in response to posters or informal conversations about my research interests at social events. Ten participants had experienced or were experiencing changed health status; one participant had a husband and daughter who had both been diagnosed with cancer within a few weeks. Although she did not fit the study criteria, she was referred to the study by a dietitian because of the fears that she expressed during nutrition counselling about whether she was somehow responsible for their changes in health status owing to how she had fed them, about how to feed them during their treatment and recovery, and about whether she was somehow being punished or tested. She was included in the study because her story added to developing an understanding of the emotions and concerns associated with the role of feeding in families experiencing illness.

An open narrative approach had been planned however, in pilot testing the interview guide, the first two test participants were confused by the invitation to share their stories. When the second asked me what I wanted to know about, I replied that I wanted to learn about what eating was like for her at that time compared to before her health status had changed, and if the experience was different, what, if any, emotions were associated with the change. She asked why I did not simply ask those questions. This approach was adopted as it built on a standard approach used by dietitians to take diet histories (e.g., "Describe what you eat on a typical day"). These three points for discussion were tested with the next two interviews and successfully yielded narratives that contained information in which I had interest. For the remaining seven interviews, I used a standardized, open-ended interview approach (Patton 438), and the three main points for discussion were:

> Describe what eating is like now
> Describe what eating was like before your health status changed
> Describe any emotions associated with any difference between eating before and now.

Because all participants had feeding responsibility for their families, asking them about eating would, I reasoned, be inextricably interconnected with feeding their families. Probing for greater detail took place during individual interviews (Patton 439). Interviews were from one to three hours in length depending on the complexity of a participant's situation. Recordings were transcribed and analyzed using content categorization (Patton 402).

All participants described "feeding rituals" and "routines," examples of what Fieldhouse describes as "Food-related activities are part of a negotiated contract, the rules of which are sometimes explicit but more often implicitly understood" (117). "Rituals" refer to the enactment of feeding roles; all household members share an understanding of who in the household has responsibility for provisioning, preparing, and offering food. "Routines" refer to the activities that ensure everyone eats within a household. Household members share an understanding of when they eat, what the typical meals are for the time of day or day within the week, and where and how they eat (e.g., eating at a table, while watching TV or while travelling to or from or while at children's activities).

FINDINGS

The analysis of narratives was complex and comprised consideration of eating-feeding choices and activities to address a participant's personal needs, their household feeding role, and any eating and/or feeding beyond the household. A conceptual framework, the Organizational Framework for Exploring Nutrition Narratives (OFFENN), emerged during the analysis. Description and discussion of the framework is beyond the scope of this paper and is reported elsewhere (Morley, "Women's Experiences"; "Development and Use of the Organizational Framework"). This paper focuses on participants' household feeding roles.

All participants had changed their diets to manage their changed health status, and two categories of experience emerged: life-altered (LA) and life-the-same (LS). With both types of condition, a person adapts to medication use, altered diets, changes in physical activity, and laboratory testing to manage their health status; however, those in the LA group experience profound change in activities of daily living (ADLs), whereas those in the LS group experience no change or minimal change in ADLs.

Those in the LS group (n=4) provided brief, simple narratives. They lived with health conditions (e.g., hypertension, Type 2 diabetes) that had not resulted in changes in activities of daily living (ADLs). They continued to work, holiday, engage in recreation and social gatherings, eat out socially, and had others to their homes for meals. All participants in the LS group had expected household members to eat according to their new diets (planned to regulate blood lipids and blood glucose); they perceived that the changes required in their diets (to manage conditions for which they had no physical symptoms) to be healthier than what they had previously eaten (lower in fat, higher in fibre, or containing more vegetables and fruit) and therefore, healthier for everyone in the family. These participants also expected family members (partners and children) to become more involved in shopping and cooking, diffusing or sharing the feeding role.

In contrast, those in the LA group (n=6) had experienced profound changes in ADLs. Participants in this group lived with conditions that included throat cancer, esophageal cancer, gut-related side effects of having had radiation therapy for ovarian cancer, metastatic breast cancer, hyperemesis of pregnancy, Crohn's Disease, and paraplegia. For most, their physical appearance changed because of weight loss or gain, the effects of therapy, or, for one person, having a feeding tube. Participants in this group were largely housebound. Four could no longer work and two had developed home-based businesses so that they could earn income while creating conditions that allowed them to manage their ever-changing, unpredictable symptoms. Participants in the LA group changed their diets to manage the symptoms of their conditions or to make the intake of food and nutrients easier. To feed the family, participants in this group made two types of meals: a meal for household members, and a meal for themselves that they could tolerate. Those in the LA group did not go out to socialize, go on holidays, or engage in recreational activities because these activities always involved eating. Either their diets were too restrictive to be safe outside of their homes or their symptoms (such as vomiting, nausea, or diarrhea) were unpredictable and difficult to manage when away from home. Participants in the LA group rarely had others into their homes for meals as these were too fatiguing and complex to host. Because the narrative of the participant who had feeding responsibility for two family members going through cancer therapy was similarly complex to those in the LA group, it was included with this group in the analysis.

The difference between the groups in expectations for preparing family meals was surprising. My expectation had been that given the severity of symptoms for participants in the LA group, another household member would adopt the feeding role and cater to the needs of the person who was sick, not that the person experiencing a life-altering condition would continue making meals for the family. When I asked participants in the LA group why, given the physical challenges of making meals, they did not delegate cooking or seek help, participants described their need to try to retain the one aspect of their lives that remained unchanged from before their health status changed: feeding their family. They viewed feeding the family as one of the only ways they could "maintain control" in their households. Three of the seven participants described a combination of feeling grateful for and resentful of others' help with household duties. One participant spoke about her mother's efforts to help with feeding the family (including her daughter, granddaughter, and son-in-law):

> *I mean, she was helpful, she really was, and I know she really tried her best, but she just wouldn't do it my way. And I guess that is just it, loss of control. It was a challenge because I had no control over it. They [daughter and husband] were just getting what people brought or what they managed to scrounge up themselves. And actually it was a challenge because I know there were times when my husband would just say, "Ew," but my mother had made it, and he would have to eat it because I couldn't make him anything. It is actually quite a difficult position to be in, and I am sure I'm not the only one who has encountered that, whether it is your mother or a neighbour or whoever, when you can't make a meal and someone brings you something you eat because that is all there is. And responsibility ... there is a word, because I felt responsible still for some strange reason. Because maybe the meal wasn't*

> *quite what they wanted? I couldn't provide anything else, but ultimately it is my responsibility as a mother to do that. So probably, yeah, I had those feelings so all of that ended up as feeling frustrated and angry. This has not been a house where other people have cooked.*

Another informant referred to her sense of servitude to others as evident in the following excerpt of our dialogue:

> Jean: *I guess, you never stop trying because you are ... you know.... Well, you want to ... it is the servitude role.*
> CM: *The servitude role?*
> Jean: *Of serving your fellow man. Yeah, you want to do it and ... it is your duty and so...*
> CM: *You want to do it, no matter how you feel?*
> Jean: *You are too tired to eat ... my family still got enough to eat.*
> CM: *Your family still ate?*
> Jean: *I was taking care of them but ... they don't know what is on the menu—they are not supposed to know.*
> CM: *Do they notice when you are ill? [with a bowel obstruction]*
> Jean: *Sometimes. They can't see what is wrong with me. I mean there will be a night of "Not tonight, I'll just have a cup of tea, Mommy's got a blockage."*

Although spoken too quietly to be picked up on the recording, she described the effort she put into hiding the pain of bowel obstructions from her sons as it upset her to upset them.

> Jean: *Yeah, it has got easier the last few years. My husband works a lot of late nights, so we don't have to have a formal dinner. When everyone was home every night for dinner, it was one of the hardest times ... the hardest times. But, you know, life is a hierarchy, and I am at the bottom of the heap [laughs].*
> CM: *You used an expression [earlier in the interview], "to be a good mother." Can you say more about that?*

> Jean: *To be a good mother—to see to the needs of everyone, to always do for others, for good or bad.*

After describing their experiences shopping and cooking, some informants were surprised to learn the importance that they had placed on their feeding roles. One participant, for example, said:

> *It is my job. I say that to my daughter. This is my job. And I do certainly see it that way. I'd like a new job, I think, but for now, this is my job. And I do try to do it very well.*

These narratives revealed a sense of duty or obligation to seek ways to have control when so much else in their lives had changed (e.g., physical appearance, bodily functions, and their ability to work or to be away from home). For these participants, maintaining their feeding role and trying to retain feeding rituals and routines provided a sense of what was familiar in their households, particularly for their children.

All participants in the LA group (except the feeder of two family members living with cancer) referred to emotions they experienced related to their awareness of the effect of their illness on their family's regular eating routine. Emotions associated with feeding the family were anger, resentment, weariness, and dispiritedness related to the constant need to consider physical limitations when planning to undertake household activities, including feeding. Three participants described how they grew weary of the need to pay attention to food composition, reminiscing about how easy making meals and eating used to be. The participant who was feeding two family members who were living with cancer reported that she always felt unsure about what she was feeding her family. She discussed her constant worry about whether the food was safe to eat (free of contaminants or cancer-producing compounds) and whether she was inadvertently helping the cancer or helping to create a healthy environment to aid her daughter's and husband's recovery.

All seven participants in the LA group expressed a sense of loneliness related to eating-feeding struggles. Despite the support of family and friends, all participants expressed feeling alone in their suffering and in their efforts to hold everything together personally and for the family. They described looking for information or guidance on the Internet and in books and magazines, but found little or nothing that reflected their experiences. Instead, they found cookbooks or what they considered as light-hearted accounts or cheerleading style encouragements about how "great" life can be when living with cancer, diabetes or bowel disease. These messages and images heightened their sense of feeling alone, even though they were living with their families.

EXPLORING MY RESPONSE TO THE NARRATIVES OF PARTICIPANTS IN THE LA GROUP

I wondered about my surprised response to learning how participants in the LA group retained their feeding roles and that some had actively discouraged family involvement. My initial response was that families should help. It did not seem right that the person in the family least physically able to cook and who was managing symptoms of their illness should cook for the family. This point of view was based on the value that I place on fairness and equality in household workload distribution, a perspective that arose from growing up in a family with five children and at a time when grocery stores closed at 6:00 p.m. My father did all the family shopping because my parents' work schedules were such that he could get to stores during the day, and my mother could not. My father cooked supper when he worked day shifts, we had '"get your own meals" when he was on afternoon shifts. Most often, making supper was shared between my mother and my brothers and me when Dad was on night shifts. It usually fell to me, the youngest, to go wake Dad up for supper—the thinking was that he would be less grumpy towards me than towards my brothers. Those night-shift dinner times were always strained because of my Dad's disturbed sleep schedule. When my brothers married, they carried with them the ritual of shared distribution of shopping and cooking, whereas I had a partner who considered shopping and cooking as "women's work," contrary to my ideal of the equal division of household work. Thus, when I heard from participants in the LA group about retaining their feeding role for their families, despite the challenges they faced, my reaction was based on my beliefs about fairness—that the person who was the least well in the household should not be the person responsible for cooking.

However, as I learned from these interviews, how a mother decided to feed her family when experiencing serious illness was not about fairness or equality; rather, it was about efforts to continue to create and nurture one's family when other possible approaches to offer this support were no longer possible. It was about trying to gain control (in the household domain) when the personal experience of eating (per the personal domain) and eating away from home (the beyond household domain [domains within the OFFENN]) became difficult to or beyond control.

I have never been seriously ill, nor have I had my daily life activities curtailed because of illness or disability, so I do not know how I might behave in a similar situation. Realizing that my response to these narratives was a result of my own upbringing and expectations led me to not impose my own beliefs about feeding the family on others when in counselling or advice-offering situations. Alternatively, I learned to create space for conversations about what will suit the situation for the person seeking advice about feeding his or her family. Furthermore, it is important to recognize that a mother who has the feeding role may not actually *seek advice* on feeding their family when they experience illness for, as DeVault indicates, the everydayness of feeding renders it invisible such that women may seek advice for another reason such as help with anxiety or feeling out of control (91).

DISCUSSION

Returning to the question I had at the outset about "what kind of help helps" when working with women (including mothers) who are experiencing illness and have feeding responsibilities for their families, two important points for consideration emerged from this study about the importance of listening to another's narrative and of finding ways to offer support that do not involve imposing one's beliefs on another. Although the number of participants in the study was small, and not all were mothers, the finding that even when sick, the mothers with feeding responsibility carried on with it speaks to the importance these women placed on this role. The mother with feeding responsibility is the central figure who creates and sustains the feeding roles, rituals, and routines that contribute to stability and daily functioning in families. Their commitment to this responsibility is something to consider when working with clients who are mothers, even when this responsibility to feed seems (to an outsider) to be adding to what is already stressful. This is certainly different than offering only nutrient-based advice, as I had been trained to do.

In considering not imposing one's own ideas and ideals about feeding in families when in a helping role, I take inspiration from Wilber:

> Over the years I've talked to a lot of people who have cancer. At first I wasn't sure what to say. The only way I could discover how to help someone was by listening. Only when I heard what they were trying to say could I get a sense of what they needed, of the issues they were confronting at the time, of the kind of help that would really help at that specific moment. (252)

and

> I remind myself that I don't have to give concrete ideas or advice to be of help. Listening is helping. Listening is giving. I try to be emotionally accessible to them, to reach through my own fears and touch them, to maintain human contact. I find there are many fearful things we can laugh at once we've allowed ourselves to be truly afraid. I try to steer clear of the temptation to define imperatives for others, even imperatives such as fight for your life, change yourself, or die consciously. I try to stay in touch with my own fear that I might one day find myself in the same situation they are in. I must constantly learn how to make friends with illness, to not see it as failure. I try to use my own setbacks and weaknesses and illnesses to develop compassion for others and for myself, while remembering

> to not take serious things too seriously. I try to stay aware of the opportunities for psychological and spiritual healing all around me in the very real pain and suffering that ask for our compassion. (255)

Listening contributes to building an understanding of what matters to the other person in feeding his or her families. Mothers with feeding responsibility and women with partners or other adults for whom they have feeding responsibility may have different views from one another and from those of the person offering counselling. "Listening is helping" (255). I observed in the interviews, especially those with mothers, that they mentioned not having thought about the importance that they placed on retaining their feeding roles. Thus, listening creates opportunities for women to express what is on their minds or what they might not realize was causing anxiety about feeding their families, what Lupton describes as a "social-psychological mesh related to eating beliefs and behaviours" ("Food, Memory and Meaning" 665).

The other point arising from this study is that although much material exists about food, cooking, and feeding families, material on sharing experiences while living with illness and disability, especially in the complex lives of mothers, is not. As health and human service professionals, as family members and friends, and as community members and neighbours, we all benefit when we find words to talk about the phenomena of feeding the family during times of illness and, specifically, about mothers who are experiencing illness. Shielded, as many Canadians are, from the everyday phenomena of illness and end-of-life processes, how families continue to be fed when the mother is sick may not be a topic with which many are familiar. As Wilber notes, if, when working with people who are experiencing health challenges, we can reach through our own fears (255), "allow ourselves to be truly afraid" (255), "steer clear of the temptation to define imperatives for others" (255)—in other words, find ways to talk about it—the experience will not be so lonely and frightening for all of us who will go through it.

There are, undoubtedly, other mothers who have feeding responsibility but do not want to continue with their feeding role when they experience changed health status. They, however, have no choice but to continue because they have no support, have time constraints, or have limited finances. How these women cope with or manage the effect of changed life circumstances on their feeding roles is subject for further inquiry.

IMPLICATIONS FOR PRACTICE, EDUCATION, AND RESEARCH

The phenomenon of mothers with feeding responsibility experiencing changed health status has implications for practitioners, educators, and researchers working in health and human services, including but not limited to nutrition and dietetics, sociology, psychology, nursing, medicine, public health, women's studies, gender studies, family and consumer studies, gerontology, and social services. Recognizing and embracing the universality of the illness experience in families draws attention to the importance of attending to mothers' feeding roles when someone in the family, including the mother herself, experiences changed health status. The taken-for-grantedness of feeding the family is such that many mothers struggle alone to find solutions that work for them. This need not be the case. Common strategies for coping with changes in eating and feeding during illness as ways to support mothers trying to feed their families while experiencing illness do exist. Such strategies include social comparison (comparing their experiences to those of others who have experienced a similar situation), creating a "new normal" (devising new feeding rituals and routine that eventually become familiar), and garnering social support (Morley, "Women's Experiences"). "Social comparison" refers to finding ways to share experiences of mothers trying to feed their families while living with changed health status. This can be through experience sharing, storytelling (in person or recorded), photovoice installations, documentary film, and other means. Creating a "new normal" refers to working collaboratively to support mothers as they find ways to continue feeding their families without overburdening themselves. Recognizing that one need not live up to an external ideal and that there are options on how to create personalized solutions can be calming and reassuring. "Garnering social support" refers to surrounding oneself with those who positively support one's decisions and behaviours while taking steps to avoid those who only offer criticism. Mothers with feeding responsibility experiencing changed health status may not have sufficient energy to find these supports, so health and human service workers can serve in this role and can connect mothers to other face-to-face and virtual sources of support. For those working in programs where food and nutrition advice is offered or where food is provided or cooking takes place, consideration of feeding roles, rituals, and routines and associated meanings opens lines of communication with participants beyond the limits of food and nutrient-oriented tips, advice, and facts. These emotionally laden aspects of daily life are rich for exploration.

In the education of future health and human service workers, educators can consider exploring with students the complexity of feeding the family, DeVault's notion of the role of mothers constituting family through feeding, and how feeding the family changes when the mother (or anyone in the family) has experienced changed health status.

Some of the research possibilities arising from this study include conducting similar interviews with greater numbers of participants, comparing the experiences of mothers feeding responsibility living in different circumstances (e.g., single mothers, mothers living with extended family members, mothers in same sex relationships), studying the determinants of health as they relate to mothers with feeding responsibility who are experiencing changed health status, and studying the phenomenon for mothers living in different parts of the world. Learning how health and human service workers apply these findings in their counselling roles is of interest, as is learning about the nature and effectiveness of mentoring students to practice with an appreciation of feeding roles and client perceptions of nutrition counselling approaches that extend beyond food- or nutrient-based information giving approaches. Findings from this study serve as a preliminary look into a complex phenomenon.

WORKS CITED

DeVault, Marjorie. *Feeding The Family: The Social Organization of Caring as Gendered Work*. Chicago, IL: University of Chicago Press, 1993. Print.

Fieldhouse, Paul. *Food and Nutrition: Customs and Culture*. 2nd ed. Cheltenham, UK: Stanley Thorne. 1996. Print.

Fischler, Claude. "Food, Self and Identity." *Social Science and Medicine* 27.2 (1988): 275-292. Print.

Fischler, Claude. *L'Homnivore*. Paris, France: Odile Jacob, 1990. Print.

Lupton, Deborah. "Food, Memory and Meaning: The Symbolic and Social Nature of Food Events". *Sociological Review* 42.4 (1994): 664-685. Print.

Lupton, Deborah. *Food, The Body and The Self*. Thousand Oaks, CA: Sage, 1996. Print.

Morley, Catherine. "Women's Experiences of Eating with Changed Health Status." Diss. University of Calgary, 2002. Print.

Morley, Catherine. "Development and Use of the Organizational Framework For Exploring Nutrition Narratives". Submitted to the Journal of Critical Dietetics, July 2014.

Patton, Michael Quinn. *Qualitative Research and Evaluation Methods*. 4th edition. Thousand Oaks, CA: Sage, 2015. Print.

Wilber, Ken. *Grace And Grit: Spirituality And Healing in the Life and Death of Treya Killam Wilber*. Boston, MA: Shambhala Press, 1993. Print.

8.
PumpMoms

Technology, Stigma and Support

TANYA M. CASSIDY

THROUGHOUT HISTORY AND ACROSS CULTURES and for a myriad of reasons, mothers have expressed their maternal milk (by hand and/or using a manual or automated device) to feed their (or other mothers') infants. Sometimes this is done to aid mothers in their own comfort (e.g. to relieve engorgement and mastitis, to increase supply, or to delegate feeding to others). Other times mothers express their milk to aid infants to nurse for some other reasons. The history of the electric breastpump is intimately linked to the expression of human milk to feed prematurely born (prior to thirty-seven week gestation) infants. The breastpump is increasingly recognized as a neonatal medically indicated intervention, ever since health care researchers (e.g. Schanler, Shulman, and Lau) demonstrated positive outcomes among prematurely born infants who receive a fortified human milk diet.[1] In countries such as Ireland, where the breastfeeding rate is one of the lowest in the world (with only 48.4 percent of mothers breastfeeding when leaving hospital) (Layte and McCrorty), mothers of infants born prematurely are told by health care providers that her milk is a potentially life-saving medicine. For some of these mothers who did not intend to breastfeed, "breastmilk feeding," or the feeding of breastmilk that has been expressed, is seen as a useful alternative form of infant feeding that they may never have previously considered. However, for those mothers of premature infants who may have wished to breastfeed, having to feed breastmilk by any means other than directly from their own breasts may be perceived as an additional personal loss following their experience of their pregnancy ending early.

Hand expression and the use of manual breastpumps have been recognized as continuing to be essential components of a breastfeeding mother's repertoire (Becker et al). The widespread use of the personal electrical breastpump did not begin until the 1990s, when the current industry leader Medela, a Swiss manufacturer, introduced a vacuum-operated pump intended specifically for home use, leading to pump sales quadrupling by 2009 (Lepore). In some parts of the world, but not in Ireland, breastpumps have become such a common parental aide that new mothers often receive them as gifts. As this expansion has occurred, there has also been an international reaction to breastmilk feeding, stating that it should not be equated with breastfeeding (Thorley). Concern involves a problematic emphasis on a product (milk), which is no longer linked to a maternal body, being delivered to an infant using some artificial means, such as a cup or a bottle and, therefore, in violation of the WHO International Code of Marketing Breastfeeding Substitutes, which was originally published in 1981. In 2008, following debate and criticism from breastfeeding advocate communities (especially some online groups), Medela issued two statements, which countered concerns regarding their compliance with WHO breastfeeding codes by claiming that their controversial production of bottles was justified as a necessary service for their customers. Meanwhile, some advocates around the world continue to see the company in violation of this code insofar as the manufacture and sale of bottles (albeit for expressed human milk) still seems opposed to a concerted anti-formula agenda.

My discussion of these issues employs complementary triangulated qualitative data (historical materials, interviews with mothers of premature infants in Ireland, and online content analysis of discussions by PumpMoms), all of which are linked to the pivotal year 2008. These three interrelated qualitative data are key to framing this discussion of mothers mediating medicalized and marketing meanings associated with infant feeding choices, which are often doubly stigmatized for the families of premature infants, some of whom look to share these experiences by seeking online support systems. After returning from my own maternity break in 2008, I received ethical approval to also conduct narrative interviews with mothers, all of whom expressed for their prematurely born infants at the Coombe Women and Infants University Hospital in Dublin. I conducted thirty-five detailed discussions about maternal experiences associated with breastmilk. As part of this project, I also obtained permission from the owners and participants of the online discussion group PumpMoms to review relevant exchanges related to breastmilk feeding. Although the moderators of this group are based in the U.S., they draw membership from all over the world, and I was informed that approximately one third of those members are mothers of premature infants. That same year, I collected a series of online materials related to the debates and criticisms circulating around the breastfeeding global community about Medela's breastpump marketing of bottles for breastmilk feeding. In addition, 2008 also marked the highest fertility rate (2.14 children) in Ireland since the end of the 1980s with over seventy five thousand live births that year. Moreover, financial analysts (in hindsight) argue that 2008 marked the beginning of the global economic crisis, and the end of nearly a decade of, not uncontroversial, economic prosperity in Ireland, then known as the "Celtic Tiger."

MEDICALIZED MOTHER'S MILK AND THE ELECTRIC MACHINE

Manual devices for expressing milk have been found in graves dating back to antiquity (Obladen), indicating their presence, use, and (unfortunately) their too often negative outcomes. These artifacts do not tell us the reasons why these devices were used. We do not know if they were used to relieve maternal issues, such as mastitis, inverted nipples, or even to increase supply, all of which are modern maternal reasons for expressing breastmilk. Alternatively, these devices may have been used for reasons linked to the infants themselves, being born early or with particular health concerns, and as such not being able to suckle for some reason. In the case of the former, recourse to maternal milk from another mother was the cultural norm in many societies throughout history, and it was not until the early parts of the twentieth century that other mothers' milk became associated with breastpumps and was linked to medicalized feeding of prematurely born infants, who were referred to officially as "weaklings" (Baker).

In both Europe and North America, hospital care for premature infants expanded at the end of the nineteenth century, and how to feed these tiniest of infants dominated many medical discussions on both sides of the Atlantic (Greer). One can argue that cultural divides regarding the use of wet nurses reflected degrees of cultural acceptance of these alternatives in these different medicalized circumstances. For instance, in Britain and some parts of North America, a more pejorative cultural construction of wet nursing existed, and there seems, therefore, to have been more support for an alternative modified (formula) animal milk product[2] (Apple; Fildes). At the same time in France, Pierre Budin, one of the earliest physicians to specialize in neonatal health care, extensively discussed the importance of mother's milk for both premature and full term infants, whether this milk came from the infant's own mother or another's mother (Sussman).

The beginning of the twentieth century also marked the beginning of what is generally now termed donor human milk banks (Cassidy), a medically controlled system of collecting, processing, and distributing human milk, in particular for premature infants. The origins of this system were to evolve in the first part of the twentieth century, with key contributions to our modern construction occurring on both sides of the Atlantic.[3] In fact, the history of the electric breastpump is directly linked to the medicalized use of human milk for prematurely born neonates. In the 1920s, Isaac Abt, a Chicago paediatrician, in conjunction with the engineer Edward Lasker (who had earlier developed bovine milking machines) developed a machine that was specifically designed to aid mothers of premature infants, and other mothers who were also supplying these infants with expressed breastmilk. In 1925, two years after the patent for this machine had been filed, an article about "Abt's Electric Breast Pump" appeared in the *American Journal of Nursing*, showing the device in use in Chicago (MacDonald).

This article has three other images of the machine in use, but in those images the nurse is the key visible figure, whereas the mother is covered up and unrecognizable. It is possible that the mother

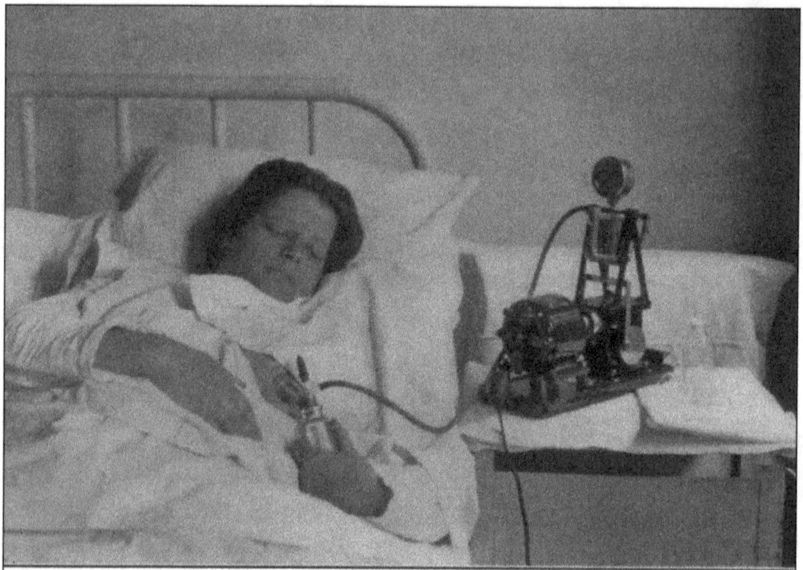

Mother Using Breast Pump—Milk Receptacle Attached

in the other pictures is the mother in the first image (whose name is not given). But it is equally likely that the other images depict other mothers who did not wish to have their face shown for some reason. Either way, it is clear that these other images (in a nursing journal article) re-enforce the medical nature of the device, encouraging nurses and other health care providers to persuade mothers to use these devices and even to help with expression themselves. These electrical devices continued to be used through most of the twentieth century within hospitals and were primarily linked to the feeding of prematurely born infants.

The historical medicalized control of maternal milk expression meant that this product could also come from a variety of mothers and once processed would be deemed a medicinal necessity for some of the most vulnerable infants in the world. However, the digital age has spawned a more communal and more networked exchange of expressed human milk and has created increasing concerns about safety and the meaning of infant feeding in this way. Health concerns on the subject of communicable diseases, such as contemporary concerns about HIV/AIDS and historical considerations regarding syphilis, are also important, a topic I have discussed elsewhere (Cassidy). Furthermore, organizations, such as Le Leche League International, continue to advocate that "breastmilk feeding" should be reserved for infants who are unable to feed directly at the breast and should not be permitted to become a normalized solution to familial feeding and maternal work issues.

"PUMPING FOR PREEMIES" IN IRELAND

Dublin has an extremely long history associated with maternal care, dating back to the eighteenth century when the Rotunda was established, the oldest continuously running maternity care hospital in the world. There are two other maternity hospitals in Dublin, including the other city centre hospital The National Maternity Hospital (which Dubliners simply call Holles Street, where it is located). The other is the Coombe Women and Infants University Hospital, located on the western edge of the city centre (very near the famed Guinness brewery), the main high risk maternity care hospital used for outside of the city. The three hospitals often work together, especially for educational programs, with each of these hospitals assisting in almost nine thousand births a year. The Coombe caters for the highest percentage of prematurely born infants and is one of the largest neonatal units in the Republic of Ireland. In May 2006, the lead clinical midwife (Barbara Whelan) and some of her colleagues started a Saturday morning neonatal post discharge support group for parents and their infants. This award winning[4] endeavour served as the recruiting venue for the mothers in my "Pumping for Preemies" project.[5]

All of the people contacted (except two) were willing to be interviewed,[6] resulting in a total of thirty five mothers telling their stories about breastmilk. All of these mothers began their stories with telling me about their pregnancies and went on to reveal the traumatic circumstances surrounding their birth experiences. They also described the alienation that they felt when confronted with the medical necessity associated with producing maternal milk for their infants who were in the NICU (neonatal intensive care unit). None of the mothers I spoke with had infants who were past thirty-two weeks in gestational age, the point at which researchers argue that infants have developed the abilities to simultaneously breathe, suck, and swallow (Medoff-Copper et al). Accordingly, all of their infants were gavage[7] fed for a period of time, some for several weeks. In line with overall national breastfeeding rates, most of the mothers whom I interviewed that were born in Ireland had not intended to breastfeed and found the prospect of being asked to express breastmilk daunting. It should also be noted, again a reflection of the maternal health care conditions in Ireland, that none of these infants made the transition fully to breast while in the hospital, and the few who were able to do this at home were among the mothers who had always intended to breastfeed, only one of whom was Irish.

Although breastfeeding rates have been slowly increasing, Ireland continues to have one of the lowest rates of breastfeeding in the EU, with the 2012 national perinatal statistics indicating that only 55 percent of mothers reported ever breastfeeding, which was up from only 43 percent in 2003. However, as Layte and McCrory discuss, these national figures are much lower when immigrant mothers are removed, who are significantly more likely to breastfeed. These low breastfeeding rates have a particular impact on Irish mothers, who are then confronted with the medically indicated necessity of human milk for their infants. Learning how to produce milk with such a machine has additional consequences for some of these mothers, whose milk may also be delayed because of the prematurity of their birth experiences. For some of these mothers, health care providers offer help in the form of donor human milk and other mothers' milk, harking back to Irish traditional milk fostering. The main public maternity hospitals in Dublin support around nine thousand births a year, which means that health care providers are tremendously stretched, a situation made worse because of the economic crisis in Ireland. For many of the mothers of premature infants, this results in a lack of support when it comes to establishing a breastfeeding relationship, and most are subtly encouraged to adopt a bottled breastmilk feeding that enables nursing staff to work quicker but makes establishing long-term feeding at the breast for these infants increasingly difficult. However, when faced with the choice of extended hospital care versus early release, many mothers and their families choose the latter. As a result, if they are to continue to provide their infant with breastmilk, it is necessary for them to breastmilk feed their infants. Some of these mothers feel this is a form of breastfeeding, but some breastfeeding advocates argue that it should not be considered breastfeeding, and so some of these mothers go online to find support.

STIGMA AND (ONLINE) SUPPORT FOR BREASTMILK FEEDING AND INDUSTRIALIZED MOTHER'S MILK

It is widely recognized that health professionals (including Cochrane reviewers Kramer and Kakuma) and global advisory groups, such as the WHO, advocate that infants should be exclusively fed breastmilk for the first six months of their lives. At this time, other solid foods can be introduced while infants continue to receive human milk as part of their diet "up to two years of age and beyond" (WHO, "Exclusive Breastfeeding"). However, as one of the mothers on PumpMoms discusses, the global logistics regarding how these recommendations can, should, and will be implemented continue to be a source of controversy and debate and something that all mothers and mothers to be (and their families) grapple with. For growing numbers of mothers internationally, these issues are further complicated when they are faced with a premature birth.

At the time I conducted my interviews in Ireland in 2008, I also reviewed discussions of the Yahoo discussion group PumpMoms, with (at that time) approximately two thousand members from around the world, and the discussion group moderators told me that they believed a third of their subscribers were mothers of premature infants. In order to ensure confidentiality, I will not quote directly from these discussions but instead will summarize some of the key issues faced by many of these mothers. All of these mothers are looking for support for their experiences (in varying degrees) as breastmilk feeding mothers.

Returning to work was the most common concern discussed by mothers on PumpMoms, along with the (not unrelated) supply issues. Being separated from an infant for an extended period of time can cause supply issues, leading some of these mothers to seek support and advice about how to continue to provide their infant with their breastmilk, especially among those women returning to work whether by choice or because their maternity leave is over. The maternal solidarity that they experience online has been helpful for many of these mothers who for whatever reason are breastmilk feeding their infants, a practise which, as Virginia Thorley has argued, should not be equated with breastfeeding, as it often involves the use of bottles (although cups and nursing systems may be used). It is important to remember that these bottles contain human milk rather than formula. It was very common for the mothers on PumpMoms to also make this distinction, especially for those who practise both breastfeeding and breastmilk feeding. Feeding their infant(s) breastmilk not directly from the breast was a necessary choice for some of these mothers, but many felt it did not replace the physical maternal infant bonding associated with breastfeeding, something that many of these mothers regretted not being able to continue because of having to return to work.

Lepore and others have argued that in the U.S. (and probably in other countries) this technology has been an inadequate solution to maternal employment issues. She also recognizes maternal regrets associated with choosing breastmilk feeding for many mothers who would have dreamed of a "successful" breastfeeding relationship with their infants. At the same time, breastfeeding advocates have been equally critical of the resulting expansion of breastmilk feeding (Thorley). These critical evaluations carry an unintended additional stigma for mothers of premature infants, a group of parents that is also expanding globally. This stigma is further complicated by the WHO international breastfeeding code , which is linked to infant bottle feeding protocols originally intended for formula, not breastmilk fed infants, and it is clear that there are important practical, policy, and political needs to address these issues about mothers, breastmilk, and technology. Recently Elizabeth O'Sullivan, an Irish doctoral candidate in the United States, has argued that many mothers who "choose" (especially in countries like the United States where maternity leave is severely truncated) to express their milk for their infants construct these actions as a form of breastfeeding and therefore need to be considered by researchers and policymakers as such. Although many of these mothers feel that their breastmilk feeding may not be ideal, they do nonetheless see it as breastfeeding.

MAKING A VILLAGE WITH THE INDUSTRIALIZED BREAST

The expanded use of the breastpump by breastfeeding mothers is linked to the notion that breastfeeding is increasingly more about the product than about the process, although obviously both are essential components involved in maternal milk infant feeding (Van Esterik). In recent years, there has been an understandable reaction to certain strands of lactivist rhetoric. The construction of breastfeeding as a form of moral imperative has resulted in some formula-feeding mothers feeling judged and stigmatized. If "breast is best," then formula-feeding mothers may feel that they are being defined as less than maternal— biologically as well as morally deficient. Lactivism may appear as one more form of over-determining coercion, another element in a war against women. Furthermore, as this chapter has shown, the traumas associated with premature birth may make breastfeeding particularly problematic. These concerns can only be accommodated and addressed if access to breastmilk is removed from the domain of individual obligation and becomes instead a societal priority. The slogan "it takes a village (to raise a child)" can be reactivated in order to demonstrate how both official and improvised networks can allow human milk to be shared, stored, and distributed on the basis of most urgent need. This conversation involves the application of twenty-first century technologies to practices that are co-extensive with recorded human history.

Also part of this story is the historical medical control of human milk in the NICU. The mothers who produce this milk are, however, at the heart of my research, and it is their experiences that form the basis of my discussion. NICUs around the world aid the mothers of these premature infants in expressing (or pumping) this milk. At the same time, a significant percentage of these mothers experience lactation difficulties as a result of the premature birth, resulting in the century-old health care intervention of donor human milk banking, specifically the use of other mothers' expressed milk. As premature birth has been expanding globally, so too have donor human milk banks, which in some areas have been linked to cultural stigma and pejorative historical and cultural constructions associated with wet nursing or "other mothers' milk." In other parts of the world, where other mothers' milk is more accepted and even culturally integrated, these expansions seem to be occurring very differently. Furthermore, in more affluent parts of the world, these altruistic expressing experiences are increasingly linked to the commercialization or, as Jill Lepore originally notes, "industrialization" of the maternal breast.

Robbie Davis-Floyd's innovative work on the medicalization of American birthing in the 1990s discussed the removal of the mother from a position of central agency and her replacement with technology and medicalized "male" meanings of female reproduction and birth. Similar medicalizations of infant nutrition led to various artificial formulas in the later part of the nineteenth century and the beginning of the twentieth century, especially in light of the cross-cultural variations and difficulties regarding the control, production, and distribution of human milk. Inherent in this tension between different forms of infant food has been the continuing feature of maternal ambivalence. This has been exploited by a global formula company's current advertising campaign in Ireland and the UK that uses the slogan "Mums, you're doing great," illustrating many of the difficulties all parents face on occasions with children, justifying this company's solution to offer artificial milk products. The "great" reference specifically reminds the audience of the "best" reference to the longstanding breastfeeding "breast is best" campaign. Australian breastfeeding advocates, such as Karleen Gribble, argue that breastfeeding should be thought of as "normal" rather than elevated to potentially unattainable heights by saying something is "gold" or out of reach of the majority of people (Berry and Gribble). The unattainable qualities underlying this message indicate how and why the formula industry has not been keen to see this use of "breast is best" eliminated but have instead used it to their advantage. Supported by health care providers, it is only recently that a number of sociologists, such as the Canadian Phyllis Rippeyoung, have asked "is breastfeeding truly cost free."

Increasingly it is recognised that women who breastfeed their children are often at professional and personal disadvantages, which contributes to increasing maternal ambivalence.

Part of this social change is linked to innovations associated with the technology for human milk removal, a history of which is again linked to providing milk to infants who were born prematurely. This technological history is linked both to the medicalization of breastmilk and to the use of other mothers' milk[8] for these vulnerable infants. The technology is directly linked to removal of maternal bodies or breasts and has increased stigma associated with mothers being identified with social prejudice and subject to pejorative constructions particularly in Britain and North America, regarding wet nursing. We should remember that some of these babies have mothers who work hard to ensure that their and other mothers' infants receive the nutritional and, sometimes, medicinal products key to their increased survival. This has also led to the global expansion of maternal generosity associated with donor human milk banks, especially within the not-for-profit system, a communal world (or "a village" as both Saloranta and Rochman argue), where all infants have the opportunity to be given the health benefits associated with maternal milk. "Other mothers' milk" becomes an option based on generosity and support rather than on exploitation and profit, despite being rightly valued as "liquid gold."

NOTES

[1]Human milk fortifier is generally made from bovine products, although there have been moves to produce human milk fortifier in order to make the entire nutrition for these infants human based.
[2]Space does not allow a detailed discussion of the history of infant formula, which is intimately connected with the history of feeding premature infants and the expansion of infant health care professions, both of which contributed to a global undermining of mothers and the feeding of their infants.
[3]I have been recently awarded an EU Horizon 2020 Marie Skłodowska Curie fellowship to study donor human milk bank, which will involve a detailed history being published in the near future.

[4]This program "Neonatal Post Discharge Support Group" was awarded an Irish Healthcare Award in the "Best Patient Education Project" category in 2007.
[5]My "Pumping for Preemies" project received ethical approval from the Coombe Women and Infant's University hospital and direct support from the midwives there, especially Barbara Whelan and the head of neonatology, at that time, Professor Martin White.
[6]Narrative interviewing was used, and these women were asked to tell me their story about breastmilk. Two women did not want to officially be interviewed, but they, nonetheless, wanted to tell me their stories. For ethical reasons, however, I have not included these in my analysis.
[7]Gavage feeding uses a tube and delivers the food directly to the stomach, bypassing the need to swallow. This form of feeding has been part of a medical regime for premature infants since the nineteenth century (Berthod), although the tools and delivery have improved.
[8]Please note that donor milk is routinely pasteurized in most countries around the world. HIV and other contaminants are killed when pasteurized. Space does not permit discussing this issue at length, but, suffice to say, there are donor banks in Norway and Germany that use unpasteurised milk. However, these later banks are required to perform a lot more testing at an additional cost that is considered prohibitive in other countries.

WORKS CITED

Apple, Rima D. *Mothers and Medicine: A Social History of Infant Feeding, 1890–1950*. Madison: University of Wisconsin Press, 1987. Print.

Baker, Jeffrey P. *The Machine in the Nursery: Incubator Technology and the Origins of Newborn Intensive Care*. Baltimore: Johns Hopkins University Press. 1996. Print.

Becker, Genevieve E, Fionnuala Cooney, and Hazel A Smith. "Methods of Milk Expression for Lactating Women." *Cochrane Database of Systematic Reviews* 12 (2011): CD006170. Web. 21 July 2015.

Berry, Nina J., and Karleen D. Gribble. Karleen D. "Breast Is No

Longer Best: Promoting Normal Infant Feeding." *Maternal and Child Nutrition* 4.1 (2008): 74–79. Print.

Berthod, Paul. Calcium and phosphorus requirements of premature infants. La Couveuse et le Gavage a la Maternité de Paris Doctoral thesis. G. Rougier Paris, France. 1887. Print.

Budin, P. *The Nursling: The Feeding and Hygiene of Premature and Full-term Infants*. Trans. W. J. Maloney London, UK: Caxton Publishing Co.,1907. Print.

Cassidy, Tanya M. "Ireland, Irish Women, and Lactation Surrogacy: Imagining a World in Which It Takes a Community to Feed a Child." *An Anthropology of Breastmilk: Challenges to Advocacy and Policy*. Eds. Tanya M. Cassidy and Tom El Abdullahi. New York: Bloomsbury Publishers. 2015. 45-58. Print.

Fildes, Valerie A. *Nursing: A History from Antiquity to the Present*. Oxford: Blackwell, 1988. Print.

Fildes, Valerie A. *Breasts, Bottles, and Babies: A History of Infant Feeding*. Edinburgh: Edinburgh University Press, 1986. Print.

Greer, Frank R. "Feeding the Premature Infant." *The Journal of Nutrition*. 131. 2 (2001): 426S-430S. Web. 9 Sept. 2015.

Kramer Michael S., and Ritsuko Kakuma. "Optimal duration of Exclusive Breastfeeding." *Cochrane Database* 8 (2012) Web. 21 July 2015.

Layte, Richard, and Cathal McCrorty. *Growing Up in Ireland Maternal Health Behaviours and Child Growth in Infancy: Analyses of the Infant Cohort of Growing Up in Ireland Study*. Dublin: Department of Children and Health. Print.

Lepore Jill. "Baby Food: If Breast Is Best, Why Are Women Bottling Their Milk?" *New Yorker Magazine*. Condé Nest, 19 Jan. 2009. Web. 21 July 2015.

MacDonald, Calvina. "Abt's Electric Breast Pump." *The American Journal of Nursing*. 25.4 (1925): 277-280. Print.

Martucci, Jessica. "Breast Pumping", *AMA Journal of Ethics* (formerly *Virtual Mentor)* 15.9 (2013): 791-797. Web. 30 July 2015.

Medoff-Cooper, Barbara, Warren Bilker, and Joel M Kaplan. "Suckling Behavior as a Function of Gestational Age: A Cross-Sectional Study." *Infant Behavior and Development*.24.1 (2001): 83–94. Print.

Obladen Michael. "Guttus, Tiralatee And Terelle: A History of

Breast Pumps." *Journal of Perinatal Medicine* 40.6 (2012): 669-675. Print.

O'Sullivan Elizabeth, S. Geraghty, and K. Rasmussen. "What Is Breastfeeding?: A Qualitative Exploration of Breast Pump Use and the Need for New Terminology." Paper presented at the Maternal and Infant Nutrion and Nurture (MAINN) Conference. UK. June 2015.

Rippeyoung, Phyllis L. F., and Mary Noonan. "Is Breastfeeding Truly Cost Free? Income Consequences of Breastfeeding for Women." *American Sociological Review* 77.2 (2012): 244-67. Print.

Rochman, Bonnie. "Breastfeeding: It Takes a Village to Help Moms to Succeed." *Time*. Time Inc, 2014. Web. 21 July 2015.

Saloranta, Emma. "It Takes a Village to Breastfeed a Child." *Huffington Post*, 2014. Web. 21 July 2015.

Schanler Richard J, Robert J. Shulman, and Chantal Lau. "Feeding Strategies for Premature Infants: Beneficial Outcomes of Feeding Fortified Human Milk versus Preterm Formula." *Pediatrics*. 103.1 (1999):1150–1157.Print

Sussman, George D. "Parisian Infants and Norman Wet Nurses in the Early Nineteenth Century: A Statistical Study." *Journal of Interdisciplinary History* 7.4 (1977): 637-653. Web. 2 Nov. 2010.

Thorley, Virginia. "The Dilemma of Breastmilk Feeding." *Breastfeeding Review: Professional Publication of the Australian Breastfeeding Association* 19.1 (2008): 5-7. Print.

Van Esterik Penny. "Forward." *Ethnographies of Breastfeeding: Cultural Contexts and Confrontations*. Eds. Tanya M. Cassidy and Tom El Abdullahi. New York: Bloomsbury, 2015. xiii – xiv. Print.

World Health Organization (WHO). *International Code of Marketing Breast-milk Substitutes*. WHO International. WHO, 1981. Web. 21 July. 2015.

World Health Organization (WHO). "Exclusive Breastfeeding." WHO International. WHO, 2015. Web. 21 July 2015.

9.
Maternal Fruit and Vegetable Consumption in Canada

Differences between Anglophones and Francophones

DAVOD AHMADI GHEIDARI, GALE E. WEST AND SIMON LANGLOIS

MANY SCIENTIFIC INVESTIGATIONS HAVE illustrated that fruit and vegetable (F&V) consumption protects humans against chronic diseases, such as coronary heart disease (CHD), stroke, hypertension, cancer, and obesity (Gunn et al.; Henry et al.). However, in 2009, only 45 percent of Canadians were consuming adequate daily portions of F&V and by 2012, this proportion had decreased to 40 percent (Canada, Statistics Canada, "Fruit and Vegetable Consumption"). Remarkably, 47 percent of Canadian females were consuming F&V five or more times daily. Since consumption of a more appropriate diet, including F&V, is embedded in family contexts and lifestyles (Schafer et al.), mothers with young children have the greatest likelihood of influencing the eating behaviours of other family members.

The different eating lifestyle of French people has been used to explain "the French Paradox," defined as "the high intake of saturated fat and the low mortality rate from coronary heart disease" (Opie 155). For example, the French eat smaller portions and take more time to eat than do Americans (Rozin et al.). In addition, fruit and vegetable intake, as part of Mediterranean diet, may decrease cardiovascular events and death (Bhupathiraju et al). In Canada, we would like to know whether there is any difference between the F&V intakes of Anglophone and Francophone mothers with children five and less than five years old. We also study the association between their intake of F&V and several lifestyle factors, subjective and objective psychological factors, and certain socio-economic characteristics.

HEALTH LIFESTYLE, PSYCHOSOCIAL, AND ECONOMIC FACTORS

Lifestyle is strongly associated with food consumption habits in general, and F&V consumption in particular. According to the theory of "epidemiological transition," humans are living in an "age of degenerative disease" (De Maio). This time period is strongly evidenced by a rapid growth of non-communicable diseases, which are mainly the consequence of lifestyles with high-calorie intakes and low physical activities (Omran; Magee et al.). Health lifestyle, as a new concept in Sociology, has been defined recently "as collective patterns of health-related behavior based on choices from options available to people according to their life chances" (Cockerham 138). Cockerham illustrates health lifestyle through such characteristics as drinking alcohol, smoking, diet choices, and medical checkups, which are evidenced in each individual's behaviour. In elaborating on lifestyle and behavioral traits, Pollard et al. emphasize the link of smoking as a major factor differentiating between women with higher and lower F&V intake. Others have emphasized that physical health status is also positively associated with F&V intakes (Steptoe et al.).

Life satisfaction, as well as life and job stress, influences individual consumption of F&V. Life satisfaction, defined as the "cognitive evaluation of one's life based on self-selected standards, is one of the key components of happiness" (Lopez 582). One previous study has indicated that "subjective well-being and happiness make a significant contribution in the variance explained for both intentions to consume F&V and actual F&V consumption" (Ding et al. 598). Furthermore, stress and depressive symptoms have been shown to determine women's food choices, including their fruit, vegetable, and meat intake (Park and Iacocca). A significant body of research has also shown that eating habits are linked to socio-economic characteristics. The main theoretical premise that explains the importance of social and economic factors as determinants of eating habits is that one's positioning in the hierarchical structure of a society governs both the quantity and quality of one's diet and, more specifically, intake of F&V (McLeod et al.; Scambler and Scambler). For example, level of education appears to have a significant association with mothers' daily F&V intakes (Franchini et al.). Others have found that marital status can also be used to characterize mothers' health behaviours and food intake (Elfhag and Rasmussen). "Being married is associated with increased intake of F&V and being single or divorced/separated is associated with low F&V intake" (Billson et al. 946). Similarly, income has a dominant effect on an individual's food choices. For example, "low-income populations have lower levels of F&V consumption than do higher-income populations" (Treiman et al. 149).

Careful attention to the determinants of mothers' F&V consumption is beneficial for the promotion of healthy food choices that can lead to healthier family diets and healthier populations (Beydoun and Wang; Ristovski-Slijepcevic et al.). The impact of healthy food choices on social cohesion, which can also improve population health, has thus far been taken for granted by food choice researchers (Berkman et al.).

MOTHERS' FRUIT AND VEGETABLE INTAKE, PSYCHOSOCIAL, AND ECONOMIC FACTORS

The current analyses are based on data from Statistics Canada's 2012 "Canadian Community Health Survey" (N=62,103) (Canada, Statistics Canada). Over half of survey participants were women (N=34,321), from which we selected the Anglophone and Francophone mothers with children five years old and under (N=3,876). Several analyses, such as descriptive, bivariate, and regression statistics, were carried out between the Anglophone and Francophone mothers in order to study the French Paradox. The association between some psycho-social and economic factors (over thirteen variables) and frequency of mothers' F&V consumption was at the front. We used the survey's questions regarding the frequency of eating salad greens, potatoes (not fried), carrots, and other vegetables. Since responses could be given on a daily, weekly, monthly, or yearly basis, whenever a mother's response was given as "number of times per week," that response was divided by 7; "number of times per month" was divided by 30; and "number of times per year" was divided by 365. The final additive scale reflects total daily frequency of consumption of the F&V named above. Scores varied from zero, indicating zero consumption per day, to a high of nineteen times per day. Furthermore, the following variables were included as predictors: having a medical doctor, body mass index (BMI) calculated from self-reported height and weight, frequency of smoking and drinking alcohol, number of minutes per day spent doing general, individual and collective sports, having heart disease, sense of belonging to community, sense of life satisfaction, declared level of life and job stress, highest level of education attained, marital status, employment status, and reported total annual household income.[1]

Results of the general characteristics of the Anglophone (N=2,291) and Francophone (N=755) mothers indicated that, when compared with Anglophone mothers, more of the Francophone mothers had higher advanced education degrees, were living as a couple, and were employed outside the home, but their households had lower annual incomes (See Appendix Table 1). In terms of F&V intakes, there was a significant difference in the frequency with which the Anglophone and Francophone mothers reported daily consumption of the F&V included in the measure. About 30 percent of the Anglophone mothers reported extremely low frequency of consumption. In contrast, 30 percent of the Francophone mothers reported consuming these F&V six or more times a day, which is higher than the Anglophone mothers (see Graphic 1). Thus, more Francophone mothers than Anglophone reported F&V consumption of six or more times per day.

Apart from descriptive analyses, some distinct associations were found between F&V intake and several psycho-social and economic factors for both Anglophone and Francophone mothers with young children (See Table 2 in Appendix). Regardless of language group, having heart disease had no significant association with reported frequency of F&V consumption. In sharp contrast, having a medical doctor and higher BMI status were both significantly associated with lower frequency of intake only among Anglophone mothers. The strength of the association between frequency of smoking and higher frequency of F&V intake was two times stronger among Anglophone mothers than Francophone mothers, but weak associations were found between frequency of

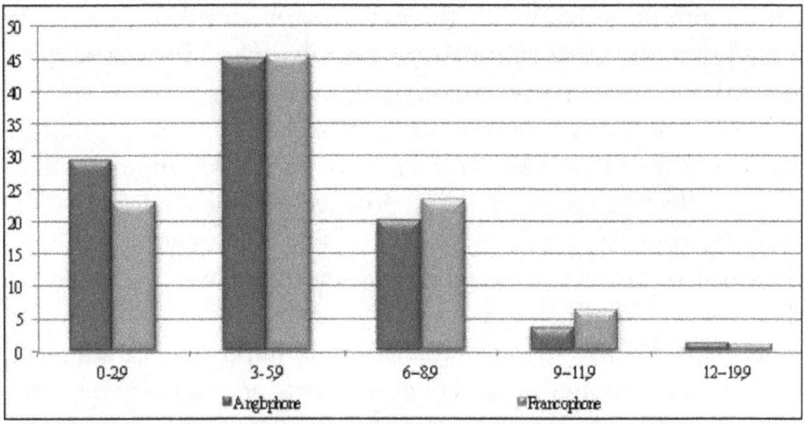

Graphic 1: Distribution percentage of daily frequency of fruit and vegetable intake among Anglophone and Francophone mothers of young children.

Chi-square test value=35,607, with degrees of freedom=8 and level of significance at p=0,000. Source: Statistic Canada, micro-data analysis of the Canadian Community Health Survey, 2012. Statistics calculated by the authors (Canada, Statistics Canada).

drinking alcohol and higher frequency of consumption of F&V for both language groups.

The associations between general physical activity and lower F&V intake were quite strong for both language groups, but doing individual sports had a strong positive association with F&V intake only among Anglophone mothers (Table 2). The association between collective sports and higher F&V consumption was three times stronger among Anglophone mothers than among the Francophone. Life stress and job stress were not associated with frequency of F&V consumption, but life satisfaction was for both language groups. Although sense of community belonging had no association with Francophone mothers' F&V intake, the association was quite strong and negative for the Anglophone mothers.

Three of the socio-economic characteristics (education, marital status, and income) had positive associations with F&V intake for both Anglophone and Francophone mothers, and the strength of the associations was similar in both language groups (Table 2). Employment status, however, was significantly associated with lower F&V intake only among the Anglophone mothers.

When combined in a multivariate regression analysis,[2] few variables continued to be significantly associated with frequency of F&V

consumption, especially for the Francophone mothers (See Table 3 in Appendix). Both frequency of smoking and involvement in general physical activity remained significant for the Anglophone mothers, but the direction of the relationship for general physical activity changed to positive. In contrast to Anglophone mothers, doing collective sport remained positively associated with F&V intake among Francophone mothers. For Anglophone mothers, the positive impact of participating in sports was captured by their general level of physical activity, whereas for Francophone mothers, collective sports remained more important. Among the subjective psychological variables, life satisfaction was no longer significant for either language group, whereas sense of community belonging reversed its significant association with frequency of F&V intake among the Anglophone mothers.[3] Educational status also remained significant for both Anglophone and Francophone mothers; as level of education increased, so did frequency of reported F&V consumption, and this was especially true for the Francophone mothers.[4]

CONCLUSION

Healthy eating habits are considered as one of the key explanations for the French Paradox. As a way to explore the possible existence of the French Paradox in Canada, this chapter has studied Francophone mothers' F&V intake in comparison to that of Anglophone mothers' intake. We also examined the potential for several lifestyle variables, as well as subjective and objective psychological and socioeconomic variables, to explain variations in the frequency of F&V consumption among Anglophone and Francophone mothers.

The analyses indicate that Anglophone and Francophone mothers in Canada who had children aged five and under did not follow the healthy guidelines for daily F&V intake put forth in the 2012 *Canadian Food Guide* (Canada, Health Canada). The majority did not report eating F&V seven and more times daily. However, Francophone mothers did report more frequent intake of F&V than Anglophone mothers. Our findings also demonstrate the importance of some lifestyle characteristics that have significant associations with both the Anglophone and Francophone mothers' F&V intake. This finding is in accordance with Annesi and Mareno, who also found that physical activity affects the frequency of F&V intakes; however, in our study, doing collective sports was consistently associated with Francophone mothers' F&V consumption, whereas general physical activity levels were important for Anglophone mothers.

Styn et al. have also emphasized that quantity and quality of food choices are determined by smoking cigarettes. Our results confirm their findings, particularly for the Anglophone mothers. Although coronary heart disease did not have a meaningful association with frequency of F&V intake among either Anglophone or Francophone mothers of young children, they are themselves quite young adults and are therefore less likely to suffer from heart disease. In general, other more detailed studies do indicate that a higher quantity F&V intake is associated with lower presence of coronary heart diseases (Bhupathiraju).

Canadians are increasingly developing chronic diseases, such as obesity and coronary heart diseases. As Walsh notes, "In modern affluent societies, the diseases exacting the greatest mortality and morbidity, such as cardiovascular disorders, obesity, diabetes, and cancer, are now strongly determined by lifestyle" (579). As a result, the necessity of addressing lifestyle variables is recognized in relation to individual health in general and eating habits in particular.

Cockerham's health lifestyle theory is pertinent to providing a sociological interpretation of the mothers' F&V intake. A healthy lifestyle is based on an individual's choices, but other contextual characteristics, such as class position, educational level, and marital status are also important. These characteristics tend to constrain individuals' actions. Types of experiences and socialization processes in life also predict healthy or unhealthy social behaviours that result from the day-to-day activities and social interactions of individuals. Healthy F&V intakes can be learned from informal relations, such as family or friends, and from formal institutions, such as the *Canada Food Guide*. In the present study, having a stronger sense of belonging to community is one of the factors that determined Anglophone mothers' frequency of F&V intake. In general, Anglophone Canadians living outside Québec have stronger ties to their communities than Canadians living within the mostly Francophone province of Québec (Vanier Institute of the Family).

The importance of the variable education for both language groups in our study suggests a more cognitive explanation. Education is an indicator of the knowledge capital that has been developed and retained by mothers. Cognition of good health practices, associated with education, appear to better explain the behaviour of mothers with young children regarding F&V consumption. The higher the educational level, the higher healthy food consumption is. More research on this observation might confirm this new interpretation of food consumption.

Although Canadians live together in one country, their family dynamics do vary somewhat by language group. The Anglophone and Francophone mothers, surveyed in 2012, reported significantly different frequencies of daily F&V consumption. There were also notable differences in the lifestyle, socio-psychological, and socio-economic characteristics associated with F&V intakes of the Anglophone versus Francophone mothers. These differences suggest that certain elements of the French Paradox potentially exist within Canada.

We would like to thank Research Assistant David Gaudreault in the Department of Sociology at Laval University, who assisted with the methodology section of this article, as well as the Social Sciences and Humanities Research Council and the Fonds de recherche du Québec—Société et culture (FRQSC) for financial support and the Centre interuniversitaire québécois de statistiques sociales (CIQSS) for access to the data.

NOTES

[1]For the bivariate analyses, all interval and continuous variables were recoded into nominal or ordinal scales, whereas the OLS regression analysis was done using unrecoded data, and dummy codes were used for having a medical doctor or heart diseases (1=yes), as well as for marital status (1=couple).

APPENDIX

Table 1. Socio-demographic characteristics of Anglophone and Francophone mothers with young children

	Anglophone	Francophone	Total
Highest level of education* **			
Less than University	56.4	55.7	53.7
Uni. Cert. or Dip.	4.8	4.0	4.9
Bachelor	28.1	26.1	29.0
Above bachelor	10.7	14.2	12.4
Marital status*			
Married or common-law	72.2	78.2	74.4
Widowed, separated, divorced	6.7	5.7	6.3
Single	21.1	16.1	19.3
Employment Status * **			
Employed	75.2	85.7	75.4
Unemployed	24.8	14.3	24.6
Family income* **			
$ 0 – $29,999	14.2	12.6	14.9
$ 30,000 – $49,999	12.6	14.0	13.8
$ 50,000 – $79,000	21.0	27.7	23.0
$ 80,000 – $99,999	14.3	15.1	13.6
$100,000 or more	37.9	30.6	34.7
Sample size	2,291	755	3,876

Chi-square significance: * = p ≤ 0.05; ** = p ≤ 0.01; *** = p ≤ 0.001
Source: Micro-data analysis of the Canadian Community Health Survey, 2012

Table 2. Bivariate associations between the independent variables and daily frequency of fruit and vegetable intake for Anglophone and Francophone mothers of young children

Independent variables	Measure of association	Anglophone	Sig	Francophone	Sig
Lifestyle variables					
Have a medical doctor (1=yes)	Cramer's V	-0.301	0.000	-0.030	0.709
BMI (from self-reported height and weight)	Gamma	-0.090	0.004	-0.075	0.175
Frequency of smoking	Gamma	0.451	0.000	0.222	0.001
Frequency of drinking alcohol	Gamma	0.095	0.003	0.128	0.018
General physical activity	Gamma	-0.328	0.000	-0.250	0.000
Do individual sports	Gamma	0.448	0.000	0.291	0.214
Do collective sports	Gamma	0.135	0.000	0.046	0.048
Have heart disease (1= yes)	Cramer's V	0.048	0.258	0.088	0.215
Subjective psychological variables					
Sense of belonging to community	Gamma	-0.253	0.000	-0.099	0.105
Life satisfaction	Gamma	0.186	0.000	0.153	0.002
Life stress	Gamma	-0.049	0.175	0.018	0.773
Job stress	Gamma	0.027	0.516	0.108	0.126
Socio-economic variables					
Education	Cramer's V	0.234	0.000	0.254	0.000
Marital status (1=couple)	Cramer's V	0.195	0.000	0.188	0.001
Employment status	Cramer's V	-0.184	0.000	-0.133	0.135
Income	Cramer's V	0.236	0.000	0.291	0.000

urce: Micro-data analysis of the Canadian Community Health Survey, 2012.

Table 3. Linear regression of the independent variables on daily frequency of fruit and vegetable intake among Anglophone and Francophone mothers of young children

	Anglophone (n=2,291) Standardized Beta	Sig	Francophone (n=775) Standardized Beta	Sig
ifestyle variables				
Have a medical doctor (1=yes)	0.043	0.164	-0.014	0.773
BMI (from self-reported height & weight)	-0.010	0.734	0.026	0.589
Frequency of smoking	**0.151**	**0.000**	0.018	0.729
Frequency of drinking alcohol	-0.038	0.213	-0.049	0.314
General physical activity	**0.185**	**0.000**	0.111	0.168
Do individual sports	0.079	0.094	0.116	0.134
Do collective sports	-0.012	0.726	**0.126**	**0.014**
Have heart disease (yes=1)	-0.029	0.327	0.024	0.613
ubjective psychological variables				
Sense of belonging to community	**0.084**	**0.007**	0.047	0.329
Life satisfaction	0.059	0.078	0.075	0.137
Life stress	0.004	0.908	-0.059	0.294
Job stress	0.020	0.533	-0.052	0.350
ocioeconomic variables				
Education	**0.076**	**0.019**	**0.183**	**0.000**
Marital status (1=couple)	0.059	0.064	-0.008	0.875

urce: Micro-data analysis of the Canadian Community Health Survey, 2012.

[2]To measure the potential of the independent variables to explain variations in the frequency of F&V consumption, two ordinary least square (OLS) linear regressions were run for both Anglophone and Francophone mothers. To avoid problems of collinearity among the independent variables, both income and employment status were excluded from these analyses due to their strong correlations with educational status.

[3]It should be noted that the R Square coefficients are 0.159 for Anglo and 0.135 for Franco Canadian mothers and are significant at the 0,000 level.

[4]The standardized Beta for Anglophone mothers is more than double that for the Francophone mothers.

WORKS CITED

Annesi, J., and N. Mareno. "Temporal Aspects of Psychosocial Predictors of Increased Fruit and Vegetable Intake in Adults with Severe Obesity: Mediation by Physical Activity." *Journal of Community Health* 39.3 (2014): 454-463. Print.

Berkman, L., et al. "From Social Integration to Health: Durkheim in the New Millennium." *Social Science & Medicine* 51.6 (2000): 843-857. Print.

Beydoun, A., and Y. Wang. "Parent–Child Dietary Intake Resemblance in the United States: Evidence from a Large Representative Survey." *Social Science & Medicine* 68.12 (2009): 2137-2144. Print.

Bhupathiraju, S., et al. "Quantity and Variety in Fruit and Vegetable Intake and Risk of Coronary Heart Disease." *The American Journal of Clinical Nutrition* 98.6 (2013): 1514-1523. Print.

Billson, H., et al. "Variation in Fruit and Vegetable Consumption among Adults in Britain. An Analysis from the Dietary and Nutritional Survey of British Adults." *European Journal of Clinical Nutrition* 53.12 (1999): 946-952. Print.

Canada. Health Canada. "Eating Well with Canada's Food Guide." *Health Canada: Food and Nutrition*. Government of Canada, 2012. Web. 8 Sept. 2015.

Canada. Statistics Canada. "Canadian Community Health Survey." *Canadian Community Health Survey—Annual Component*. Government of Canada, 2012. Web. 8 Sept. 2015.

Canada. Statistics Canada. "Fruit and Vegetable Consumption, 2012." *Health Fact Sheets*. Government of Canada, 2012. Web. 8 Sept. 2015.

Cockerham, W. C. "Bourdieu and an Update of Health Lifestyle Theory." *Medical Sociology on the Move: New Directions in Theory*. Ed. W. C. Cockerham. New York: Springer Publication, 2013.127-154. Print.

De Maio, F. *Global Health Inequities: A Sociological Perspective*. London: Palgrave Publication, 2014. Print.

Ding, T., et al. "Does Subjective Well-Being Predict Health-Enhancing Behavior? The Example of Fruit and Vegetable Consumption." *British Food Journal* 116.4 (2014): 598-610. Print.

Elfhag, K., and F. Rasmussen. "Food Consumption, Eating Behavior and Self-Esteem among Single v. Married and Cohabiting Mothers and Their 12-year-old Children." *Public Health Nutrition* 11.9 (2008): 934–939. Print.

Franchini, B., et al. "Fruit and Vegetables: Intake and Sociodemographic Determinants among Portuguese Mothers." *Annals of Nutrition and Metabolism* 63.1-2 (2013):131–138. Print.

Gunn, C., et al. "Midlife Women, Bone Health, Vegetables, Herbs and Fruit Study. The Scarborough Fair Study Protocol." *BMC Public Health* 13.23 (2013):13-23. Print.

Henry, H., et al. "Associations of Decisional Balance, Processes of Change, and Self-Efficacy with Stages of Change for Increased Fruit and Vegetable Intake among Low-Income, African-American Mothers." *Journal of the American Dietetic Association* 106.6 (2006): 841-849. Print.

Lopez, S. *Encyclopedia of Positive Psychology.* London: Blackwell Publishing, 2009. Print.

Magee, M., et al. "Commentary: Co-occurrence of Tuberculosis and Diabetes: New Paradigm of Epidemiological Transition." *International Journal of Epidemiology* 40.2 (2011): 428-431. Print.

Omran, A. "The Epidemiologic Transition: A Theory of the Epidemiology of Population Change." *The Milbank Memorial Fund Quarterly* 49.4 (1971): 509-538. Print.

Opie, L. "Invited Editiorial: The French Paradox: Are 'They' Really So Different?" *Dialogues in Cardiovascular Medicine* 13.3 (2008): 155-158. Print.

Park, C., and M. O. Iacocca. "A Stress and Coping Perspective on Health Behaviors: Theoretical and Methodological Considerations." *Anxiety, Stress, & Coping* 27.2 (2014): 123–137. Print.

Pollard, J., et al. "Lifestyle Factors Affecting Fruit and Vegetable Consumption in the UK Women's Cohort Study." *Appetite* 37.1 (2001): 71-79. Print.

Ristovski-Sliijepcevic, S., et al. "Being a 'Good Mother': Dietary Governmentality in the Family Food Practices of Three Ethno Cultural Groups in Canada." *Health* 14.5 (2010): 467-483. Print.

Rozin, P., et al. "The Ecology of Eating: Smaller Portion Size in France than in the United States Help Explain the French Paradox." *Psychological Science* 14.5 (2003):450-454. Print.

Schafer, R., et al. "Marital Food Interaction and Dietary Behavior." *Social Science & Medicine* 48.6 (1999): 787-96. Print.

Scambler, G., and S. Scambler. "Marx, Critical Realism, and Health Inequalities." *Medical Sociology on the Move: New Directions in*

Theory. Ed. W. C. Cockerham. New York: Springer Publication, 2013. 83-103. Print.

Steptoe, A., et al. "Quality of Life and Self-Rated Health in Relation to Changes in Fruit and Vegetable Intake and in Plasma Vitamins C and E in a Randomized Trial of Behavioral and Nutritional Education Counselling." *British Journal of Nutrition 92.1* (2004): 177-184. Print.

Styn, M., et al. "Cue-Induced Cigarette and Food Craving: A Common Effect?" *Addictive Behaviors* 38.3 (2012): 1840–1843. Print.

Treiman, K. "Attitudes and Behaviors Related to Fruits and Vegetables among Low-Income Women in the WIC Program." *Journal of Nutrition Education* 28.3 (1996): 149-157. Print.

Vanier Institute of the Family. *Families Count: Profiling Canada's Families*. Ottawa, Ontario: Vanier Institute of the Family, 2010. Print.

Walsh, R. et al. "Lifestyle and Mental Health." *American Psychologist* 66.7 (2011): 579-592. Print.

III.

FOOD SECURITY IN INSECURE CIRCUMSTANCES

10.
Cooking to Win the War

Canadian Mothers in the Second World War

TRACEY LEIGH DOWDESWELL

IN THIS AGE OF FAST-FOOD OUTLETS, big-box supermarkets, food fads, and food activism, it is easy to forget that mothers have not always had such a wide range of choices or such ease of access to nutritious food. During World War II, a significant amount of Canada's domestic food production was diverted to the export market, resulting in food rations and price controls (Auld 1). The strategies were designed to produce a sufficient supply of food while also maintaining adequate nutrition at home. I have divided these strategies into three main categories: to ration what was produced, to repurpose food supplies so that they could be put to better use, and to increase production across society. Of course, much of this work fell to Canadian housewives to perform, which changed dramatically how many of them grew, cooked, and prepared foods. At the time, women's domestic labour was filtered through the lens of gender, and the term "housewives" included working women, single, and childless women as well as grandmothers, and this paper attempts to tease out from the historical record the experiences and reflections of the mothers who carried out these tasks. In many ways, more work needs to be done to re-examine the record through the lens of mothering, as mothers and children are often obscured within it.

The Canadian government and its partners in the private media were all encouraging housewives to "do their part" for the war effort. Their labour was needed, not for the welfare of Canadian children, but to supply food for Britain, for soldiers fighting overseas, and for men working in essential industries at home.

Canadian housewives had been told that they were cooking to win the war, and they took this to heart. The Canadian government's centrally-planned wartime economy could only be made operational by the concerted actions of millions of Canadian women acting *locally* (Bruce vii). So, too, did Canadians rise beautifully to the challenge: food production and preservation increased dramatically during the war years, and Canadians were not only consuming more calories but they were also eating a more nutritious diet, including far more fruits, vegetables, and milk than they had been during the Depression (Mosby, "Food on the Home Front"). In this, Canadian mothers were helping not only their own children but their neighbours' children as well as other mothers' hungry children in Britain and Europe, in what was an enormous collective effort.

Fortunately, Canadians never experienced the full brunt of the food shortages and ration systems imposed in Britain, and certainly not the outright hunger and even starvation that ravaged many parts of the world during the war years. Canada's scarcity was in many ways a manufactured one, and the strategies that Canadian housewives used to cope were remarkably successful but also have much to teach today, as potential calamity looms every day: well-stocked big-box stores and their "just-in-time" supply chains belie the scarcity that could ensue should they ever be disrupted; the threat of continuing drought in global breadbaskets like California (Hanson et al.) and Brazil (Winter et al.) threaten food shortages and price inflation in our own time; and the environmental ravages of the "3000-mile-salad" (Kunstler) have left people today looking for alternatives to conserve resources and increase local production. This paper hopes to draw on some of these lessons and to use the wisdom developed by Canadian mothers during the war to inspire solutions to the challenges of food security faced today.

MOTHERS AND FOOD CONSERVATION

The main goal of the Canadian government's food policy during the war was to assist Britain in maintaining adequate food stocks (Auld 1). In this, Canadian efforts were ultimately successful. At the end of 1945, British Minister of Food, Sir Ben Smith, said,

"One of the reasons why Hitler failed to starve us into defeat was the wonderful supplies we got from Canada" (Auld 1).

The efforts of Canadian housewives were crucial to this success. In 1941, Canada's National War Services Minister, J.T. Thorson, told the House of Commons that the "women who keep the heart of the nation sound by doing their daily tasks in the homes and the communities are doing war service of the highest possible order" (Bruce 1). Mrs. John Scott, a pioneering suffragette, stated that for her, cooking was the most important contribution that women could make; she opined that "most of the troubles of the world might be solved if 'everyone got three square meals a day'" (qtd. in Bruce 2). Indeed, very few of the problems of the world can begin to be tackled when this not the case. This was the context within which Canadian housewives found renewed meaning in their daily tasks.

The ration books that housewives took shopping must surely be one of the more familiar wartime measures that governments instituted, but rationing was only one of several policies designed to control prices and distribute scarce food supplies. The Wartime Prices and Trade Board (WPTB) was given sweeping powers to control the price, supply. and distribution of all of the "necessaries of life" in Canada (Auld 10). In 1942, the Canadian government, perhaps thinking that this was an excellent way to reach out to Canadian housewives, named Byrne Hope Sanders, the long-time editor of *Chatelaine* magazine, as director of the Consumer Branch of the WPTB (Bruce 3). The WPTB was authorized under the *War Measures Act*, which "erected the greatest structure of administrative controls ever experienced by Canadians. The objective was the early attainment of mobilization of the nation for war" (Auld 5). A lead editorial in *Chatelaine* magazine told housewives that they possessed the "power to sabotage" Canada's war against inflation and, thus, the war effort as a whole (Editorial, Chatelaine 76).

Only a small number of consumer goods were actually rationed, and government policies were primarily concerned with managing shortages and curbing inflation (Fahrni 3). Rationed goods included commodities that were particularly wanted in Britain, such as sugar, tea, coffee, meat, milk, and butter (Bruce 7). Ration coupons and shortages made obtaining necessities much more laborious than it had been before the war and added to housewives' daily chores. As Keshen states:

> As materiel shortages and rationing became more prominent features of daily life from 1942 onwards, shopping grew more difficult. Strict controls over petrol consumption and the purchase of tires resulted in the discontinuation of store delivery services. Women found themselves on long bus rides or even on bicycles, trudging from store to store in search of often scarce goods. (245)

With a rise in single mothers in the workforce and with even mothers of very young children being encouraged to work to do their patriotic duty, the daily burdens on mothers increased (Bruce 109). Cooking and child care tasks increasingly fell to those housewives who were not employed and who, therefore, assumed a greater share of these tasks. Gwen Lambton, a single mother who worked night shifts at a factory in Toronto, recalls how lucky she was to find a landlady who could look after her two children while she worked and who often fed the family when money was scarce. She remembers how her landlady, "out of the goodness of her heart, sometimes slips me a baloney sandwich," before Gwen went out, exhausted, to work the graveyard shift (Latta 31).

The government's policies were not carried out by bureaucrats but by cadres of housewives volunteering their support. Some of these networks were formal and organized by the government. As Fahrni states, "[t]he consumer Branch of the Wartime Prices and Trade Board in fact secured the official cooperation of 16,000 women across the country, all of whom agreed to monitor prices and report back to the board" (3).

At the same time that these activities were promoted using the trope of the housewife as the good consumer and household manager, these same activities also helped to empower mothers by making their roles public and visible and by highlighting the true importance of their unpaid labour. As Fahrni explains, "[t]hese women, acting in the name of wives and mothers, targeted the state as well as shopkeepers, and claimed gendered citizenship rights" (1). This made families' and mothers' claims visible in the public sphere and assisted women in organizing during wartime around consumer issues; this also helped women to claim gendered rights of economic citizenship during the post-war reconstruction period (Fahrni 2).

RATIONS AND CONTROLS

As Mosby reminds us, rationing was only part of a much larger set of government interventions into the wartime kitchens of the nation (Mosby 7, "Food Will Win the War"). Many of the activities that housewives were now asked to perform—conserve food, save scraps, and improve nutrition—had an even bigger impact on how they cooked and prepared food. As Anne Fromer wrote in *Saturday Night* in 1942, "Canada has determined to change the eating habits of a nation, because she [Canada] has learned that efficient production of food is only half the victory. It takes efficient consumption, too, to give full meaning to the slogan, 'Food will win the war'" (qtd. In Mosby 3, "Food Will Win the War," citing Anne Fromer, "Is Food the Answer to Increased Production?" *Saturday Night* 12 December 1942: 42-43).

One key task of housewives was to collect salvage materials—bones, bottles, rags, rubber, paper, glass, metals, and fats and oils—that were needed to produce war supplies (Bruce 4). Collecting fat scraps for ammunition was particularly important for the war effort, and it is here that the militarization of housework becomes most evident. Canadian housewives were told to conserve these materials so that each could be "a munition maker right in your own kitchen" (qtd. in Mosby 109, "Food Will Win the War"). One advertisement claimed that each pound of fat a housewife saved supplied "enough glycerine to fire 150 bullets from a Bren gun" (Mosby 109).

Canadian housewives were also encouraged to feed their families more in wartime and to cook and serve more nutritious foods. Nutrition experts had found that 60 percent of the Canadian population was suffering from some form of vitamin deficiency—a legacy of the poverty and crop failures of the Depression—and this was causing alarming rates of medical rejections from the military (Mosby, "Food on the Home Front"). Perhaps it was this rather than a concern over the health of poorer children that prompted the government to improve nutrition. The federal government launched the Canadian Nutrition Program in 1942, including a widespread advertising campaign, urging "Eat right, feel right—Canada needs you strong!" (Mosby 21. "Food Will Win the War"). This campaign also included the first edition of "Canada's Official Food Rules," which would later become the *Canada Food Guide*, and included the now-familiar food groups and proportions needed to maintain a healthy diet (Buswell, "Winning Through").

Canada's "Official Food Rules" from 1942 and 1944 do reference children, stating that children required one pint of milk per day versus half a pint for adults (Health Canada). Elsewhere, children were relatively absent from the public discourse, as it was directed towards housewives. One advertisement urged Canadians, "In wartime eat one more slice of bread each meal" (Advancement of Canadian National Health). This ad draws heavily on the gendered stereotypes of the period. The message is ostensibly directed at men, telling them, "Today, you're burning up more energy and you need more energy food. Two slices of bread a meal are *not enough*. You can't work longer hours, do heavier wartime jobs on your peacetime energy quota." In the accompanying illustration, a housewife serves this extra slice of bread to a man adjusting his tie, getting ready to go to work, and looking entirely too tidy to perform much heavy labour in a wartime industry. What is most surprising is that this is an advertisement for baker's bread, complete with a picture of a smiling—male!—baker. Here, women's traditional skills are devalued and obscured, and the woman is depicted as a servant, a willing conduit between one working man and another. This presents a gendered and idealized image of an increasingly consumerized upper-middle class household. This advertisement also suggests that the housewives' role in feeding their families at this time was largely about producing healthy workers, not healthy children. For those mothers for whom food was scarce, a question arises as to whether they felt pressure to distribute food to working male family members rather than to young children.

Housewives were also presented with a wealth of new recipes that better conserved scarce and rationed foods. One of the most popular was "war cake," a milk-less, egg-less and butter-less fruit cake that stored well for use in overseas care packages. Mosby has located one version of this cake from Mrs. Charles Regis who, due to the length of time she had been using this recipe, likely devised it during the First World War (Regis). Mrs. Regis states that, "If made one month before using this will be found a very moist cake, and may be kept any length of time" (Regis). Grandmothers, who had prior experience in food rationing in World War I, seem to have found that their recipes were now of assistance to a new generation of mothers feeding their families in another world war.

Other advertisements of the time urged housewives to change their cooking habits to conserve resources, while drawing on traditional gendered stereotypes. One French-language poster wisely urges mothers to cook in ways that guard against vitamin loss, such as using a minimum amount of water and then reusing the water for soups and sauces (Metropolitan Life). Another advertisement urges housewives to make scarce meat "go further by cooking s-l-o-w-l-y" to reduce shrinkage (Swift). Further tips on preparing and cooking meat are presented by what the ad terms the "famed home economist" Martha Logan, underscoring the fact that many of the nutrition experts and domestic scientists of the day were themselves women. This ad also serves as a reminder of the militarization of housework by proclaiming "Meat is material of war!", reminding housewives that "Canadians are going to need every ounce of meat we can produce if we are to fulfill our wartime obligations to our allies and armed forces and supply the basic needs of our civilian population" (Swift). Again, children are obscured, and one wonders what it meant for mothers to relate to their children as members of the "civilian population."

MOTHERS AND FOOD PRODUCTION: VICTORY GARDENS AND URBAN FARMS

Household gardens were as important to Canada's food security in World War II as they had been during World War I. Despite the successful precedent set in the First World War, the federal government initially discouraged these Victory Gardens, as they were called. This may have been due to a shortage of seed and fertilizer supplies in the early days of the war (Auld 69), which had led to panic buying and a depletion of supplies (Auld 59). Auld is here referring to commercially produced seeds and inorganic fertilizers, suggesting that at the outbreak of the war, Canada was already relying heavily on these inorganic methods of farming. In 1939, Walter James (Lord Northbourne) had already written a treatise critiquing these industrial methods of agriculture, coining the term "organic farming" (James). Just how much of the Victory Garden movement relied on organic methods is a question that requires further investigation.

Shirley Buswell tells the story of Victoria's "intrepid Victory Garden Brigade." Headed by Emily Schofield as president and Elizabeth MacKenzie as secretary, "Victory Gardens were needed, they said, to offset labour shortages in the food industry, and to release food supplies for shipment overseas" (Buswell, "The Garden Warriors"). Although these goals were in line with federal government policies, the Victory Garden Brigade was at first rebuffed (Buswell, "The Garden Warriors"). The deputy minister of agriculture sent the Brigade members a pamphlet entitled "Home Vegetable Gardening," which warned that a home vegetable garden should not be undertaken unless conditions were favourable, as seed, inorganic fertilizers, and energy could not afford to be wasted, and gardening was best left to those who were experienced (Buswell, "The Garden Warriors"). Buswell writes that "[a]lmost forty years later, no musty filing system can stifle the personalities of Schofield and MacKenzie, two women who refused to be daunted by red tape or silenced by official handouts, even in time of war" (Buswell, "The Garden Warriors"). Schofield and MacKenzie wrote back to the minister of agriculture:

> In Victoria we have proved that amateur gardeners, even on land newly broken, have been able to keep themselves in fresh vegetables for the last two or three months, to have some for winter use and some to give away. In addition, the money saved has been used to buy War Bonds, or put towards increased taxation. The general verdict has been "Well worth while." But every citizen must endeavour to grow more vegetables in order to make an appreciable

> difference in the situation that confronts us, and we claim that this is a war effort of primary importance. (Buswell, "The Garden Warriors")

Finally, at the end of 1942, Gardiner's Department reversed its policy and issued a pamphlet entitled "The Wartime Garden," that now urged Canadians that "[t]here is a greater need for home food production of vegetables now than at any time during the war. Every available bit of land that is suitable should be put into a garden. Those with experience should help their neighbours who wish to start" (Buswell, "Winning Through"). One poster by Hubert Rogers promoting the Victory Garden campaign depicts a young woman sporting a snood and gardening gloves, while she holds up a trowel alongside two men similarly armed with guns. The poster proclaims, "Attack on all fronts!" (Rogers). Victory Gardens were now a part of the war effort, and gardening had become as fully militarized as any of the other tasks that housewives performed.

Victory gardening went alongside other activities designed to maximize local food production, including keeping backyard chickens for a fresh supply of eggs and garnering the fields and woods. Joy Trott recalls that some strange things turned up in salad bowls in England, and "[d]andelion greens were pronounced delicious and full of good minerals" (qtd. in Latta 125). Home canning and pickling to store all of this new produce were also very popular during the war (Mosby). One *Household Bulletin* from the Department of Agriculture includes wartime canning recipes for canning fruits without using sugar, by just boiling the fruit in water and processing the jars for 5 minutes of sterilizing time (Department of Agriculture 6). Using and preserving every available food resource is sadly less common today.

By 1943, the Victory Garden campaign was a success. There were then 209,200 Victory Gardens in Canada, each producing an average of 550 pounds of produce (Buswell, "Winning Through"). One in seven victory gardeners was a city dweller (Buswell, "Winning Through"). Greater Vancouver was particularly productive, having fully 52,000 Victory Gardens by the end of 1943, producing four million dollars' worth of food (Buswell,

"Winning Through"). With the end of the war, the liberation of the camps, and the numbers of starving and dispossessed children in Europe becoming more evident, Victory Gardens became more needed than ever. Buswell writes what all mothers know: "War," she states, "is fought against children, and its strongest weapon is starvation" (Buswell, "Winning Through"). Victory Gardens were also about self-sufficiency and as Buswell reminds us, "the closer to home we can bring our sources of food, the greater control over them we have" (Buswell, "Winning Through").

CONCLUSION

The role of Canadian mothers in cooking to win the war was a contradictory mix of newfound roles and old gender stereotypes. Mothers' domestic labour was made visible and important; at the same time, they were being squeezed into an increasingly idealized vision of upper-middle class domesticity. Some of the examples of housewifely thrift used during the war are models for modern sustainability and food security: urban and community gardening, keeping backyard chickens, garnering wild fruits for canning and pickling, slow cooking to reduce vitamin loss, and reusing scraps as well as oil and water from cooking instead of throwing them away. Perhaps something can be learned from some of the failures of the era, as well. Although it is clear that government policies can rapidly be formulated around mothers and their domestic labour, it is equally clear that these policies will not necessarily *favour* mothers or their children. Victory Gardens were a "bottom-up" movement, and one that the government was pressed into supporting, which showed the great potential of mothers' efforts in social organizing. On the other hand, organic and sustainable methods of farming were not necessarily part of the conversation, and it seems likely that the war, in the drive for speedy and massive food production, set this burgeoning movement back. In the end, one of the most significant lessons that we can learn from mothering during the war is to remind ourselves that as mothers, we make our greatest contribution to food security as *producers* rather than the consumers that we have been encouraged to become.

WORKS CITED

Advancement of Canadian National Health. "In Wartime Eat One More Slice of Bread Each Meal." *Chatelaine* March (1944): 23. Print.

Auld, Hedley F. *Canadian Agriculture and World War II: A History of the Canada Department of Agriculture and its Wartime Boards and Agencies*. Ottawa: Canada Department of Agriculture, 1953. Print.

Bruce, Jean. *Back the Attack! Canadian Women During the Second World War—At Home and* Abroad. Toronto: Macmillan, 1985. Print.

Buswell, Shirley. "The Garden Warriors of 1942." *City Farmer* 3.2 (1980) [Part 1]. Web. 29 Feb. 2016.

Buswell, Shirley. "The Garden Warriors of 1942: Winning Through in '43." *City Farmer* 3.2 (1980) [Part 2]. Web. 29 Feb. 2016.

Editorial, *Chatelaine*. June 1944: 76. Print.

Department of Agriculture. "Wartime Canning: Jams and Jellies." # 751 *Household Bulletin* No. 20 (1943): 5-15. Print.

Fahrni, Magda. "Counting the Costs of Living: Gender, Citizenship, and a Politics of Prices in 1940s Montreal." *The Canadian Historical Review* 83:4 (2002): 1-13. Print.

Hanson, R. T., et al. *Hydrologic Models and Analysis of Water Availability in Cuyama Valley, California*. U.S. Geological Survey, Scientific Investigations Report 2014-5150 (2014). Print.

Keshen, Jeff. "Revisiting Canada's Civilian Women During World War II." *Histoire sociale/Social History* 30.60 (1997): 239-266. Print.

Kunstler, James H. *The Geography of Nowhere: The Rise and Decline of America's Man-Made Landscape*. New York: Touchstone, 1994. Print.

Latta, Ruth. *The Memory of All That: Canadian Women Remember World War II*. Burnstown, Ontario: General Store Publishing House Inc., 1992. Print.

Metropolitan Life Insurance Company. "Avez-vous déjà goûté une vitamine?" *War Posters*. McGill Digital Library. 19 Mar. 2014. Web. 29 Feb. 2016.

Mosby, Ian. "Food on the Home Front during the Second World

War." *Wartime Canada*. University of Western Ontario, 20 Mar. 2014. Web. 29 Feb. 2016.

Mosby, Ian. *Food Will Win the War: The Politics, Culture and Science on Canada's Home Front*. Vancouver: UBC Press, 2014. Print.

Regis, Mrs. Charles. "This Weeks' Best Wartime Recipes: Fruit Cake." *Windsor Daily Star*, 14 March 1942: 19. Print.

Rogers, Hubert. "Attack on All Fronts." *War Posters*. McGill Digital Library. 20 March 2014. Web. 29 Feb. 2016.

Swift Canadian Co. Limited. "Make Meat Go Further by Cooking S-l-o-w-l-y." *Chatelaine,* March 1944: 20. Print.

War Measures Act, R.S.C. c. 206. 1927 Print.

Winter, Brian, et al. "Record Brazil Heat Pressures Crops, Energy Prices, Government." Reuters, 31 January 2014. Web. 19 August 2014.

11.
Secrets of a Food Storage Mom

Mormonism, Motherhood, and the Mainstreaming of Emergency Preparedness

DEBORAH WHITEHEAD

THE 2012 *NEW YORK TIMES* ARTICLE "Dining through Disaster" explores the "growing demand for survivalist fare" in the United States today, "as Americans become increasingly anxious about natural, economic, and geopolitical disorders" (Murphy). In the wake of 9/11 and devastating natural disasters such as hurricanes Katrina in 2005 and Sandy in 2012, emergency preparedness supplies are no longer a niche product. Registering annual sales growth rates of 20 to 100 percent in recent years, these products are now widely available online as well as sold in major store chains such as Costco and Walmart. With a broadening consumer base and no sign of receding demand, long-term food storage is not just for "gun fanatics and political extremists" anymore, as more Americans seek security in having the ability to provide for their families in case of a catastrophic event; indeed, "more than motherhood or religion, it's fear and uncertainty that drive people to invest in emergency food" (Murphy). But while fear may be driving demand, motherhood and religion may provide one answer. A new generation of family-centered survivalists—people with regular jobs, homes and families who are actively preparing for large-scale emergencies—are increasingly looking to the expertise of Mormon mothers and their traditional practices of food storage to help them prepare for disaster.

Survivalism extends well beyond the National Geographic Channel's "Doomsday Preppers" television series or religious groups with apocalyptic beliefs and is becoming more common among families from all walks of life. Popular media often depicts survivalism as an almost exclusively male enterprise, associated with stockpiling weapons, building bunkers, braving the wilderness, and protecting helpless women and children (Wagner). Yet the mainstreaming of survivalism today is driven by a growing number of women who view the tedious work of planning for disaster as specifically *maternal* labour. These newer discourses around survivalism often reflect gendered assumptions about the proper allocation of domestic labour and maternal care, stressing that it is the unique responsibility of mothers to protect and provide for their families both now and in perpetuity. "Survival is a Mom's job," proclaims "Survival Mom" blogger Lisa Bedford, who also advises fellow mothers to "worry less and enjoy life more" through preparedness. "It's okay not to know why you're prepping," she says in a recent video; whether one fears a sudden job loss, natural disaster, terrorism, EMP (electromagnetic pulse) attack, power outage, pandemic, zombie apocalypse, or final judgment day, being prepared for the worst will help to ensure the safety and well-being of one's family now and in the future (Bedford).

To aid in their preparations, Bedford and other "survival moms" have drawn from the extensive resources of the Church of Jesus Christ of Latter-day Saints (LDS), popularly known as "Mormons." Founded by Joseph Smith in 1830 in New York, the LDS Church has long embraced a culture of physical provision, prudent living, and preparedness, including the practice of storing emergency food and water supplies. Today, a majority of internet-based food storage companies are located in Utah, where the church is headquartered, and terms once used only internally within the Mormon community—such as the "72-hour kit," a grab and go bag with a three day supply of food, water, clothing, fuel, and other personal necessities to be used in an emergency— are now widely used. Journalist Ted Koppel devotes three chapters in his recent book *Lights Out* to the LDS Church's "extraordinary" levels of preparedness, contrasting it with the woefully underprepared general public (Koppel). But it is more specifically Mormon women, historically highly active in church welfare and relief efforts, who have led the way in food storage as a central element of preparedness. In the LDS tradition, food storage has constituted a unique form of women's labour that prepares and provides for the long-term health and well-being of individuals, families, and the community. In order to accomplish this work, LDS women have had to develop skilled, creative, and extensive methods and systems for preparing, storing, and using long-term food supplies. Although these "secrets" of food storage have traditionally been passed down from grandmothers and mothers to daughters within the community, today Mormon women's food storage practices are acquiring new contexts and audiences via the mainstreaming of emergency preparedness and the affordances of social media.

Although many religious traditions espouse practices of charity, in the LDS faith "the saving of the physical body has been seen as an obligation in the same sense as the saving of the soul," with the goals of "preventing poverty and improving the lives of members" remaining constant throughout the Church's history (Arrington vii). The Mormon dietary code, known as the Word of Wisdom, emphasizes a diet of fruits, vegetables, grains, and limited meat, and is found in the *Doctrine and Covenants* (D&C), a book of canonized scripture. To accomplish the goals of physical health and well-being, every church member is expected to follow this diet as well as to cultivate values of self-reliance and care for others. The expectation that the community is living in the "latter days" before the second coming of Christ has fueled the imperative for preparedness: believers are commanded to "prepare ye, prepare ye for that which is to come," to prepare so that "notwithstanding the tribulation which shall descend upon you ... the church may stand independent," and to understand preparedness as a means of providing comfort and peace, such that "if ye are prepared ye shall not fear" (D&C 1:12, 78:14, 38:30). As both a belief and a practice, preparedness extends to individuals and the larger community. Mormon storehouses to consolidate community resources to provide for the poor were established as early as 1832 (D&C 78:3). Although the concept is rooted in scripture, its meaning has been indelibly shaped by historical events; during the Mormon migration westward to Utah territory in 1846-47, each member was required to bring particular goods that were then stockpiled by church leaders in storehouses. The difficulties of sustaining a large community in the Great Basin's arid environment, combined with water scarcity and natural disasters causing devastating crop and cattle loss, led church leaders to emphasize practices that would ensure long-term community survival. In 1876, Church President Brigham Young counselled members to "store food, particularly grain, against times of personal difficulty or famine in their own storehouses," a practice that foreshadowed the "modern counsel to store food and water" (Mangum and Blumell 66). Interestingly, Young's instructions were mostly ignored until they were taken up by the Relief Society, an auxiliary organization for adult women within the LDS Church, and "grain storage eventually became an enormously successful long-term Relief Society project" (Mangum and Blumell 66).

During the Great Depression and the New Deal, church authorities began to develop their own community welfare program to care for all members "exclusive of government relief and to assist them in placing themselves on a financially independent basis" (Mangum and Blumell 134-35). Today, Salt Lake City's Welfare Square, built between 1938 and 1941, comprises an entire city block and boasts an employment centre as well as a 46,000 square foot central storehouse. Practically speaking, it is the church welfare program's emphases on "frugality, hard work, food storage, and work on behalf of others" that have had the most impact on the Mormon diet generally and food storage practices specifically, including keeping a "one- to two-year supply of emergency food," "rotating food storage staples into everyday cooking, and avoiding luxury items," and making "inexpensive meals from food storage staples like whole wheat and powdered milk, using inexpensive ingredients like peanut butter, canned garden produce, and seasoning mixes" (Holbrook 204).[1]

During World War II, food storage acquired new emphasis and urgency from church leaders. Families were encouraged to "build up a year's supply of essential foodstuffs, homegrown, as much as possible," both to "provide security for the family" and to assist the war effort (Mangum and Blumell 150). The church provided detailed instructions and booklets on gardening, food preparation, and storage in addition to constructing dozens of canning facilities, which LDS women used during the war to preserve an estimated fifty million cans of food. In the post-war, Cold War period, fears of pending nuclear threat influenced church leaders to adopt a more apocalyptic tone, exemplified by Ezra Taft Benson's 1974 statement that "the revelation to store food may be as essential to our temporal salvation today as boarding the ark was to the people in the days of Noah" (Benson). Today, the tone is less apocalyptic, but the Church continues to emphasize food storage as obedience to scripture as well as a prudent expression of the core virtues of preparation and self-reliance. Under the heading "Provident Living" on the LDS website are over a dozen separate topics, including the church welfare program, financial planning, home storage, and emergency preparedness. "Members of the Church have been counseled for many years to be prepared for adversity," the website says. "Preparation, both spiritual and temporal, can dispel fear. With the guidance of Church leaders, individual members and families should prepare to be self-reliant in times of personal or widespread emergency" (LDS, "Provident Living").

Food storage as practiced within the LDS church is an expression of the core values of self-reliance and avoiding debt, no matter what one's income level. Crucially, these values distinguish LDS food storage from the massive stockpiling or hoarding that is often associated with survivalism in popular media.[2] In a 1998 General Conference address to the "boys and men" of the Church, then-Church President Gordon Hinckley, himself a child of the Great Depression, instructed them to "set your houses in order": "If you have paid your debts, if you have a reserve, even though it be small, then should storms howl about your head, you will have shelter for your wives and children and peace in your hearts," he counseled (Hinckley, "To the Boys and to the Men"). The Church now has extensive holdings across the United States in canneries, dairies, factories, cattle ranches, orchards, and granaries, in addition to its 143 megastore-like regional storehouses and the massive Bishops' Central Storehouse in Salt Lake City. Yet, Hinckley argued, despite the great scope and scale of church resources, self-reliance begins at home:

> None of us knows when a catastrophe might strike. Sickness, injury, unemployment may affect any of us. We have a great welfare program with facilities for such things as

> grain storage in various areas. It is important that we do this. But the best place to have some food set aside is within our homes, together with a little money in savings. The best welfare program is our own welfare program. Five or six cans of wheat in the home are better than a bushel in the welfare granary. (Hinckley, "To Men of the Priesthood")

Hinckley advised families to practice frugality and to build up their home storage a week, a month, and three months at a time, until bit-by-bit, they accumulated a long-term reserve. A 2007 address by Bishop Keith McMullin echoed the focus on family preparedness, urging men to "lay up in store" for the times ahead. He emphasized that "wives are instrumental in this work, but they need husbands who lead out in family preparedness. Children need parents who instill in them this righteous tradition. They will then do likewise with their children, and their stores will not fail" (McMullin). His words acknowledge the essential role of LDS mothers in not only doing the work of food storage within the household but also passing down this knowledge and tradition to their children.

Although contemporary LDS food storage practices draw on these broader historical and theological traditions, they also entail a significant investment of time and a concrete set of practical skills that one must learn from others. To this end, the Church provides an extensive set of both print and online resources on the topic. Food storage is introduced on the LDS website with these words:

> Our Heavenly Father ... has lovingly commanded us to "prepare every needful thing" [see D&C 109:8] so that, should adversity come, we may care for ourselves and our neighbors, and support bishops as they care for others.
>
> We encourage members worldwide to prepare for adversity in life by having a basic supply of food and water and some money in savings. We ask that you be wise, and do not go to extremes. With careful planning, you can, over time, establish a home storage supply and a financial reserve. (LDS, "Food Storage")

The site provides basic advice on how to begin and how, where, and how long to store food and water, with an emphasis on avoiding hoarding and debt. In this way, food storage "is within everyone's grasp. The first step is to begin. The second is to continue" (LDS, "FAQ," "Home Storage"). An oft-cited 2007 pamphlet outlines the "basics of family home storage," namely a three-month supply of food, a supply of drinking water, a financial reserve, and a longer-term supply "that will last a long time and that you can use to stay alive, such as wheat, white rice, and beans" (LDS, "All Is Safely Gathered In"). The three-month food supply should be regularly rotated and drawn from for everyday meals, whereas the longer-term supply should keep for twenty or thirty years and is for use only in an extended emergency situation.

The website provides a number of additional resources, including guidelines for calculating adequate amounts of food, recipes and videos for cooking with food storage items (both to rotate supplies and ensure freshness as well as to acclimate your family to the different tastes and textures of stored food), family teaching materials, key quotes from church leaders on the topic, guidelines for water storage and purification, and detailed instructions on long-term food storage, including shelf life estimates, product and packaging recommendations, and how to use oxygen absorbers and PETE bottles to store dry goods for decades (LDS, "Longer Term Food Supply"). Accompanying videos prominently feature LDS women talking about how food storage has helped their families, stressing that these practices are both a matter of obeying commandments as well as practicality and provision. One woman, Maureen, is shown in her home preparing meals using food storage supplies with her children; she urges other women not to make excuses, such as lack of time and space, and to "just do it." She then shows how she has rearranged her small home to find every possible space for long-term food storage, including in her closets and under her children's beds. "It gives you a sense of peace when you have all of your food storage," says Maureen. "If you want to follow the Prophet [Joseph Smith], just do it" (LDS, "Family Home Storage—Meet Maureen"). Another video features Jean, a young woman who was unexpectedly forced to live on her food storage for eight months when her husband lost his job. "It's such a great blessing that in times of need, that Heavenly Father has provided us all these things so we could use it," she says, crying. "You never know when it could happen to you" (LDS, "Family Home Storage—Meet Jean"). Both videos emphasize how investing in long-term food storage is not for the wealthy only; rather, particularly for those struggling economically, the practice enables women to practice daily care for their families in literally life-saving ways.

The LDS food storage calculator found on the Church's website is a practical tool for computing the amounts and types of food needed to feed a family for one year, based on number and ages of family members, and is widely used and praised by Bedford and other survivalist moms. Supplies can be purchased directly via the Church's online store, where family self-reliance guides, 220-volt converters, water filtration kits, and cases of powdered milk, potato flakes, sugar, beans, and grains, among other long-term storage items, are all available to Mormons and non-Mormons alike (LDS, "Self-Reliance"). For those who prefer to pick up their supplies in person as well as to purchase a wider variety, one can print and fill out an order form and take it to one of the over one hundred LDS Home Storage Centers across the U.S. and Canada, designed to "help Church members and others build a basic supply of food for their longer-term home storage needs" (LDS, "Home Storage Centers").

The Church counsels food storage for all of its members, including young adults, singles, and adults with grown children. But in its published materials, there is a particular emphasis on food storage as maternal labour, a practice wives and mothers undertake for their families. This emphasis is also reflected in Mormon mothers' food storage blogs, such as *Secrets of a Food Storage Mom*, *Prepared LDS Family*, and *Simply Living Smart*. Mormon women's food storage blogs exist at the busy intersection of food blogging, the Mormon blogosphere (often termed the "bloggernacle"), and women's family or parenting blogs. Food storage blogs can be considered a subset of the larger category of "mommy blogs" and share a similar demographic (Friedman). As these Mormon mothers chronicle and share their own unique, detailed, and time-tested approaches to food storage via their blogs, they draw inspiration from church teachings and traditions as well as practices inherited from their own mothers and grandmothers. Yet even as they reinforce traditional gender roles and assumptions about women's labour in some respects, these blogs also have a distinctly modern, even feminist air. This is not your mother's or grandmother's food storage; there are no time-consuming canning guides or instructions to store forty-pound drums of wheat and honey in your basement indefinitely. Instead, these blogs emphasize efficiency, practicality, skill, health, frugality, ease and convenience, and advocate the rotation, integration, and regular replenishment of food storage supplies with daily meal preparation routines for today's busy moms. *Simply Living Smart's* tagline is "Be Organized. Be Healthy. Be Empowered." *Prepared LDS Family's* tagline is "Practical Food Storage and Preparedness Ideas." *Secrets of a Food Storage Mom*, from whose blog I borrow the title of this chapter, features the tagline "Food Storage and Other Adventures in Motherhood." Blogger Heather Buzbee explains, "This blog is about my adventures in motherhood, trying to stretch a dollar, raise healthy kids and be a good mom. I share stuff that I think will be helpful to other parents out there" (Buzbee). These blogs emphasize the frugality of buying in bulk and cooking with staples as well as the health benefits of feeding whole grains to their families. Besides a wealth of information and tips, they feature colourful designs, photos, videos, lists, printable resources, calculators, and recipes; sometimes, they sell books and equipment, such as food processors and grain mills.

Food blogs typically have two distinctive features: "a desire to make something that both documents their own process of self-formation through food and shares their knowledge of this material object with others" (De Solier 152). Mormon mothers' food storage blogs also engage in personal self-documentation and the public sharing of knowledge. *Simply Living Smart* author Anitra Kerr describes her own experience of growing up in a large LDS family when her self-employed father was diagnosed with cancer. Although this could have been an incredibly stressful time for her family, Anitra tells her readers that it was not, because of "the confidence that came from my mother because she had learned the skills [of food storage and preparation]" (Kerr). Heather of *Secrets* self-identifies as "a mom [of three children], a nurse, a feminist, a runner, a vegetarian, a grad school student," and says "I'm pretty savvy when it comes to food storage" (Buzbee). Valerie, author of *Prepared LDS Family* and self-identified "semi-homemade prepper," says, "I'm a Utah mom [of seven] and grandma [of five] who loves to share what I learn about preparedness. With consistency, you CAN do this [too]"; she adds, "I am an expert in the knowledge that preparedness brings peace [and] a way to share hope with my brothers and sisters around the world" (Albrechtsen). Each of these blogs establishes their authors' expertise through their role as Mormon mothers and their particular experience with food preparation and storage, and each emphasizes a "can-do" attitude, showing readers how they, too, can acquire this sense of peace and specialized knowledge to care and provide for their families. To this end, the blogs weave personal experience with step-by-step tips for smart shopping and meal planning, preparedness checklists, and great tasting recipes using inexpensive storage staples.

The mainstreaming of emergency preparedness into popular culture has led Mormon food storage blogs to acquire audiences well beyond the LDS community. Two well-known "prepper" blogs, *Survival Mom* and *Food Storage Moms*, both reference LDS resources and embrace many of the same practices. Describing the process of being interviewed for the "Dining through Disaster" article, Kendra and Linda, authors of the popular *Food Storage Moms* blog, wrote: "They asked if we did food storage because of religious beliefs. We both said no. We both believe in being prepared for the unexpected times in our lives" (Food Storage Moms). Kendra was able to feed her family of seven for a month with her food storage when her husband lost his job. *Survival Mom* Lisa Bedford says that although she is religious, she is not Mormon, "although when I first started talking about food storage, some of my friends thought I had converted!" (Bedford). And Heather, of *Secrets*, recently decided to leave the Church, yet still believes that "food storage is a good idea, even if you are an ex-Mormon" (Buzbee).[3] Judging by the readership of Mormon food storage blogs, many mothers agree with her.

Longstanding LDS food storage practices are acquiring new audiences and contexts as part of a broader cultural trend of women- and family-centered survivalism. This is a process in which legacy and digital media have played a central role, by publicizing real and imagined disasters, generating greater interest in survivalism, and providing access to a growing number of products and resources to address those fears. "People's uncertainty isn't going away," says one food storage company CEO, so it seems likely that there will continue to be a thriving market for preparedness and survivalism (Murphy). By making the "secrets" of this rich religious and cultural tradition accessible via social media, Mormon mothers are leading the way as today's survivalism experts.

NOTES

[1]This explains why Mormon recipes have tended to use wheat instead of all-purpose flour, evaporated or powdered milk instead of fresh milk, home garden produce, and ingredients with longer shelf lives (Holbrook 207).

[2]This emphasis on the LDS teachings of frugality, avoiding debt, and gradually building up a supply within one's means provides essential context for understanding the practice of Mormon food storage, and differentiates it from the massive and expensive practices of hoarding or stockpiling military food rations practiced by many survivalists outside the Church, such as those on the "Doomsday Preppers" series.

[3]Buzbee officially ended her blog at the end of 2014, writing:

> My life really isn't about food storage anymore ... This blog was helpful to me as I researched issues with the LDS Church and processed my own feelings and I hope that it was helpful for many of you also. (Ok, I know it was helpful for several for many because you told me so, while many members of the LDS Church were thinking "Wat [sic] in the world is going on here? I thought this was supposed to be about food storage.")

WORKS CITED

Albrechtsen, Valerie. *Prepared LDS Family*. Food Storage Organizer, 2015. Web. 15 April 2015.

Arrington, Leonard. "Foreword." *The Mormons' War on Poverty: A History of LDS Welfare*, 1830-1900. Ed. Garth Mangum and Bruce Blumell. Salt Lake City: University of Utah Press, 1993. vii-xi. Print.

Bedford, Lisa. *The Survival Mom*. The Survival Mom, 2015. Web. 15 April 2015.

Benson, Ezra Taft. "Prepare Ye." *The Church of Jesus Christ of Latter-day Saints*. Intellectual Reserve, n.d. Web. 15 April 2015.

Buzbee, Heather. *Secrets of a Food Storage Mom*. N.p. n.d. Web. 15 April 2015.

Church of Jesus Christ of Latter-day Saints. "All Is Safely Gathered In." *The Church of Jesus Christ of Latter-day Saints*. Intellectual Reserve, n.d. Web. 15 April 2015.

Church of Jesus Christ of Latter-day Saints. "Family Home Storage—Meet Maureen." *The Church of Jesus Christ of Latter-day Saints*. Intellectual Reserve, n.d. Web. 15 April 2015.

Church of Jesus Christ of Latter-day Saints. "Family Home Storage—Meet Jean." *The Church of Jesus Christ of Latter-day Saints*. Intellectual Reserve, n.d. Web. 15 April 2015.

Church of Jesus Christ of Latter-day Saints. "Food Storage." *The Church of Jesus Christ of Latter-day Saints*. Intellectual Reserve, n.d. Web. 15 April 2015.

Church of Jesus Christ of Latter-day Saints. "Food Storage Calculator." *The Church of Jesus Christ of Latter-day Saints*. Intellectual Reserve, n.d. Web. 15 April 2015.

Church of Jesus Christ of Latter-day Saints. "Frequently Asked Questions: Family Home Storage." *The Church of Jesus Christ of Latter-day Saints*. Intellectual Reserve, n.d. Web. 15 April 2015.

Church of Jesus Christ of Latter-day Saints. "Home Storage Centers." *The Church of Jesus Christ of Latter-day Saints*. Intellectual Reserve, n.d. Web. 15 April 2015.

Church of Jesus Christ of Latter-day Saints. "Longer Term Food Supply." *The Church of Jesus Christ of Latter-day Saints*. Intellectual Reserve, n.d. Web. 15 April 2015.

Church of Jesus Christ of Latter-day Saints. "Provident Living: Self-Reliance and Welfare Resources." *The Church of Jesus Christ of Latter-day Saints*. Intellectual Reserve, n.d. Web. 15 April 2015.

Church of Jesus Christ of Latter-day Saints. "Self-Reliance." *The Church of Jesus Christ of Latter-day Saints*. Intellectual Reserve, n.d. Web. 15 April 2015.

Church of Jesus Christ of Latter-day Saints. "Word of Wisdom." *The Church of Jesus Christ of Latter-day Saints*. Intellectual Reserve, n.d. Web. 15 April 2015.

De Solier, Isabelle. *Food and the Self: Consumption, Production and Material Culture*. New York: Bloomsbury, 2013. Print.

Friedman, May. *Mommyblogs and the Changing Face of Motherhood*. Toronto: University of Toronto Press, 2013. Print.

Hinckley, Gordon B. "To the Boys and to the Men." *The Church of Jesus Christ of Latter-day Saints*. Intellectual Reserve, n.d. Web. 15 April 2015.

Hinckley, Gordon B. "To Men of the Priesthood." *The Church of Jesus Christ of Latter-day Saints*. Intellectual Reserve, 2002. Web. 15 April 2015.

Holbrook, Kate. "Good to Eat: Culinary Priorities in the Nation of Islam and the Church of Jesus Christ of Latter-day Saints." *Religion, Food and Eating in North America*. Eds. Benjamin Zeller, Marie Dallam, Reid Neilson, and Nora Rubel. New York: Columbia University Press, 2014. 195-213. Print.

Kerr, Anitra. *Simply Living Smart*. N.p., n.d. Web. 15 April 2015.

Koppel, Ted. *Lights Out: A Cyberattack, A Nation Unprepared, Surviving the Aftermath*. New York: Crown Publishers, 2015. Print.

Loosli, Linda and Kendra Wright. *Food Storage Moms*. N.p., n.d. Web. 15 April 2015.

Mangum, Garth and Bruce Blumell, eds. *The Mormons' War on Poverty: A History of LDS Welfare, 1830-1900*. Salt Lake City: University of Utah Press, 1993. Print.

McMullin, Keith B. "Lay Up in Store." *The Church of Jesus Christ of Latter-day Saints*. Intellectual Reserve, n.d. Web. 15 April 2015.

Mormon Channel. "How to Begin Your Short-Term Food Storage." *Mormon Channel Blog*. Intellectual Reserve, 10 Jan. 2015. Web. 15 April 2015.

Mormon Channel. "Self-Reliance: Three-Month Food Storage – Store What You Eat, Eat What You Store." *Mormon Channel Blog*. Intellectual Reserve, 24 Jan. 2015. Web. 15 April 2015.

Murphy, Kate. "Dining through Disaster." *The New York Times*, 3 Nov. 2012. Web. 15 April 2015.

Wagner, Rachel. "God, Games, and Guns: The New Apocalypticism." Presentation at Media and Religion: The Global View. Boulder, Colorado. January 2014, Boulder. Unpublished conference paper. Print.

12.
Mothers as Managers of Scarcity

Poverty and Food Security in Brazil

SIMONE BOHN AND LUCIANA VEIGA

UPON REFLECTING ABOUT THE ISSUE of mothers and food, one immediately starts to envision mothers going at great lengths to ensure that their children consume the daily recommended amount of fruits and vegetables, refrain from indulging in sugary drinks, and have strictly limited access, if any, to the candy store. For mothers, child obesity and all its related ailments are a real, legitimate threat. Yet a substantial number of mothers fight a rather distinct kind of the battle. These mothers live in households where food security—basically understood as stable access to sufficient nutrition to maintain a healthy life—is not a reality.

The goal of this chapter is to uncover the reality of food management in this context of scarcity. How do mothers cope with irregular access to nutrition? Do they put "maternal buffering" practices in motion? What strategies do they deploy in these situations? Do they sacrifice food quality in order to maintain a minimum quantity for everyone in the family? Do they abstain from eating to guarantee their kids' basic nourishment? How do they decide who eats and who does not in situations of extreme decrease in food supply?

This text draws on the case of the participants of the *Bolsa Família* program (BFP) from Brazil. What is the BFP? It is considered to be the largest governmental conditional cash transfer (CCT) program in the world. As of the first quarter of 2014, it benefitted approximately fourteen million families in all the regions of Brazil. The monthly cash transfer (received through a debit card) has a clear gender component: it is given to the mother of the family or the oldest adult daughter, in the absence of the mother. Fathers are in charge of the benefit primarily in the cases of single-parent families devoid of adult daughters. Benefits vary based on the number of kids (zero to fifteen years) and adolescents in the family (sixteen- and seventeen-year olds). The program targets poor and extremely poor families, and it is headed by the federal government of Brazil. The chief criterion for selecting participants is low income: per capita monthly family income of up to BRL 77 or approximately USD 29 (all conversions into dollars use rates from January 1, 2015). There is a basic benefit of USD 77 and a variable benefit that varies according to family type. Families with pregnant women, children, and youth up to fifteen years of age receive a variable benefit of USD 13 for a maximum variable benefit of USD 66. Families with adolescents of up to seventeen years are entitled to a variable benefit of USD 16, up to the maximum variable benefit of USD 32. Beneficiaries must fulfill a series of conditions in order to remain in the program, such as child vaccination, prenatal care (in the case of pregnant women), and school attendance. As the BFP targets poor families, its study enables one to have access to the reality of destitute mothers who frequently face the context of food insecurity.

The analysis utilizes a mixed-method approach: it has a quantitative component—a survey with four thousand beneficiaries—as well as a qualitative one, which stems from thirty-nine in-depth interviews with the program's participants from all the five regions of Brazil. These two streams of research took place in 2008, and with the objective of gauging the preliminary accomplishments of the first two years of the program, they provide powerful insights into the beneficiaries' description of the impact of the BFP on their lives before and after they started to receive the benefit.

The chapter concludes by showing the depth and heterogeneity of poverty and the high degree of uncertainty that disadvantaged mothers face in their task of managing food supply. When confronted with a decline in food quantity, they uniformly put in motion a hierarchy of eaters and abstainers and place themselves at the very bottom of the scale. Once a steadier flow of produce is attained, poor mothers adopt a kids-centric approach and invest heavily in food diversification for their children.

FOOD INSECURITY AND THE MANAGEMENT OF SCARCITY

Even though some argue that food security is a basic human right (ADA), approximately 12 percent of the world's population still experience hunger on an almost daily basis (FAO, IFAD and WFP). Several factors have been used to account for this calamity, such as the cost of food (particularly fruits and vegetables), access to markets, precarious employment conditions, and poor housing (Singh). Barring situations of social cataclysm, there is a growing consensus that at the societal level food insecurity stems more from a deficiency of "entitlements" (i.e., structural factors that shape access to food) than from a "crisis of provisions" (i.e., lack of sufficient food for all) (Dahrendorf).

At the household level, the sustained lack of adequate food intake has been associated with low child growth, increased propensity of dental cavities among children, suboptimal child language development, household violence, and maternal depression (Chilton, Rabinowich, and Woolf; Frazão et al.; Gewa, Oguttu, and Yandell; Huddleston-Casas, Charnigo, and Simmons; Saha et al.). Food insecurity is also said to have distinct consequences in the countries of the Global North as compared to the ones from the Global South, particularly when it comes to the amount and quality of nutritional intake (Rosas et al.).

In households where food insecurity is a reality, adults, particularly mothers, have been shown to resort to the so-called maternal buffering behaviour (Piperata et al.), whereby parents reduce their food intake to ensure that their kids eat. This kids-centric safeguarding behaviour involves several different strategies that can be placed on a continuum of responses to distinct degrees of food scarcity: for instance, from family meal differentiation (i.e. offering different foods to distinct family members), to portion-size reduction, to occasional meal skipping, and to facing hunger (Stevens). However, this is a controversial matter, as there are authors who argue that maternal buffering does not always occur in situations of food insecurity. Abdullah and Wheeler, for example, after studying household food distribution in the context of rural Bangladesh, suggest that there is no decrease in mothers' food intake during moments of depression in the overall food availability.

In the face of these contradictory findings, this chapter's main goal is to verify whether there is evidence of maternal buffering among the *Bolsa Família* mothers. The data under examination here, particularly its qualitative module, captures the mothers' self-reflection on their distinct decisions regarding food allocation in their households. Do they decrease their own food intake to feed their children? If so, how do they do the latter? What strategies compose their maternal buffering behaviour? Before analyzing these issues in detail, a note about the data and methods is necessary.

DATA, METHODS, AND *BOLSA FAMÍLIA*

This text makes use of a dataset created by the Institute Datauff from Brazil's Federal Fluminense University in 2008. The quantitative component is comprised of face-to-face interviews with four thousand *Bolsa Família* participants using a structured (closed-questions) questionnaire; it is based on five regional subsamples of eight hundred households, has a 95 percent confidence level, and the margin of error is ±1.8 percent. The qualitative component has two modules; the first one consists of thirty-nine in-depth interviews carried out in twenty-one municipalities, which cover the five different regions of Brazil and municipalities of different sizes (see Table 2 in the Appendix). The interviewees of the quantitative survey were BFP recipients who in 2008 had been participants of the program for at least two years. Besides program participants, the qualitative survey also interviewed social workers involved with the administration of the benefit, including those with direct contact with the beneficiaries (twenty-nine additional interviews, i.e. the second module). Nevertheless, this text only focuses on the narrative of beneficiaries.

In order to gauge how *Bolsa Família* mothers cope with scarcity, this chapter uses a scale of food *in*security, adapted from the Brazilian Scale for the Measurement of Food Insecurity (or EBIA, see Segall-Correa and Salles-Costa). The EBIA scale had to be adapted because the quantitative survey on which this work is based lacked questions about food quality for both before and after participants joined the CCT program. Only the qualitative survey taps into this dimension of food diversity.

As Table 1 shows, households are classified into four categories based upon concern over access to food and whether adults and children eat on a regular basis:

Table 1. *Levels of food insecurity*

Level	Food access and quantity	Household food distribution
Food security	No serious concern with food	Kids and adults eat on a regular basis
Low food insecurity	Uncertainty over near-future access to food	Kids eat on a regular basis; adults resort to portion-size reduction
Moderate food insecurity	Persistent concern with access to staples; meagre supply of food	Kids eat skimpy meals; adults skip meals
Severe food insecurity	Finding food is a daily priority; frequent food shortages	Hunger is a common occurrence for adults and a high possibility for kids

Source: Adapted from Segall-Correa and Salles-Costa.

How did *Bolsa Família* participants fit into these categories? Responses to the questions about food security from the quantitative survey were used to determine the participants' level of food insecurity both before their becoming beneficiaries of this conditional cash transfer policy and after they already had the benefit for two years.[1] The graph below displays these changes.

Figure1 highlights some important points. First, the data suggest that program is well targeted. At their entry into the BFP the bulk of the participants faced either moderate or severe level of food insecurity. Second, these self-reported data indicate that program does seem to aid in the reduction of hunger. After receiving the benefit, the group of families facing a severe level of food insecurity decreased substantially. Other authors—such as Miller and colleagues—have shown the same in relation to cash transfer programs elsewhere.

Figure 1. Participants' self-reported level of food security before and after joining Bolsa Família program

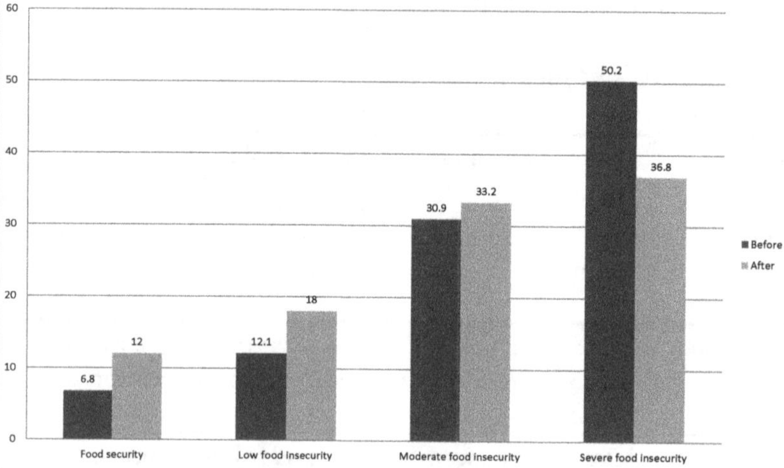

Source: Calculation from the authors based on the data from Datauff's Research on the *Bolsa Família* program.

Perhaps more importantly (for the purposes of this work), the data show that poor families are far from being homogenous: they vary from those with relatively no concerns when it comes to maintaining a steady supply of food to those for whom having access to a meal is an everyday concern. The qualitative interviews clearly illustrate these differences. Among the marginally poor families, for example, was the case of a mother from São Carlos, a city in the countryside of the state of São Paulo (Beneficiary Number II, São Carlos, São Paulo). As a mother of five kids, she described that her family never faced hunger. Her illiterate husband sold ice-cream in the street; her household lost income when she stopped working (as a cleaner) to take care of an alcoholic son with mental health issues, who formerly had been in charge of supervising her smaller kids. Another mother of five kids (Beneficiary Number II, Joinville, Santa Catarina) had a different experience. When her husband lost his job, he and she resorted to several informal odd jobs, but they could not make ends meet and, as a consequence, the family had almost no food supply for days in a row. Finally, at the end of the spectrum is the case of a single mother of seven kids (three adults, and four still living with her, plus an ailing mother), who was originally from the countryside and, once in the city, used to wash soldiers' uniforms for a living (Beneficiary Number IV, Corumbá, Mato Grosso do Sul). She described her situation before receiving the benefit as being extremely precarious:

> *Yes, I faced hunger many times. There were days in which we only had cornmeal porridge to eat ... until the school director helped us. She would come to our house with a basket of goods, as we were not able to get up from bed.* (Beneficiary Number IV, Corumbá, MS)[2]

In other words, the quantitative and qualitative materials clearly reveal distinct levels of poverty and food insecurity. What do these data mean for the purposes of this chapter? Do mothers across food insecurity levels vary in their management strategies? Or, more precisely, do mothers who experience the most severe levels of food insecurity implement maternal buffering strategies that the marginally poor mothers do not have to resort to? The qualitative material sheds light on these questions and reveals important differences, as highlighted by the interviews below.

MANAGING FOOD SCARCITY

The qualitative data indicate that maternal buffering is highly visible in families facing severe food insecurity. When faced with severe scarcity, the strategy of meal skipping is put in motion. Under these circumstances, mothers (and fathers, where present) overwhelmingly choose to refrain from eating to allow their kids to have the bare minimum to survive:

> *It happened that I would refrain from eating to feed my daughters. I do not have the courage of seeing a child in need of food, being hungry, and to serve food to myself, and leave her looking at me.* (Beneficiary Number II, Serra Talhada, PE)[3]

> *Me and my husband would not eat to leave food for the children.* (Beneficiary Number II, Joinville, Santa Catarina)

> *I would not eat to save food for my daughters.* (Beneficiary Number I, Petrolina, Pernambuco)

Maternal buffering does not limit itself to the households facing the most extreme situations of scarcity. Beneficiaries from distinct levels of food insecurity point to the existence of a clearly defined hierarchy of eaters. In cases of moderate food insecurity, for instance, where food supply is rather limited, children have the priority over adults and smaller kids over their bigger siblings. The mother below (with a husband and two kids) makes this point clear. When answering the question about whether hunger occurred in her household, she said that she privileges the younger kids over the older ones as a necessity, and uses family meal differentiation as a coping strategy:

> *Look, to face complete hunger, thanks be to God, no one at home has ever faced. I mean not to have absolutely anything to eat. Of course, if you have skimpy meals at hand, of course ... you will give the best [items] to the smallest children.* (Beneficiary Number II, Raimundo Nonato, PI)

Other strategies to manage scarcity include the controlling of portion size, the purchase of the cheapest staples available, and the offering of highly nutritional food items only on specific days:

> *I would buy a notebook. But then there was no [money to buy a] snack [for kids to take to school]. We would portion things off to make sure we would have bread.*(Beneficiary Number III, Maceió, Alagoas)

> *Look, if I tell you that we never lacked food, I would be lying. I believe that poor people always lack food, don't they? We have to face the reality and to live with what we have. Today we have meat, and tomorrow we don't; today we have beans, and tomorrow, we don't. This is how we cope.* (Beneficiary Number II, Porto Alegre, Rio Grande do Sul)

> *Every day, yes I buy something; a kilogram of bean, which lasts for two or three days, because I portion it off. And then, I buy the cheapest rice; buy two [Brazilian] Reals of ground beef. Sometimes, I buy sausage. This is the way we move along. Today we had rice and beans, and I went to the store to buy three Reals of sausage; I fried a little piece for everyone. The children say: "Mummy, let us always have at least beans"; they like beans.* (Beneficiary Number III, Corumbá, Mato Grosso do Sul)[4]

Once households started to receive the cash transfer, mothers continued to display a kids-centric pattern of spending. Given the difference in their poverty level, however, mothers from moderate to low levels of food insecurity are able to invest massively in food diversification for their children:

> *I buy fruit, milk, Mucilon [breakfast cereal for infants], these little things for children, do you know? Crackers, fruits. This one here eats a lot of banana, she loves bananas.* (Beneficiary Number III, Pien, Paraná)

> *Banana, apple, a [Brazilian] Real worth of apples, one Real of bananas, these things that people did not buy before.* (Beneficiary Number II, Maceió, Alagoas)

> *I have never bought milk for my children before receiving the benefit, and now I buy milk.* (Beneficiary Number III, Corumbá, Mato Grosso do Sul)

> *Now my children drink milk; we never run out of milk for them. And if the money is for them, I buy what serves for them. For me, it is one or other expenditure, and this way there is food for everyone* (Beneficiary Number III, Fortaleza, Ceará)

Whereas the additional income enables mothers from food-insecure households to focus on food quality for their children, marginally poor mothers (most of whom experienced food security even before receiving the benefit) put the extra revenue to different use. They purchase cooking gas, pay water or electrical bills, buy medicine that is not already available for free distribution at the public health clinics, and purchase school supplies as well as uniform clothes and shoes for their children:

> *It [the Bolsa Família benefit] helps a lot, because before she [the interviewee's daughter]wanted to buy things that I could not afford. She wanted to buy a notebook, a book that she would see, and she could not have them because I could not buy them. Sometimes she wanted a beautiful little pencil, and I could not give her.* (Beneficiary Number II, Maceió, Alagoas)

> *With the money from Bolsa Família, I can afford to buy clothes for them, shoes, tennis shoes. They go to the farmers' market and buy pants, shorts. I can afford to buy school supplies.*(Beneficiary Number III, Corumbá, Mato Grosso do Sul)

Several of the families that remained in the situation of severe level of food insecurity or whose conditions deteriorated despite receiving the benefit share a host of similar circumstances: the sudden unemployment of the father and/or the mother, the hospitalization of a family member, illnesses that call for expensive drugs, and other emergencies. These families seem to lack rainy-day funds, and when difficulties befall them, the immediate consequence is the worsening of the food insecurity in their household. When these moments occur, mothers (and fathers as well, where present) put in motion a series of strategies to manage food scarcity. The in-depth interviews reveal that the inverse is also true. Severely insecure families move up the scale of food insecurity primarily when they can access additional income, such as when an unemployed family member finds work, an ex-husband pays alimony, a mother is able to make extra money on the side (for instance, from arts and crafts), or a grandparent receives a retirement benefit. Finally, the beneficiaries' narratives also show that intricate informal social networks (neighbours, relatives, acquaintances, and owners of small food stores) are paramount to the reduction of hunger in households affected by severe food insecurity.

CONCLUSION

Even though this chapter's empirical material has the limitation of being based on self-reported behaviour (instead of observed, externally measured behaviour, which has limitations of its own), the data presented here unequivocally indicate that mothers from underprivileged homes are extremely resilient. They respond to the context of food scarcity by putting in motion different coping mechanisms. All these strategies entail some degree of maternal buffering, whereby mothers reduce or modify their nutritional intake in order to protect their children. Evidently, as most interviewees were women, it is not possible to know unequivocally whether in fact parental buffering—instead of just maternal buffering—also takes place.

In addition, it also became clear that once household income increases (after families started to receive the *Bolsa Família* benefit), mothers across poverty levels display a kids-centric behaviour, including those who were just marginally poor when their homes were recruited to participate in the cash transfer program.

One of the key implications of this study is that accessing additional income seems essential to decreasing the constraints that mothers from disadvantaged homes face. Owing to their maternal buffering behaviour, mothers will spend these supplementary resources in ways that increase the well-being of the future generations. As the beneficiary below describes, securing steady employment is central to the stabilization of the family's finances and to the improvement of its overall situation. Once this occurs, she, who is a mother of five kids (with an unemployed husband desperately seeking work), will leave the *Bolsa Família* program, in order to open up space for families that she deems poorer than her. When asked if she thought her financial situation would improve to the point that she could leave the program, she replied:

> *I believe so. We always try our best. Our intention is to refrain from becoming dependent upon outside sources.*

I only enrolled in the Bolsa because my children were underweighted back then, but the tendency is to improve more, so that we are not as dependent, as out there, there could be families that are needier than ours. (Beneficiary II, Joinville, Santa Catarina)

APPENDIX

Table 2. ***Number of beneficiaries interviewed, by city and state.***

Region	State	City	Estimated Population in 2009	HDI (PNUD 2000)*	Number of interviews
Centre-West	Mato Grosso	Cuiabá	550,562	0.63	2
	Mato Grosso do Sul	Corumbá	99,467	0.77	4
North-east	Alagoas	Maceió	936,314	0.74	3
	Ceará	Fortaleza	2,505,552	0.79	4
	Pernam-buco	Petrolina	281,851	0.75	4
		Serra Talhada	80,294	0.68	4
North	Piauí	São Raimundo Nonato	32,215	0.68	4
South-east	São Paulo	São Carlos	229,463	0.84	4
South	Paraná	Pien	11,811	0.75	3
	Rio Grande do Sul	Porto Alegre	1,436,123	0.87	3
	Santa Catarina	Joinville	497,331	0.86	3

*HDI: Human Development Index, for each of the cities.

NOTES

[1]The six questions from the quantitative survey used here are as follows. First, *Question 30. Before receiving the Bolsa Família benefit, would your household lack food before you had money to buy more supplies?*, whose answers are "yes," "no," and "NS/NR" (does not know/did not answer). Second, *Question 32. Before receiving the Bolsa Família benefit, would somebody refrain from eating because there was not enough food for everyone?*, whose answers are "yes," "no" and "NS/NR." Third, *Question 39. Before receiving the Bolsa Família, how long would food last in your house?*, whose answers are "one week," "two weeks," "three weeks," "four weeks (the whole month)," and "NS/NR." Questions 29, 31 and 38 have identical wording but refer to the period after the participant started to receive the CCT.
[2]All translations are the authors'.
[3]Program participants are not identified by name in the dataset; rather they are just "Beneficiary Number X, city Y, and state Z."
[4]To contextualize some of these statements, it is important to mention that the average meal of the Brazilian is composed of rice, beans, meat, potatoes, vegetables and/or salad. Furthermore, there tends to be a progression from just rice and beans; to rice, beans, vegetables or salad; to rice, beans, vegetables, salad, and finally meat. Thus, when the daughter of this last interviewee asks her mother to always offer beans, she is, in fact, requesting that the bare minimum is always made available.

WORKS CITED

American Dietetic Association (ADA). "Position of the American Dietetic Association: Addressing World Hunger, Malnutrition, and Food Insecurity." *Journal of the American Dietetic Association* 103.8 (2003): 1046-57. Print.

Abdullah, Mohammad, and Erica Wheeler."Seasonal Variations and Intra-household Distribution of Food in a Bangladesh Village" *American Journal of Clinical Nutrition* 41 (June 1985): 1305-13. Print.

Chilton, Mariana M., Jenny R. Rabinowich, and Nicholas H. Woolf.

"Very Low Food Security in the USA is Linked with Exposure to Violence." *Public Health Nutrition* 17.1 (2014): 73-82. Print.

Dahrendorf, Ralph. *Revolutions of Modernity. The Modern Social Conflict. An Essay on the Politics of Liberty.* London: Weidenfeld & Nicholson. 1988. Print.

Food and Agriculture Organization of the United Nations (FAO), The International Fund for Agricultural Development (IFAD), and the World Food Programme (WFP). *The State of Food Insecurity in the World 2013.The Multiple Dimensions of Food Security. Food and Agricultural Organization of the United Nations.* FAO, 2013. Web. 8 Sept. 2015.

Frazão, Paulo, Maria H. D. Benicio, Paulo C. Narvai, and Marly A. Cardoso "Food Insecurity and Dental Caries in Schoolchildren: A Cross-Sectional Survey in the Western Brazilian Amazon." *European Journal of Oral Sciences* 122.3 (2014): 210-5. Print.

Gewa, Constance A., Monica Oguttu, and Nanette S. Yandell. "Maternal Nutrition in Rural Kenya: Health and Socio-Demographic Determinants and its Association with Child Nutrition." *Maternal & Child Nutrition* 8 (3) (2012): 275-86. Print.

Huddleston-Casas, Catherine, Richard Charnigo, and Leigh Ann Simmons. "Food Insecurity and Maternal Depression in Rural, Low-Income Families: A Longitudinal Investigation." *Public Health Nutrition* 12.8 (2009): 1133-40. Print.

Miller, Candace, Tsoka, Maxton. and Reichart, Kathryn, "The Impact of the Social Cash Transfer Scheme on Food Security in Malawi." *Food Policy* 36 (2011):230-238. Print.

Piperata, Barbara, Kammi Schmeer, Craig Hadley, and Genevieve Richie-Eiwing. "Dietary Inequalities of Mother—Child Pairs in the Rural Amazon: Evidence of Maternal-Child Buffering?" *Social Science & Medicine* 96 (2013): 183-91. Print.

Saha, K. K., F. Tofail, E. A. Frongillo, K. M. Rasmussen, S. E. Arifeen, L. Å Persson, S. N. Huda, and J. D. Hamadani. "Household Food Security is Associated with Early Childhood Language Development: Results from a Longitudinal Study in Rural Bangladesh." *Child Care, Health and Development* 36.3 (2010): 309–316. Print.

Segall-Correa, Ana Maria and Rosana Salles-Costa. "Novas Possibilidades de Alimentação a Caminho?" *Democracia Viva* 39

(June 2008): 68-73. Print.

Singh, Sumanjeet. "Global Food Crisis: Magnitude, Causes and Policy Measures." *International Journal of Social Economics* 36.1/2 (2009): 23-36. Print.

Stevens, Christine. "Exploring Food Insecurity among Young Mothers (15–24 Years)" *Journal for Specialists in Pediatric Nursing* 15.2 (2010): 163-71. Print.

13.
Feeding the Family in the Face of Climate Change

Mothers of Rural Southwestern Uganda

FLORENCE KYOMUGISHA, BERNADINE ATUGABIRWE,
AND CAROLINE NSHEMERIRWE

IN 2011, ELEVEN MILLION OUT OF A TOTAL population of thirty five million people in Uganda experienced food insecurity and 19 percent of the population, mostly children, were classified as malnourished (Uganda Ministry of Agriculture, Animal, and Fisheries). Uganda's rural population largely depends on subsistence agricultural farming for its livelihood, and most of the agricultural food production in rural communities is done by women. The food that that women (mostly mothers and grandmothers) grow is used to feed children, and any surplus food is sold to earn income to maintain their families. During the past decade, rural communities have experienced the degradation of agricultural farm land due to rapid population growth, deforestation, and climate change. Particularly in the last seven years, rural communities have experienced an increased vulnerability to seasonal food shortages due to erratic rain seasons, accompanied by floods and drought that often result in significant soil degradation, erosion, depletion of top soil, and loss of nutrients. These environmental conditions create enormous challenges for rural communities to grow food, which frequently result in food insecurity periods, thus making famine a possibility in the near future (FAO 5-9). The challenges of growing food are further exacerbated by women's lack of control of land on which they grow food (FANTA and USAID 36-37). Despite this, women are charged with most of the responsibility of producing food and feeding their children; the Ugandan traditions of male ownership and custodianship of land, however, challenge women's opportunities, skills and abilities to grow food to feed their children and maintain their families. This paper describes efforts to address the challenge of food insecurity in rural communities in southwestern Uganda. The paper focuses on the new and important role mothers are currently playing in agricultural food production for domestic consumption, subsequently improving the nutritional needs of their children.

In 2009, Gender and Development (GAD) a local non-governmental organization partnered with women at grassroots level in an effort to acquire new knowledge and new skills to tackle the challenge of feeding their families. Working with GAD, women's efforts to address the food situation included adopting (1) a new culture about how mothers should properly feed the family and especially children; and (2) new methods and innovative practices of agricultural food crop farming that are now seen as the most effective means of supporting and maintaining the health and well-being of families. GAD's food security projects concentrated on food production at the family and community level and diversifying sources of income for women in farming rural communities. This paper focuses on banana and sweet potato production, which was identified by women in the local population as the immediate targeted food security intervention for their rural communities. For most mothers, green and yellow bananas as well as sweet potatoes are the ideal food items on the daily menu for children.

RATIONALE FOR FOOD SECURITY PROGRAMS

Food security is "when all people at all times have access to sufficient, safe, nutritious food to maintain a healthy and active life" (WHO). Food security is an assumed desired goal for any family or society. Despite an economy based on the agricultural sector, rural Uganda in the past decade has increasingly experienced food insecurity—a situation of insufficient nutritious food resulting from weakening agricultural production combined with relatively high rates of population growth. Food insecurity has negative implications for the well-being of a society, especially young children. Generally health research shows that access to adequate and nutritious food in a family and community decreases the incidence of illnesses in childhood and later in adulthood. In addition, good nutrition in the family benefits the health of women, especially pregnant women and mothers who are lactating and breastfeeding and whose nutrition status significantly affects the health and well-being of babies (Eggebretsen et al. 2). Furthermore, improvements in women's agency and their socio-economic status have a positive impact on their ability to feed and to maintain their families as well as their communities (WHO).

Unfortunately, the food insecurity in Uganda' rural community has exacerbated the health situation among women and children. Reports from health professionals who work with children show that malnutrition is a significant risk factor for morbidity and mortality in most diseases of children. Micronutrient deficiencies are evident in most children, which could hamper a robust immune response to infections, such as malaria, respiratory infections and even HIV (Caulfield et al 195-197). Reports by health professionals at a children's hospital in southwestern Uganda document that 55 percent of the illnesses are attributable to malnutrition (HICH Report). Generally, in populations characterized by malnutrition, younger children are more likely to be underweight; there are higher rates of diarrhea, low-birth weight, and even death among children; and there higher rates of morbidity among pregnant women (Eggebretsen, et al. 10-12; FANTA and USAID 2, 7). The 2012 World Bank Report documented that "Low birth weights and childhood exposure to disease have been linked to lower cognitive development, school attainment, and learning in adolescence. Less healthy children are at an elevated risk of becoming less healthy adults" (105). The Ugandan government acknowledges the nutritional challenges and their health implications for children and mothers. In 2009, a Uganda Ministry of Health report stated:

> Data from the Uganda Demographic and Health Surveys (UDHS) leaves no doubt that malnutrition is prevalent in Uganda. According to the 2000/2001 UDHS, stunting rates were at 39%, wasting rates were at 4% and the rate of underweight children was at 23% among the under-five year olds included in the survey. The more recent UDHS 2006 offers little consolation: stunting was at 38%, wasting

> was at 6%, and underweight at 16% among all children surveyed in the same age bracket. These rates of malnutrition contribute to over half of the high infant mortality rate of 76 deaths per 1000 live births. (Uganda, Uganda Ministry of Health, 14)

Although Uganda's rural communities experience the health challenges associated with malnutrition among children, this is not a unique situation on the African continent. For instance the United Nations 2010 Millennium Development Goals progress report documented that although there have been improvements worldwide, child mortality rates continue to be high in Africa, where one in seven children died in 2008. This is a troubling phenomenon considering that globally six million of the eleven million deaths in children each year could be prevented by low-tech and cost effective measures, such as simple food security and nutrition programs.

TACKLING THE CHALLENGE

We, the authors, concur with health professionals who suggest that many health risks in children can be remedied by targeted food security programs. Furthermore, many people in the Ugandan rural community, especially mothers, fully understand the association of food security and the maintenance of health in children. Moreover, we believe that mothers in Uganda should heed the recommendations of health professionals who suggest that targeted food production and nutritional programs will go a long way to remedy many health risks in children (HICH Report). Coming from that perspective, GAD, in 2009 partnered with rural women's groups to address the challenges of food insecurity and malnutrition in rural communities of southwestern Uganda. GAD was born out of the conviction that any population can be empowered to improve its condition. Guided by this conviction, GAD conducted food security and nutrition programs that were developed under the umbrella of GAD's larger three year project. Its aim was to improve the living conditions of families, raise their health status (through improved hygiene, sanitation, and nutrition), increase available household income (through sale of agricultural produce), and harmonize relations between men and women in the family and community to enhance the effectiveness of joint planning and implementation of development activities (Queiroz and Azuba 16-17). Two of the authors are members of GAD. They conducted training in the skills and methods of farming bananas and potatoes as well as provided information about nutrition to 890 families that participated in the food security and nutrition programs in rural southwestern Uganda. The third author worked on the intervention in summer 2012.

GAD employed a participatory learning and action model (PLA) aimed at strengthening self-help capacities and forming agency among the local population to work collectively to improve the communities' livelihoods, especially in the area of food security and nutrition in families. This approach and focus are rooted in the belief that the success of food security and nutrition programs depend on the congruence between the innovations in food production and the social (education), economic, and psychological characteristics of men and women in rural communities.

GENDER GROUPS

In a society where women have very limited control or access to land and other economic resources, GAD's approach to empowering communities is rooted in raising women's consciousness to understand that their greater control over household resources leads to more investment in children's human capital, with dynamic positive effects on economic growth (FANTA and USAID 54-58). Therefore, it has been GAD's priority to build rural women's agency because

> Agency is about one's ability to make choices—and to transform them into desired actions and outcomes.... Women's agency influences their ability to build their human capital and take up economic opportunities.... Women's agency also matters for the welfare of their children.... Women's greater public voice not only benefits women and children but can also benefit men. (WHO 105)

GAD worked with women in rural communities to develop and establish gender groups, which are mostly composed of mothers. Men had to be part of this effort because although women grow the food, prepare it, and feed the family, men who own the land on which the food is grown and, therefore, their support for some food projects was paramount for the success of food programs in rural communities. GAD's program began with addressing mother's concerns about feeding their families and gender relations as well as with emphasizing the involvement of both women and men in food projects. The effort started with the raising of consciousness on gender issues in the home and the community. GAD conducted PLA exercises that addressed gender barriers related to intra-household communication in addition to addressing gender roles, especially those related to reproductive work in an effort to strengthen building capacity needed when a community is embarking on group projects, such as food production. The PLA exercises specifically emphasized constant exchange of information and effective flow of information between men and women because good communication was vital for collective action and the adoption of innovative techniques for improving the way of life. Hence, PLA exercises strived to install the belief that mothers and fathers working collectively to improve food production is critical to providing the viability of nutrition that can sustainably support livelihoods of families. The food program addressed the health component of food and emphasized the goal of achieving food security as being vital in the prevention of stunted populations, childhood diseases, and death. The food program included hands-on-training in skills that enable mothers to maintain good hygiene in their families, prepare nutritious food, and properly feed their children.

GAD's program encouraged women to take up leadership positions in their gender groups and the community. They emphasized the strengthening and sustaining of mothers' leadership and collective action while focusing on understanding "concrete experiences" from the women's standpoint, which is crucial for community building, a skill derived from women's unique role of feeding and caring for children (Collins). It was important to enhance women's agency and also make women the leaders in the group food projects, mainly because women are the implementers—they cultivate, prepare and serve food—and if deliberate effort had not been done to ensure that both women and men participated in the projects, conventional mobilization would have excluded women. As mentioned above, it was crucial that men be deliberately mobilized to increase their involvement in food crop production, considering that men own the land and are culturally the decision makers. Therefore, their consent on land utilization is paramount in increasing food production (FANTA and USAID 37).

COMMUNITY NEEDS ASSESSMENT

As mentioned in the introduction, due to a rapid increase in population in Uganda, there is a shortage of land for farming. For instance, rural households of eight to eleven people on average now own two to three acres of land for a homestead as well as farming, and this amount of land is not sufficient for growing enough food for the maintenance of a household of eleven people. Consequently not having adequate farming land has several negative outcomes, including loss of soil fertility because of continuous cultivation of the same plot season after season, soil erosion due to poor methods of farming, bush burning, and clearing of vegetation for firewood and lumber. These conditions combined with the challenges associated with climate changes have made food shortages a reality for many rural communities. Using PLA exercises, gender groups at grassroots level identified the needs of the community, defined their priorities, and set the agenda for development projects in their communities.

Gender groups identified the low yield of the banana crop to be the main challenge of feeding their families. Ideally, green bananas are the main staple for southwestern Uganda. This region of Uganda grows different types of banana crops for different uses. One type of banana crop, locally known as *amenvu* is eaten ripe as a fruit; another type locally known as *embire* is processed to produce juice and a local alcoholic brew, which is a source of income. The third type of banana crop locally known as *matooke* is the most popular—while still green it is cooked and eaten almost daily as the main dish for lunch and supper, especially for children. Surplus bananas are sold to generate income for families. Although this is the ideal situation, erratic climate and environmental changes have created low banana yield periods, and families have found themselves in situations where they have had to harvest the bananas before they matured, and immature bananas produce less nutritious meals. Also, during periods of food shortages, many families do not process the *embire* to make juice or a local alcoholic brew for income. Rather, they make meals out of the *embire*, producing a banana meal that is locally known as *empate*, which is a less desired, less nutritious meal and quite inadequate for children.

Faced with these circumstances, gender groups concluded that they needed to develop strategies for improving the quality of the banana yield and to promote a supplement staple food, sweet potatoes. Hence, the GAD program made bananas and sweet potatoes focal crops in their quest to attain food security. Mothers and some fathers pledged to collaborate with GAD farming specialists and to acquire knowledge and skills training in "best and effective methods" in farming while using local and familiar resources to grow bananas and sweet potatoes and feed their families with nutritious food. To enhance effective development and implementation of food security projects, couples (mothers and fathers) participation was recommended as a prerequisite to ensure the sustainability of food projects and food security in the community as a whole. In addition, couples formed small working groups made up of households of the same socio-economic level, which enhanced active participation and a sense of corporate responsibility. At the same time, the households pooled resources and provided encouragement and mutual support during the implementation of these new and innovative sustainable agricultural technologies that were time and labor demanding.

BANANA AND SWEET POTATO PRODUCTION

Individual households in rural communities plant bananas, a perennial crop, in small groves close to the homesteads. Once the banana grove is established, it requires minimum maintenance, which is mostly done by mothers who use it for food for their families. Therefore, a family's banana grove should produce sufficient bananas to sustain the family throughout the year. Hence, the rejuvenation of the banana crop is vital for the survival of many families, and GAD's farming specialists introduced new sustainable agriculture practices—such as using organic manure and utilizing innovative soil and water conservation methods of farming—to accomplish this. In addition, GAD provided gender groups with hands–on-training in new skills that enabled the local population to implement banana crop management practices. These practices included the following: hand picking of weeds to reduce soil compaction, erosion and re-germination; pruning to remove dead fibers and male buds, which if not removed could spread pests and diseases, such as the banana bacterial wilt; and spacing banana plants ten feet apart to enable their access to light and nutrients to ensure healthy shoots. The farming practices during the rainy season included uprooting the banana plant stumps to eliminate pests and allow banana plants access to both water and nutrients; conserving soil through slicing uprooted stumps into small pieces to be composted into humus or to be used a mulch; and conserving water by harvesting rain water in trenches around the banana grove. The new and innovative farming methods improved the quality of the banana crop; however, due to the existence of erratic climate changes, the annual banana crop yield is still low and not sufficient. As a result, the rejuvenation of the potato crop was necessary to provide food for mothers to adequately feed their families.

Eighteen months after the banana crop farming started, gender groups embarked on rejuvenating the sweet potato. Prior to this project, sweet potatoes had been one of the many other foods—including cassava, yams, corn and millet—that are part of the diet in southwestern Uganda. However, the rural population preferred matooke and millet and, therefore, spent most of their time and labor maintaining *matooke* groves and millet gardens (matooke is popular for children, whereas millet is popular among adults). GAD farming specialists provided information about sweet potatoes' nutrition value. For instance, mothers learned that the sweet potato crop, which previously they did not value, is actually good for cardiovascular health and is a rich source of flavonoid anti-oxidants, dietary fiber, minerals, and vitamins, especially vitamin A. In addition, sweet potatoes are ideal for feeding children, especially since their sweet and starchy nature is a good source for calorie. Moreover, they are sweet to taste buds and, thus, are liked by children. Mothers also learned about the different ways of preparing potatoes to make them more appealing to children, including making sweet potato chips and sweet potato pies and breads as well as using them as a healthier snack for children to replace the common snacks, which are loaded with sodium and fructose. Furthermore, prior to the potato project, many rural communities did not know that potato leaves were edible as a vegetable or were a good source of iron, vitamin C, vitamin K, folates, and potassium. After acquiring this additional knowledge about the nutrition value of the sweet potato, mother began to rejuvenate the sweet potato crop as a supplement for bananas. Moreover sweet potato gardens withstand the winds, rains, and draught much better than any other food crop.

In an effort to improve the quality of the potato yield gender groups acquired innovative farming methods and practices, including preparing the land for potato planting during the dry season, breaking the cycle of weeds, and making interlocking big round mounds of soil, ideal for eventual rain water conservation. In addition, the mounds of soil had to be large enough to accommodate four to six vines with seven inches between the vines, Also, the garden was divided into plots for different types of potatoes because different varieties of potato crops mature at different times, ranging from three to twelve months. The gender groups also learned that the vines for planting should be selected from mature high-yielding potato gardens and that the vines should be cut with a knife to avoid tearing and damaging the vine, which can lead to the vines rotting. Before they were planted, the vines were to be kept in a shaded area for several days so that as they started to wither, they would shoot out roots allowing the vines to set quickly in the ground. Gender groups learned about the value of periodic weeding, thinning, and removing the mature sweet potatoes to give space to the young ones. They also learned that piece meal harvesting using a stick instead of a hoe enabled a continuous supply of food as well as the removal of the diseased potatoes and vines, which is vital to the potato gardens' sustainability.

ACHIEVEMENTS

Food projects that started in 2009 are ongoing and may have become the norm in some communities in rural southwestern Uganda. At the end of 2012, approximately 870 families in southwestern Uganda had participated in the banana and sweet potato food program. The majority of the mothers and grandmothers in the families that played a dominant role in the food program are experiencing some degree of food security. Families are experiencing a level of sustainable food supply, improved food intake on a daily basis as well as improved socio-economic status, thus bringing some relief and comfort to the mothers who are responsible for feeding children and maintaining the well-being of their families.

Sustainability. Rural families are now able to sustain their banana groves and sweet potato gardens by applying the newly acquired farming methods and practices, which have improved food crop yields without significant financial investment. Sweet potatoes have supplemented bananas, enabling mothers to harvest mature bananas and other food crops to feed their children. In addition, the number of months that families received insufficient food previously has been reduced from eight months to three months in a year, and this a significant relief for pregnant mothers and for mothers raising very young children, who need a steady intake of food to develop and grow. Furthermore, the adoption and replication of new methods and practices of growing and processing food have been a collaborative effort among families in the community, thus acknowledging that the reproductive role is the joint responsibility of all mothers in the community. The collaborative effort on food projects has been possible because women have established systems of mobilizing members of the community to maximize their participation in food security projects. For instance, members of a gender group pay annual membership dues, establish gender group bylaws, and hold periodic meetings, during which they brainstorm, strategize, and devise the means of how to proceed on food projects in their communities.

Food intake and nutrition. During a follow-up visit three years after the food program started, many mothers expressed how their communities had adopted a new culture of feeding children.

Families have increased the number of meals in a day—from one meal a day to at least two meals a day. More meals per day are now possible because, for instance, of the improved yield and increase in the size of a bunch of bananas—one big bunch provides an average family of six with two meals instead of one meal. The larger size potatoes also enable feeding a family with fewer potatoes, which now involves less labor for preparation. Being able to provide adequate food for the family is a big relief for mothers, since it is vital that children eat several times in a day to develop both mentally and physically. The majority of the mothers are consistently employing the new methods and skills of feeding their children. More mothers now properly clean fruits and raw vegetables before they feed them to their children. They are using the new skills of preparing food so to retain its nutrients and so not to overcook certain foods as well. Mothers are consistently sharing the best effective methods and practices of feeding their children to maximize their nutrients intake, including providing nutritious snacks of yellow bananas, sweet potato chips, and fresh fruits and vegetables. In addition, mothers are now adding the potato leaves vegetable to their families' diet, increasingly providing their families with a more nutritious and balanced diet. Family meal times are becoming more important to ensure not only that young children get adequate food intake but also that mother and children can spend quality time eating together.

Income. Good yields of potatoes and bananas are providing families with opportunities to sell the surplus food for money. Furthermore, families' reduced expenditure on food is making money available for other projects in the family. Many mothers and grandmothers, who are the main caretakers in the family, now have some extra money to buy medicine and other health services for their children as well as to pay their school fees. Also, a few members have used their gardens of potatoes as collateral for credit to develop their food projects and other income-generating projects.

Social status. Many families have indicated that they gained some social status in communities when they have well maintained banana groves, sweet potato gardens, and other food gardens around their homesteads. In addition to the improved social status of the family, the existence of well-maintained food gardens combined with the continuous availability of food in families has further enhanced positive relationships among families. Many families are now able to share food with neighbors and friends. For instance, mothers are reporting that they can now make effective contributions to friends' and neighbors' special events and celebrations, such as the christening of children, weddings, as well as funerals.

CONCLUSION

Much work and effort are still needed to implement the food program throughout rural Uganda, but for now, there have been improvements in food security in this region of southwestern, Uganda. The food security programs initiated by GAD, which are ongoing, have helped to reshape the culture of feeding the family, with improved and nutritious food replacing the inefficient traditional practices of feeding families in rural southwestern Uganda. We recommend GAD food programs to be a model for other rural communities because they will alleviate mothers' challenges for feeding children. We are seeing enhanced agency and self-help capacity among women in addition to cohesiveness among mothers in promoting nutritional health and well-being within their families, which will strengthen the vitality and sustainability of health projects and food security projects in their communities. Because of the approach of this study, we did not collect the hard data on health outcomes of the food program. Nevertheless, most mothers have indicated that their children are now healthier because of the improved food situation, and we believe that very real health gains are possible when the entire family and the community are involved as well as knowledgeable about how to improve the quality of their lives. The increased availability of food, especially the reintroduction of sweet potatoes to the diet, alleviated the concern and anxiety of many mothers and is giving them an opportunity to feed their children with food enriched with vitamins, minerals, and fiber which are essential for optimal health. Mothers' increased participation in the development and implementation of food security projects and other related economic activity is seen by GAD as one step towards achieving a sustainable improved quality of health for their children and enhancing women's skills for leadership in the community and subsequently increasing women's representation in the political system, which will improve women's chances for reshaping public policy related to children's well-being and social views related to gender roles, particularly in balancing work and family. GAD's focus on enhancing women's agency is widely acknowledged by women as vital for the health and well-being of children, as it is emphasized in the WHO's *World Development Repot 2012*, "women more strongly favour investments in children's human capital. Women's control of income and assets is important as an instrument for child welfare." (151). Despite living in society that significantly marginalizes women, the mothers in these rural communities have raised their consciousness and are collectively devising the means to improve the conditions of their families, especially their children. What we are seeing in southwestern Uganda can also be captured in the words of Patricia Hill Collins, "women's innovative and practical approaches to mothering under oppressive conditions often bring power and recognition" (234).

WORKS CITED

Caulfield, Laura, Marcedes de Onis, Monica Blössner, and Robert Black. "Under-Nutrition as an Underlying Cause of Child Deaths Associated with Diarrhea, Pneumonia, Malaria, and Measles." *American Journal of Clinical Nutrition* 80.1 (2004): 193-8. Print.

Collins, Patricia Hill. *Black Feminist Thought: Knowledge, Consciousness, and the Politics of Empowerment.* Boston: Unwin Hyman, 1990. Print.

Eggebretsen, Ingunn Marie, Thorkild Tylleskar, Henry Wamani, Charles Karamagi and James Tumwine. "Determinants of Infant Growth in Eastern Uganda: a Community-Based Cross-Sectional Study." *BMC Public Health* 8 (2008): 418. Web. 27 Feb. 2013.

Food and Agricultural Organization of the United Nations (FAO). *Climate Change Implications for Food Security and Natural Resources Management in Africa.* FAO, 2010. Web. 26 February 2013.

Holy Innocents Children's Hospital (HICH). *Holy Innocents Children's Hospital Report 2011.* Print.

Against Malaria. Against Malaria Foundation, 2011. Web. Feb. 2012.

Queiroz de Souza, Andrea, and Rose Azuba. Cross-Section Evaluation of MISEREOR Supported Gender Projects in Uganda. Aachen, Germany: MISEREOR, 2010. Print.

Uganda. Ministry of Agriculture, Animal, and Fisheries. "Sector Performance FY 2011-2012." *Ministry if Agricultural, Animal, and Fisheries*. Government of Uganda, 2012. Web. 9 June 2014.

Uganda. Uganda Ministry of Health. "Policy Guidelines on Infant and Young Child Feeding." *Uganda Ministry of Health*. Government of Uganda, 2009. Web. 9 June 2014.

United Nations. *UN Millennium Development Goals Report 2010*. New York: United Nations, 2010. Print.

Food and Nutrition Technical Assistance (FANTA) and United States Agency for International Development (USAID). *The Analysis of the Nutrition Situation in Uganda*. *FANTA III: Food and Nutrition Assistance*. USAID, 2010. Web. 26. Feb. 2013.

World Health Organization (WHO). *Global Database on Child Growth and Malnutrition. Uganda Profile Based on WHO Growth Standards*. WHO, 2009. Web. May 27 2013.

World Bank, *World Development Repot* 2012. Washington, DC: World Bank, 2012. Print.

14.
When Mothering Does Not "Measure Up"

Breastfeeding in the Context of Obesity and Income-Related Food Insecurity

S. MEAGHAN SIM, MEGAN ASTON, AND SARA F. L. KIRK

THE ABSENCE OF CONTINUED, EXCLUSIVE breastfeeding among mothers, the perception of increasing body weight among both women of childbearing age and children, and the prevalence of income-related food insecurity are considered among the most urgent contemporary maternal-child health issues within Canada. Of particular interest to health stakeholders are the breastfeeding practices among mothers considered to be "at risk" (Millar and Maclean), including those experiencing income-related food insecurity and who visibly carry excess body weight. Accordingly, public health strategies prioritize the infant-feeding practices of "vulnerable" mothers with the goal of shifting their "behaviours." Traditionally, this has been achieved through initiatives that include aspects of breastfeeding promotion, support, and education (Public Health Agency of Canada). Although these approaches are well meaning, they may unintentionally exclude myriad social and institutional contexts that also impact breastfeeding practices. A critical social perspective offers a different understanding of how maternal identity may be profoundly affected by dominant discourses[1] that construct and reinforce contemporary understandings of breastfeeding, food (in)security, and obesity.

Discourses that circulate within the health system both affirm understandings about a concept and influence other aspects of social life. In particular, dominant discourses play a key role in shaping subjectivity—how people understand themselves and others across the social field and how they, consequently, experience their lives (Lupton). Discursive tactics within the health field—such as observation, measurement, assessment, and classification—construct how health stakeholders "know" people by assigning meaning to these classifications that are contextualized through health and labeling people and their actions as "healthy" or not. Constructing health practices as "good" or "normal" or "other" create mirroring identities based on the health practices to which one subscribes, where individuals position themselves in pursuit of "good" health practices while minimizing "risky" ones. As a result, individuals experience themselves and their actions as rational (moral) or deviant (Coveney).

We suggest that mothers who "measure up" engage in normative health practices or strive for them. Their health-related actions become the measure of their capabilities and capacities for mothering and play a role in constructing the normative maternal subject, which positions mothers as nurturers and caregivers with primary responsibility for the family's well-being.[2] As such, gender is a key component of the broader discourse of maternal identity such that the "ideal" mother is one who, by virtue of being born female and bearing children, is represented as having a natural desire to breastfeed, avoid poverty, and feed her family well while managing her body weight and that of her children.

As part of a broader investigation of how breastfeeding practices are experienced among mothers classified with overweight and income-related food insecurity, we explore dominant discourses of these issues, supplemented with participant voices from our recently completed study,[3] in order to support critical reflection regarding mothers who may deviate from normative expectations of mothering. We neither present an exhaustive review of the evidence nor intend to persuade the reader towards a unitary understanding of these issues. We use this exploration to consider the implications for those mothers whose health-related practices and decisions do not "measure up" to culturally defined standards.

"TRUTHS" ABOUT BREASTFEEDING, OBESITY, AND FOOD (IN)SECURITY

Our review of the biomedical literature suggests that women classified as low income (linked with food insecurity) and also experiencing excess body weight are regarded as being less likely to initiate or maintain breastfeeding and are, subsequently, a group under focus from health stakeholders. Breastfeeding beliefs, values, and practices may be shaped by experiences of pregnancy, poverty, and excess maternal weight (Amir and Donath; Laraia, Siega-Riz, and Gundersen), suggesting that any meaningful understanding of these issues requires an attendance to the lived experiences of those situated within these circumstances.

Breastfeeding, obesity, and food (in)security are all matters situated within an era of intense, scientific mothering, where health issues are framed through rationality and risk, children's welfare is paramount, and mothers seek advice from experts. The implication is that breastfeeding (among other parenting practices) is medicalized and that the capabilities of mothers are measured through the lens of "good motherhood" (Knaak; Kukla; Lee; Murphy; Schmied and Lupton).

Breastfeeding is positioned as the ideal or "normal" practice of infant feeding— unequalled for its benefits to mother, infant and, broader population health; conversely, artificial feeding is represented as inferior or "risky" (INFACT Canada). Evidence of associations between breastfeeding and potential health outcomes is used to legitimize breastfeeding's position. In some cases, the associations are strong (e.g., morbidity due to gastrointestinal illness), whereas others are less conclusive (e.g., reducing overweight and/or obesity in breastfed babies, impact of breastfeeding on weight loss among nursing mothers) (Ip et al.; Kramer and Kakuma). Irrespective of the asserted strength of the evidence or the well-known methodological challenges with breastfeeding research, the "benefits" of breastfeeding are central to its promotion (Wolf).

Breastfeeding as a medicalized discourse also normalizes surveillance-like strategies that objectify the practice (e.g., timing or frequency of feeds, voids or wet diapers, and even colour and consistency of an infant's stool). An infant's ability to meet weight-gain benchmarks becomes one measure of how "successful" breastfeeding is, while another is the ability for mothers to meet public health recommendations for breastfeeding.[4] Even describing the process of lactogenesis as "supply and demand" echoes neoliberalist ideology—mothers doing their best for their babies *and* the state (Dykes).

We are not dismissing breastfeeding's important health impacts. Rather, we observe that breastfeeding discourse favours these perspectives while silencing alternative experiences. Scholars have persistently challenged dominant breastfeeding ideologies, calling for a greater attendance to the socio-political and historical circumstances that shape women's lived experiences in relation to infant feeding (Groleau, Sigouin, and d'Souza; Knaak; Kukla; Murphy; Wolf). These alternative and potentially resistant discourses largely intersect with structural and social inequities to play a defining role in the breastfeeding experience, and may provide valuable insight to why breastfeeding practices occur the way that they do (Law). Less visible are discourses that construct breastfeeding as laborious and socially isolating, as detrimental to other family relationships, or as impacting a mother's career or her physical and emotional health—particularly if breastfeeding intentions do not align with experiences (Borra, Iacovou, and Sevilla; Dykes; Gatrell; Lavender, McFadden, and Baker; McCarter-Spaulding; Schmied and Lupton). Lynn—a study participant, who identified as partially breastfeeding—was challenged with integrating breastfeeding into her life as a lone mother:

> It is just ... too hard to be completely with breastmilk ... there is no schedule and it's because of that ... if she needs anything—I'm the one who has to run and get it.... I'm doing this all by myself so instead of sitting down and breastfeeding for four hours, you know, it's one of those things that's ... don't get me wrong, it would be worth it to do it. But where it's just me here? I don't think it's very ... conducive?

Breastfeeding practice is also contextualized through experiences of mental illness, abuse, and body dysmorphia (Barnes et al.; Dennis and McQueen; Kendall-Tackett; Wood and Van Esterik) and is also racialized and classed (Millar and Maclean). In our culture, a woman's breasts continue to be regarded as sexualized objects. Thus, breastfeeding is a potentially "embarrassing" act that when delegated to private spaces, reinforces the discourse of female domestication (Johnston-Robledo and Fred; Mahon-Daly and Andrews). Lynn further described that a history of living in group homes and of "people not being so good" to her shaped her perceptions of breastfeeding; thus Lynn expressed a desire to limit personal exposure. She said that she would consider "appropriate boundaries" when breastfeeding her baby—including for how long (until what age) and where (public versus private breastfeeding).

Similarly, the "naturalness" of breastfeeding suggests a dominant, essentialist perspective on female bodies and "mothers" having primary responsibility for feeding the family (Meyer and De Oliveira). This responsibility becomes clouded within the constraints of living with material and social deprivation and when challenges arise. Lee, another study participant, stated in our initial interview: "I assume [breastfeeding is] just gonna work. I just assume that it'll be innate and instinctual and natural and that it will just work." Lee went on to experience challenges with breastfeeding, even after accessing resources, such as lactation consultants and pharmacologic intervention. She reflected on breastfeeding within the context of her own food insecurity: "I never thought of, you know, my body barely subsisting on what I have put into it having an effect on my ability to breastfeed." She continued, "What they [health care providers] eventually determined is ... I was not making enough [breastmilk]. Yeah totally shocking to me! I didn't know that could happen. I just figured you breastfeed and it works!"

The dominant discourses of obesity and income-related food insecurity also shape understandings about "normal," good mothering practices. Through these discourses, mothers are regarded as "targets of concern" and their health-related practices are scrutinized (Keenan and Stapleton).

Obesity is represented as a medicalized issue of epidemic proportions, resulting from an imbalance between "energy in" (diet) and "energy out" (physical activity), which puts one's health at "risk" (Sobal). Individual "choice" frames the reason why people gain weight and stay overweight, and normative body weight standards are achieved through one's ability to self-regulate behaviours. Discursive strategies naturalize and pathologize obesity (e.g., linking "natural" factors such as gender to "risk" of developing obesity, using surveillance techniques to understand obesity and to identify subgroups at risk), but they also construct obesity as something that must be avoided. Although the role of environmental, social, and political contexts in the development of obesity is mentioned within these strategies, obesity prevention and treatment interventions continue to prioritize individual behaviour modification (Lau et al.). Thus, individuals have the potential to identify themselves as "normal" or deviant with corresponding effects on their subjectivity. For Jennifer, another study participant, this discourse shaped her own self-surveillance as she started to gain weight in her pregnancy: "so this being the first month I've gained weight, the past week I've been thinking more about it. I'm going through every day—what am I eating? What am I eating correctly? What am I not eating correctly?"

Obesity is also viewed as a "complex" condition. This discourse circulates within the public health field where practitioners are actively working to prevent obesity, specifically among youth. This reflects not only child-centred discourse but also the understanding that children with excessive weight are more likely to remain so as adults (Lau et al.; Wall), which is another means of reinforcing normative mothering practices. It is not just children who are engaged in practices putting themselves at risk for obesity; it is, also, the practices of their mothers, which are open to critique (McNaughton) and surveillance. Because maternal obesity is suggested as the strongest predictor of obesity in children, mothers are consequently positioned to either perpetuate or end the cycle of obesity within their families through their health-related actions (Klohe-Lehman et al.; Whitaker et al.). Subsequently, breastfeeding is represented as an ideal means for mothers to support healthy weights in their children, especially for mothers living with excess body weight (Salsberry and Reagan).

Discourses that construct obesity as a failure of personal responsibility result in negative stereotypes about individuals experiencing excess weight, characterizing them as lacking willpower, uneducated, lazy, and with poor compliance to health-related recommendations. These biases are pervasive throughout the social field, even among health practitioners (Puhl and Heuer), which reinforces the dominance of downstream approaches[5] to obesity management, such as self-regulation. The socio-political considerations regarding obesity get lost within an audience that values autonomy and willpower as central to public health issues (Dorfman and Wallack). Tracy, another study participant, spoke about experiencing excess body weight throughout her life: "you're judged very differently ... my self-image was completely in the toilet ... people have associated people being overweight with their being dumb, not smart at all ... 'sloppy,' I guess is the best word."

Those experiencing poverty and income-related food insecurity are commonly associated with higher risk of obesity. Income-related food insecurity is understood as a situation whereby an individual's or household's lack of economic resources affects food access; among women, food insecurity may lead to excess body weight (Townsend et al.). The link between food insecurity and excessive body weight is attributed usually through diet quality or the types and healthfulness of foods that are accessible to, and chosen by, families under material resource constraint (Drewnowski).

Women living in poverty are thus situated among conflicting and shifting discourses related to financial and health self-governance. Described by Daykin and Naidoo as "responsibility without power" (63), beliefs and values about obesity and food insecurity that have been constructed in these dominant discourses represent women living in poverty as both victims and villains. Equally "vulnerable" to food insecurity and its effects, they are also represented as placing their children in precarious circumstances because of their "failure" to properly raise and adequately nourish them, according to normative maternal standards (Bell, McNaughton, and Salmon; Fineman; McIntyre et al). These "realities" send mothers to the "margins of motherhood and personhood" (Cassiman 1692) and conceal alternative ways of understanding the subjectivity of those constituted as food insecure and how food insecurity can be addressed. Although it is suggested that obesity and food insecurity are connected through diet quality, perhaps the pervasive representation of fat women as lazy, stupid, and less-than (Murray) hinders the ability for these women to be economically secure so that they can purchase the types of foods they wish to feed themselves and their children (Olson and Strawderman).

CONCLUSION

We offer a viewpoint from which to begin to examine maternal subjectivity for those who experience collective societal disadvantage—by their income, weight status, and infant-feeding practices. Exposure to dominant discourses may lead to conflict, guilt, stigma, and shame for those mothers who cannot, or choose not to, meet expectations represented within those discourses (Newhook et al.).

As health practitioners, we are committed to not perpetuating blame and judgment for our role in these constructions. We do suggest, however, that health-related initiatives that are developed based on incomplete understandings of these issues have the potential for more harm than good. Discourse has its own effects in silencing alternative ways of understanding health, which may result in a "partial and misinformed" perspective (Travers 214). When dominant discourses are strongly supported by numerous social institutions, alternative or resistant discourses face an uphill challenge. This leads to a polarization of viewpoints; efforts to seek common ground or workable solutions are resisted, impacting the actions we take as health stakeholders to understand and support all families in their journey of early parenthood. Dominant discourses also influence the research evidence and ongoing inquiries into these issues, further distorting "truths" about these concepts. In addition to its representation as a "natural" and "healthy" way to feed an infant or child, breastfeeding should equally be represented as a complex and socially relational practice. Breastfeeding requires ongoing negotiation between a nursing woman, her child, and her significant others, which is further contexualized within the prevalent discourses surrounding gender, motherhood, class, socio-economics, social perceptions of body weight, and health.

Augmenting the conversation about breastfeeding to include discussion and action about structural and social issues may have a more lasting impact on infant-feeding decisions beyond promoting the "benefits." These conversations must include considerations about housing and income security, ending physical and emotional violence against women, and reframing discourses about body weight. At the same time, we must be sensitive to the diverse circumstances in which mothers are situated and not malign them for their infant-feeding choices. It is our obligation to reflect on the demands of early parenting and to be mindful of the specific challenges for families when material resources are inaccessible or limited. We must not take for granted that there is one best way, or absolute experience, of mothering. Finally, we must consider that multiple, fragmented, and contradictory perspectives are represented within society. People have agency to resist the discourses to which they are exposed and to reshape other and alternative subjectivities. From this perspective, understandings of breastfeeding, obesity, and income-related food insecurity should be grander than the hegemonic perspectives that currently occupy the discourse within our health system for the betterment of professional practice.

NOTES

[1]Foucault describes discourse as the repeated use of language in relation to an object; it is not neutral but is constitutive. His concept of power operating through discourse suggests that discourses compete for legitimacy ("truth"), resulting in some becoming hegemonic, whereas others are positioned as alternative or rejected (49). Across the health field, dominant discourses have developed over time to create a particular "reality" that affects the beliefs, values, and practices of people.

[2]Essentialism or biologic determinism is embedded throughout contemporary health discourses and operates discursively to constitute, naturalize, and shape identity rather than the "reason" for identity itself (Weedon 49).

[3]"Choice or circumstance? An exploration of breastfeeding practice among obese, low income, food insecure Nova Scotian mothers" CIHR doctoral scholarship (2011-2014); NSHRF doctoral award (2009-2011).

[4]Exclusive breastfeeding for six months with continued breastfeeding up to two years and beyond (Public Health Agency of Canada).

[5]The upstream-downstream analogy is frequently used in the public health field. Downstream strategies are analogous to those that aim to pull people out of a downstream river before they drown (e.g., individual-level modifications), whereas upstream approaches

signify those that address the reasons why people fell into the water in the first place (e.g., policy in attendance to social, political, environmental affects on health) (Dorfman and Wallack).

WORKS CITED

Amir, Lisa H., and Susan Donath. "A Systematic Review of Maternal Obesity and Breastfeeding Intention, Initiation and Duration." *BMC Pregnancy and Childbirth* 7.1 (2007): n.pag. Web. 29 Aug. 2014.

Barnes, J., et al. "Extreme Attitudes to Body Shape, Social and Psychological Factors and a Reluctance to Breast Feed." *Journal of the Royal Society of Medicine* 90 (1997): 551-559. Web. 29 Aug. 2014.

Bell, Kirsten, Darlene McNaughton, and Amy Salmon. "Medicine, Morality and Mothering: Public Health Discourses on Foetal Alcohol Exposure, Smoking around Children and Childhood Overnutrition." *Critical Public Health* 19.2 (2009): 155-170. Web. 29 Aug. 2014.

Borra, Cristina, Maria Iacovou, and Almudena Sevilla. "New Evidence on Breastfeeding and Postpartum Depression: The Importance of Understanding Women's Intentions." *Maternal and Child Health Journal* (2014): 1-11. Web. 21 Aug. 2014.

Cassiman, Shawn. A. "Resisting the Neo-liberal Poverty Discourse: On Constructing Deadbeat Dads and Welfare Queens." *Sociology Compass* 2.5 (2008): 1690-1700. Web. 29 Aug. 2014.

Coveney, J. "The Government and Ethics of Health Promotion: The Importance of Michel Foucault." *Health Education Research* 13.3 (1998): 459-468. Web. 29 Aug. 2014.

Daykin, Norma, and Jennie Naidoo. "Feminist Critiques of Health Promotion." *The Sociology of Health Promotion: Critical Analyses of Consumption, Lifestyle and Risk*. Eds. Robin Bunton, Sarah Nettleton, and Robert Burrows. New York: Routledge, 1995: 57-69. Print.

Dennis, Cindy-Lee, and Karen McQueen. "The Relationship between Infant-Feeding Outcomes and Postpartum Depression: A Qualitative Systematic Review." *Pediatrics* 123.4 (2009): e736-751. Web. 29 Aug. 2014.

Dorfman, Lori, and Lawrence Wallack. "Moving Nutrition Upstream: The Case for Reframing Obesity." *Journal of Nutrition Education and Behavior* 39.2 (2007): S45-50. Web. 29 Aug. 2014.

Drewnowski, Adam. "Obesity, Diets, and Social Inequalities." *Nutrition Reviews* 67. Suppl. 1 (2009): S36-9. Web. 29 Aug. 2014.

Dykes, Fiona. "'Supply' and 'Demand': Breastfeeding as Labour." *Social Science & Medicine* 60.10 (2005): 2283-2293. Web. 29 Aug. 2014.

Fineman, Martha L. "Images of Mothers in Poverty Discourses." *Duke Law Journal* 1991.2 (1991): 274-295. Web. 29 Aug. 2014.

Foucault, Michel. *The Archeology of Knowledge and the Discourse on Language*. Rpt. New York: Vintage, 1982. Print.

Gatrell, Caroline Jane. "Secrets and Lies: Breastfeeding and Professional Paid Work." *Social Science & Medicine* 65.2 (2007): 393-404. Web. 29 Aug. 2014.

Groleau, Danielle, Catherine Sigouin, and Nicole Anne d'Souza. "Power to Negotiate Spatial Barriers to Breastfeeding in a Western Context: When Motherhood Meets Poverty." *Health & Place* 24 (2013): 250-259. Web. 7 July 2014.

INFACT Canada. *Risks of Formula Feeding: A Brief Annotated Bibliography*. INFACT Canada, 2006. Web. 29 Aug. 2014.

Ip, Stanley, et al. *Breastfeeding and Maternal and Infant Health Outcomes in Developed Countries, Evidence Report/Technology Assessment No. 153*. Tufts-New England Medical Center Evidence-based Practice Center, Contract No. 290-02-0022. Rockville, MD: Agency for Healthcare Research and Quality, April 2007. Print.

Johnston-Robledo, Ingrid, and Victoria Fred. "Self-Objectification and Lower Income Pregnant Women's Breastfeeding Attitudes." *Journal of Applied Social Psychology* 38.1 (2008): 1-21. Web. 29 Aug. 2014.

Keenan, Julia, and Helen Stapleton. "Bonny Babies? Motherhood and Nurturing in the Age of Obesity." *Health, Risk & Society* 12.4 (2010): 369-383. Web. 29 Aug. 2014.

Kendall-Tackett, Kathleen A. "Violence against Women and the Perinatal Period: The Impact of Lifetime Violence on Pregnancy, Postpartum, and Breastfeeding." *Trauma, Violence, & Abuse* 8.3 (2007): 344-353. Web. 29 Aug. 2014.

Klohe-Lehman, Deborah M., et al. "Low-Income, Overweight and Obese Mothers as Agents of Change to Improve Food Choices, Fat Habits, and Physical Activity in their 1-to-3-Year-Old Children." *Journal of the American College of Nutrition* 26.3 (2007): 196-208. Web. 29 Aug. 2014.

Knaak, Stephanie J. "Contextualising Risk, Constructing Choice: Breastfeeding and Good Mothering in Risk Society." *Health, Risk & Society* 12.4 (2010): 345-355. Web. 29 Aug. 2014.

Kramer, M.S., and R. Kakuma. "Optimal Duration of Exclusive Breastfeeding (Review)." *Cochrane Database of Systematic Reviews* 1. (2002): n.pag. Web. 29 Aug. 2014.

Kukla, Rebecca. "Measuring Mothering." *International Journal of Feminist Approaches to Bioethics* 1.1 (2009): 67-90. Web. 29 Aug. 2014.

Laraia, Barbara A., Anna Maria Siega-Riz, and Craig Gundersen. "Household Food Insecurity Is Associated with Self-Reported Pregravid Weight Status, Gestational Weight Gain, and Pregnancy Complications." *Journal of the American Dietetic Association* 110.5 (2010): 692-701. Web. 29 Aug. 2014.

Lau, David C.W., et al. "2006 Canadian Clinical Practice Guidelines on the Management and Prevention of Obesity in Adults and Children." *CMAJ* 176.8 Suppl (2007): n.pag. Web. 29 Aug. 2014.

Lavender, Tina, Catherine McFadden, and Lisa Baker. "Breastfeeding and Family Life." *Maternal & Child Nutrition* 2.3 (2006): 145-55. Web. 29 Aug. 2014.

Law, Jules. "The Politics of Breastfeeding: Assessing Risk, Dividing Labor." *Signs* 25.2 (2000): 407-50. Web. 29 Aug. 2014.

Lee, Ellie J. "Living With Risk in the Age of 'Intensive Motherhood': Maternal Identity and Infant Feeding." *Health, Risk & Society* 10.5 (2008): 467-477. Web. 29 Aug. 2014.

Lupton, Deborah. *Food, the Body, and the Self*. London: Sage Publications Ltd, 1996. Print.

Mahon-Daly, Patricia, and Gavin J. Andrews. "Liminality and Breastfeeding: Women Negotiating Space and Two Bodies." *Health & Place* 8.2 (2002): 61-76. Web. 29 Aug. 2014.

McCarter-Spaulding, Deborah. "Is Breastfeeding Fair? Tensions in Feminist Perspectives on Breastfeeding and the Family." *Journal of Human Lactation* 24.2 (2008): 206. Web. 29 Aug. 2014.

McIntyre, Lynn, et al. "Food Insecurity of Low-Income Lone Mothers and their Children in Atlantic Canada." *Canadian Journal of Public Health*. 93.6 (2002): 411. Web. 29 Aug. 2014.

McNaughton, D. "From the Womb to the Tomb: Obesity and Maternal Responsibility." *Critical Public Health* 21.2 (2011): 179-190. Web. 29 Aug. 2014.

Meyer, Dagmar Estermann, and Dora Lúcia De Oliveira. "Breastfeeding Policies and the Production of Motherhood: A Historical–Cultural Approach." *Nursing Inquiry* 10.1 (2003): 11-18. Web. 29 Aug. 2014.

Millar, W. J., and H. Maclean. "Breastfeeding Practices." *Health Reports* 16.2 (2005): 23-31. Web. 29 Aug. 2014.

Murphy, Elizabeth. "'Breast is Best': Infant Feeding Decisions and Maternal Deviance." *Sociology of Health & Illness* 21.2 (1999): 187-208. Print.

Murray, S. "(Un/Be) Coming Out? Rethinking Fat Politics." *Social Semiotics* 15.2 (2005): 153-163. Print.

Newhook, Julia Temple, et al. "Infant-Feeding among Low-Income Women: The Social Context that Shapes their Perspectives and Experiences." *CJNR* 45.3 (2013): 28-49. Web. 29 Aug. 2014.

Olson, Christine M., and Myla S. Strawderman. "The Relationship between Food Insecurity and Obesity in Rural Childbearing Women." *The Journal of Rural Health* 24.1 (2008): 60-66. Web. 29 Aug. 2014.

Public Health Agency of Canada. *Protecting, Promoting and Supporting Breastfeeding: A Practical Workbook for Community-based Programs, 2nd Edition*. Ottawa, ON: Minister of Health, May 2014. Print.

Puhl, Rebecca. M., and Chelsea. A. Heuer. "The Stigma of Obesity: A Review and Update." *Obesity* 17.5 (2009): 941-964. Web. 29 Aug. 2014.

Salsberry, Pamela J., and Patricia B. Reagan. "Taking the Long View: The Prenatal Environment and Early Adolescent Overweight." *Research in Nursing & Health* 30.3 (2007): 297-307. Web. 29 Aug. 2014.

Schmied, Virginia, and Deborah Lupton. "Blurring the Boundaries: Breastfeeding and Maternal Subjectivity." *Sociology of Health & Illness* 23.2 (2001): 234-250. Web. 29 Aug. 2014. Sobal,

Jeffery. "The Medicalization and Demedicalization of Obesity." *Eating Agendas: Food and Nutrition as Social Problems.* Ed. Donna Maurer, and Jeffery Sobel. New York: Walter de Gruyter, (1995): 67-90. Print.

Townsend, Marilyn S., et al. "Food Insecurity Is Positively Related to Overweight in Women." *The Journal of Nutrition* 131.6 (2001): 1738-1745. Web. 29 Aug. 2014.

Travers, Kim D. "Do You Teach them How to Budget? Professional Discourse in the Construction of Nutritional Inequities." *Eating Agendas: Food and Nutrition as Social Problems.* Eds. Donna Maurer and Jeffrey Sobel. New York: Walter de Gruyter, 1995. 213-240. Print.

Weedon, Chris. *Feminist Practice and Poststructuralist Theory.* 2nd Edition. MA: Wiley-Blackwell, 1997. Print.

Whitaker, Robert C., et al. "Predicting Obesity in Young Adulthood from Childhood and Parental Obesity." *New England Journal of Medicine* 337.13 (1997): 869-873. Web. 29 Aug. 2014.

Wolf, Joan B. *Is Breast Best? Taking on the Breastfeeding Experts and the New High Stakes of Motherhood.* New York: New York University Press, 2011. Print.

Wood, Karen, and Penny Van Esterik. "Infant Feeding Experiences of Women Who were Sexually Abused in Childhood." *Canadian Family Physician* 56.4 (2010): 136-141. Web. 29 Aug. 2014.

IV.
REPRESENTATIONS, COMMUNICATION, AND MEDIA

15. Mothers as Trickster Figures Who Hide Vegetables in Kids' Food

VIVIAN HALLORAN

IN FOLKLORE, MYTH, AND POPULAR CULTURE, "trickster figures" are characters of small or unimposing stature but great mental ability, who outwit their more powerful opponents through the use of cunning or trickery. According to the prefaces of what I am calling "anxious mom" cookbooks—such as Jessica Seinfeld's *Deceptively Delicious: Simple Secrets to Get Your Kids Eating Good Food* and Missy Chase Lapine's *The Sneaky Chef: Simple Strategies for Hiding Health Foods in Kids' Favorite Meals* and so-called mommy blogs such as Tracy Gibb's *Less Than Perfect Parents*—a family's children, rather than the parents, wield all the power at mealtime throughout American households. Children's regular tantrums, whining, and complaints about the unappetizing nature of the meals their mothers prepare for them can ruin dinnertime for all concerned, especially because the expectation is that cooking and eating should both be quick, simple, and easy affairs at the end of a busy day. Faced with the prospect of yet another predictable confrontation at the dinner table, Seinfeld, Lapine, and Gibbs decide to turn the tables on their picky eaters by resorting to culinary trickery and "sneaking" vegetables into child-friendly entrées that have proven popular in the past. The books and blogs that they publish about their struggles constitute a public celebration of the successful ruse, what Seinfeld calls the "loving deception" (Seinfeld 13) of one's children. These harried mothers understandably wish to create a more peaceful atmosphere for their families to enjoy their time together, as they fuel their bodies after a long day. The trickery advocated within these books and blog offer the promise of being able to turn the tables, something that resonates deeply with an eager audience of fellow moms similarly besieged by their willful offspring. Although Seinfeld, Lapine, and Gibbs all confess to feeling powerless in the face of their children's ability to ruin mealtimes for the entire family—"I had begun to dread mealtime," as Seinfeld writes (10)—I contend that by assuming the role of "trickster figure," these mothers redefine the context of their mealtime battles as conflicts over nutritional imperatives, which due to their youth, gullibility, and lack of culinary know-how, the children are bound to lose.

This essay argues that "anxious mom" cookbooks and "mommy blogs" foster a sense of inter-parental solidarity through the exchange of strategies of culinary subterfuge, which affirm the women's shared sense of mission at the expense of their relationship with their children. Rather than offering a complex system for retraining their children's palates or educating or persuading them of the benefits of healthful foods, these texts promote the benefit of control—whether exercised over the kids' food intake or over one's home environment—without the emotional cost of having to impose more self-discipline on the children or grant them more agency as eating subjects. These cookbooks and the blogs perpetuate a disenabling discourse of female anxiety about food, nutrition, and health that aligns the maternal duty to nourish one's young with the citizen's duty to adhere to the nutritional guidelines issued by the United States Department of Agriculture for recommended daily allowance of fruits and vegetables, and with the orthorexic's obsession to only eat "healthy" food. These texts equate the consumption of produce with proof of one's patriotism, for nothing, after all, is as American as motherhood and apple pie.

TRICKING THE KIDS—STRATEGIES IN CONTEXT

The concern these women feel about the potentially harmful consequences of their children's idiosyncratic eating behaviour is not new, although the "anxious mom" cookbook is, indeed, a novel manifestation of this age-old American concern. Parents who felt similar anxieties about their children's aversion to vegetables in the 1990s turned to highly processed nutritional supplements, such as the canned shake Pediasure (Byrd-Bredbenner & Grasso), as a corrective to any nutritional imbalance that they might have. Earlier generations of nervous parents had done the mixing themselves, adding powdered mixes such as Ovaltine (Koerner) or Carnation Instant Breakfast (Yach 81) to fortify the beverages with extra nutrients. These parents' nutritional supplementation demonstrated their era's faith in science and chemistry that facilitated micronutrient fortification via processed (and sweetened) powders and shakes. Seinfeld's, Lapine's, and Gibbs's twenty-first century approaches to enhancing their finicky children's meager consumption of fruits and vegetables also reflect the spirit of the current "foodie" era, which advocates the consumption of organic produce, humanely raised beef, chicken and pork, and a return to home cooking as solutions for the high incidence of childhood obesity in the United States.

These affluent women who self-identify as nutrition-conscious mothers have managed to turn their concerns about their children into thriving careers by carving out their own niches within the new media landscape, whether by giving rise to the "mommy" cookbook genre or by cross-promoting their "brand" across multimedia platforms (books, websites, and TV appearances). Gibbs has turned a profit from her mommy blogs by sharing parenting tips based on her personal experiences raising her family. All three of these mothers promote steaming and puréeing fruits, vegetables, and legumes and incorporating these additives into their children's favourite meals, something even people who have only moderate cooking skills or talent can easily accomplish. Since Gibbs' blog covers other issues than just strategies for handling picky eaters, I will focus my analysis on the longer works. With the benefit of hindsight, Lapine confesses in the preface of her second book in the *Sneaky Chef* series that the prime motivation for developing her "sneaking" system was her growing sense that her children's picky eating not only reflected poorly on her mothering skills, but it also seriously imperiled their well-being. Speaking of her group of friends, she explains that a sense of shame pervaded even their communal conversations about their kids' lives and kept them from collaborating on developing strategies for confronting this problem: "What we didn't share with each other was how deeply it bothered us that our kids weren't getting the nutrients they needed. Their health was in our hands, and we were letting them down because we didn't know how to counter their irrational and unreasonable food aversions" (Lapine, *Sneaky Chef to the Rescue* 16). Luckily, however, the publication of her first book changed that for the better, among not only her immediate social circle but the wider context of her readers and avid fans as well. For her part, Seinfeld credits a whole team of professional food workers—from a chef to the same nutritionist who helped her lose weight after her pregnancies—for ensuring the duplicability of the recipes contained in her volume, since she is careful to acknowledge that she is "not a professional chef—far from it." Her ingenuity, coupled with her collaborators' impeccable credentials, reassures readers of her book that the recipes are easy to prepare and that their nutritional content meets the recommended daily allowance, as outlined by the United States Department of Agriculture.

In stressing how much the book's recipes accord with "proper eating," Seinfeld and her team imply that mothers who follow the "loving deception" preached by the volume perform their civic duties as American citizens. Indeed, food studies scholar Anita Mannur advances the concept of "culinary citizenship" to explain the complex ways through which people understand their relationship to their country through food and eating. Mannur defines this type of food-based citizenship as "that which grants subjects the ability to claim and inhabit certain identitarian positions via their relationship to food" (Mannur 29). In this specific context, the nutritional guidelines, which figure so prominently in Seinfeld's accounting of the healthy nature of her "tricks," are disseminated by government agencies, such as the USDA and its subsidiaries and the website Nutrition.gov. Thus, by resorting to "sneaky" or "deceitful" strategies, both Seinfeld and Lapine perform their civic duty to the United States of America.

All the help and support Seinfeld receives from the women who comprise her team contrasts with how she portrays her interaction with her children, the unwitting recipients of all this innovative culinary scheming. Appearing as caricature drawings at the end of the recipe for "avocado spread" (Seinfeld 136), Seinfeld's son declares that he likes the recipe on his tacos, whereas her daughter professes her dislike of it. Rather than engaging her children in dialogue, the drawing of Seinfeld that accompanies her children is depicted with her index finger held up to her lips, in a conspiratorial gesture of silence, next to a statement clearly aimed at her mom readers: "Shhh! She has it [avocado spread] in her quesadillas." This is a small betrayal.

MOTHER KNOWS BEST: CULINARY TRICKERY AND NICHE MARKETING

These successful lifestyle publications are all based on the premise that the base readership for this genre—mothers of young picky eaters—will not continue to replenish itself as soon as the next wave of toddlers begins eating table foods. In order to succeed at promoting their particular brand of culinary subterfuge as a parental strategy worth imitating, these authors need to strike a balance between using the rhetoric of deceit and trickery, on the one hand, and conveying their love and concern for their children's health and well-being, on the other. To that end, Seinfeld uses first person singular narration to convey her daily struggle with getting her children to eat the food that she prepared for them and also to highlight her own ingenuity in finding a solution for the problem that had presumably eluded other mothers as well: "It worked! The kids, entirely innocent of my deceit, plowed happily through their dinners. I was beside myself with joy. I couldn't stop smiling at the knowledge that my kids had eaten vegetables without a word from me" (Seinfeld 10). This passage's juxtaposition of the mother's joyful "deceit" and the vulnerability of the "entirely innocent" kids is rather heartbreaking, especially because the mother's jubilation is described as excessive. Seinfeld soon switches gears rhetorically by using the more inclusive first-person plural narration, which suggests that readers of *Deceptively Delicious* share a similar background and life experience with the author: "All we want is to make simple, fast, nutritious meals that our kids will actually eat. But after just one experience of watching a child throw our best efforts onto the floor, or refuse to eat, we just want to give up. Who has that kind of time—and food—to waste?" (Seinfeld 11). Key among Seinfeld's concerns, and by extension, those of her readers, is the perception that time is a limited resource that should not be wasted either in food preparation or consumption. The passage cited above presents "fast" food as an ideal and sees "time" as a commodity wasted by children who push back against the meal choices their parents offer them. The trade-off that she proposes—a few more minutes of food preparation via purée making ahead of time—translates into meals that can be enjoyed even more quickly during the week, both because there is less to do when cooking and less to argue about during dinner. Although she claims to use the extra time to talk with her family during dinner time, Seinfeld only measures her parenting success through what goes into her children's stomachs.

Whereas Seinfeld's narrative strategy features a shift from the private, first-person singular "I" to the communal, first person plural "we," Lapine's narrative alternates between first (I) and third (they) person points of view. However, the sense of dread Lapine feels about time's relentless march forward is darker than Seinfeld's—time is not merely a wasted commodity in *The Sneaky Chef* but a co-conspirator with illness and disease. She recalls her breaking point after her children threw a tantrum because two foods touched each other on their plates: "So ... I couldn't use logic, but I couldn't afford to give up either. Their bodies were continuing to develop whether they were taking in adequate nutrients or not. Somehow I had to outwit them and get them to eat right in spite of themselves" (Lapine, *The Sneaky Chef* 24). Although the children are not the nemesis in this particular family dynamic, Lapine nonetheless portrays them as foes who must be "outwit[ted]," as she fights a battle against time for their health. This desperate view of the high stakes meals have in her household suggests that a mother's duty is to purposefully alienate a child from his or her body, whose worth is measured in terms of its nutrient intake or lack thereof. More so than does Seinfeld, Lapine sees herself as the custodian of her children's physical well-being, not merely a model for good eating habits. When not directly engaged in "outwitting" her stubborn kids, Lapine promotes a medicinal approach to food preparation and the feeding of children that further de-couples the act of eating from any sense of gustatory pleasure. Rather than emphasize how appetizing the meals that she makes for them are, Lapine instills in them a utilitarian view of food as fuel that facilitates superior performance in other arenas: "I tell my kids how much faster they'll run when they're playing soccer or how much smarter they'll be in math class. I tell them that while other kids are getting sick, they'll feel great because their immune system will fight off the germs. And that they'll probably spend less time in the dentist's chair" (Lapine, *Sneaky Chef to the Rescue* 19). Although this line of argument is directly aimed at her own children, by repeating it within the book, Lapine plays to every mother's insecurity and competitive instinct. After all, none of her readers want their children to be sickly, dumb, or have a mouth full of cavities.

ORTHOREXIA AND THE ACCEPTANCE OF "KID FOOD" AS A CATEGORY

If getting children to eat more fruits and vegetables, whether they are aware of doing so or not, were a universally agreed-on standard through which to assess a woman's parenting skills, then these mothers would indeed be "winners." Instead, Lapine's and Seinfeld's insistence on ensuring that their children eat only "healthy" food in spite of themselves closely parallels some of the characteristics associated with the condition of "orthorexia nervosa," an obsession with healthy eating. According to the National Eating Disorders Association, "Self-esteem becomes wrapped up in the purity of orthorexics' diet and they sometimes they feel superior to others, especially in regard to food intake" (Kratina). Although I am not suggesting that either *The Sneaky Chef* or *Deceptively Delicious* contributes to orthorexia, I think the rhetoric of one-upmanship—whether it is directed at one's children, anyone eating an unhealthy diet, or fellow mothers—sets up adversarial dynamic that could have unforeseen negative consequences.

Although Seinfeld and Lapine both try to change the stakes of the nutritional battle they wage with their small children, the culinary subterfuge that they deploy so happily depends for its very success on adult acceptance of the existence of two distinct sociocultural categories of sustenance: normal "adult food," which is presumably healthy and full of vegetables, and "children's special food," which is less so. In fact, the concept of "kids' food" was first developed by, and promoted through, corporate advertising (Elliott, "Junk Food" 133). Campaigns associating meals for children either with sweetness or else with non-nutritive value added, such as playfulness or "fun," promote processed foods as suitable to both feed and entertain (hence the eponymous concept of "eatertainment") young children (Elliott, "Eatertainment" 547). Since *Deceptively Delicious* and *The Sneaky Chef* both contain recipes for macaroni and cheese, chicken nuggets, pizza and brownies, it can be argued that the authors' children still have the upper hand in determining the family's gastronomic choices, regardless of how many vegetable purées they unwittingly consume.

Not all mothers are willing to let their children dictate what is for dinner, however. A former "anxious mom" who took up the challenge of revamping her entire family's eating habits is Canadian Karen Le Billon, whose book *French Kids Eat Everything: How Our Family Moved to France, Cured Picky Eating, Banned Snacking, and Discovered 10 Simple Rules for Raising Happy, Healthy Eaters* rejects the very premise that adults and children should eat or like entirely different types of food. Le Billon advocates a more honest parental strategy of celebrating the pleasures of the table as a family by partaking of the same delicious meal. She invokes the example of "good" eating behaviour modelled by French children and encouraged by no-nonsense French mothers, rather than diagnosing the American dinnertime family dysfunction as a problem that must be remedied quickly. This Canadian academic was herself a picky eater whose two daughters had experienced dinnertime meltdowns and food boycotts similar to Seinfeld's and Lapine's children. During a year spent living abroad near relatives in France, both the parents and their children alter their previous approach to cooking, eating, and even buying food, and they discover the pleasure of eating and trying new things together. Their French relatives, neighbours, school teachers, and even perfect strangers at the market serve as eager mentors for Le Billon, as she tries to understand why food plays such a central role in French culture. By emphasizing both the family's shared commitment to changing the their eating habits as well as by lauding the rewards of the leisurely family meal where everyone has a role to play, Le

Billon offers a vision of children as informed eaters rather than ignorant dupes, as Seinfeld's and Lapine's cookbooks imply.

French Kids Eat Everything is less a cookbook than it is a memoir of a year spent living abroad in her husband's boyhood village, punctuated by "10 simple rules" anyone can follow to enjoy eating a broad variety of foods together with their family. Le Billon leverages France's storied national cuisine as an assurance to the reader that her advice leads to very good eating indeed rather than offering any assurances about the nutritional impact of these dishes. In France, Le Billon soon learns that the two cultural frameworks with which she is familiar interpret the role of food according to radically different criteria. Food, or "*aliment*" (Le Billon 81), for the French is primarily a source of sensory pleasure—through its aroma, its taste, and its texture. Le Billon and her family learn to appreciate these aspects of the food and ingredients that they shop for, prepare, and bring to the table. Rather than rushing to cook, eat, and clean up as Seinfeld does, Le Billon advocates taking things more slowly and thinking of family meals as pleasant and leisurely occasions involving the same pomp and circumstance—like tablecloths and fancy glasses—as holiday fare. Most importantly, Le Billon describes French children's eating education as a collective undertaking that extends outside of the home space and into the school cafeteria, where peer pressure is put to work so as to reinforce the sense that eating is a rewarding gustatory and social experience simultaneously: "At school, under the influence of peers, children taste and eat things that would have them turning up their noses at home (peer-induced behavioural change is also confirmed by American research). The French system is actually a highly perfected peer-pressure-driven food diversification program" (Le Billon 42). What Le Billon brings back to North America from Europe, then, is the knowledge that children's palates need to be trained over time to appreciate food in its natural or unadulterated form rather than being tricked into unwittingly consuming superfoods inside their "fun" junk food. She and her family learn to live to eat rather than eat to live.

By not resorting to trickery and actually engaging her children in an open dialogue about the meals they share, how they taste, what they are made of, and how they arrived in their home, Le

Billon asserts her authority as the parent all the while respecting the children's developmental stages as eaters in formation. Le Billon celebrates the pleasure of the table through a shared exploration of the variety of appealing textures, luscious tastes, and enticing aromas inherent in the meals the family will share; thus, *French Kids Eat Everything* is more adaptable than either *Deceptively Delicious* or *The Sneaky Chef*, both of which limit themselves to a narrow selection of bland vegetables, whose taste and texture can be easily disguised. The rules that Le Billon advocates are not limited to French food but are general principles inspired by the French approach to eating: no snacking between meals, family meals are eaten together, everyone eats the same dishes, and mealtime is for relaxation.

Since Seinfeld and Lapine also claim to have raised "happy, healthy eaters" who eventually eat vegetables of their own free will, as do Le Billon's kids, there is no objective standard by which to judge one approach to be better than the other. After all, Le Billon's publishers, William Morrow, are courting the very reader base of "anxious moms," created by Lapine's *Sneaky Chef* and Seinfeld's *Deceptively Delicious*. Her more honest approach, however, might lend itself better to older children who are hungry for something beyond the kiddie pizza, chicken nuggets, and brownies on offer in these earlier texts.

WORKS CITED

Byrd-Bredbenner, Carol, and Darlene Grasso. "Trends in US Prime-Time Television Food Advertising Across Three Decades." *Nutrition & Food Science*. 30.2 (2000): 59-66. Print.

Elliott, Charlene. "Eatertainment and the (Re)classification of Children's Foods." *Food, Culture and Society* 13.4 (2010): 539-553. Print.

Elliott, Charlene. "'It's Junk Food and Chicken Nuggets': Children's Perspectives on 'Kids' Food' and The Question of Food Classification." *Journal of Consumer Behaviour* 10.3 (2011): 133-140. Print.

Gibb, Tracy. "20 Ways to Sneak Vegetables into Kids (sic) Food." *Less Than Perfect Parents*, 29 July 2013. Web. 21 Aug 2014.

Koerner, Brendan. "What is Ovaltine, Please?" *Slate*. Slate, 22 Nov. 2002. Web. 21 Aug. 2014.

Kratina, Karin. "Orthorexia Nervosa." *National Eating Disorders Association*. National Eating Orders Association. n.d. Web. 27 Aug. 2014.

Lapine, Missy Chase. *The Sneaky Chef: Simple Strategies for Hiding Healthy Foods in Kids' Favorite Meals*. Philadelphia: Running Press, 2007. Print.

Lapine, Missy Chase. *The Sneaky Chef to the Rescue: 101 All-New Recipes and "Sneaky" Tricks for Creating Healthy Meals Kids Will Love*. Philadelphia: Running Press, 2009. Print.

Le Billon, Karen. *French Kids Eat Everything: How Our Family Moved to France, Cured Picky Eating, Banned Snacking, and Discovered 10 Simple Rules for Raising Happy, Healthy Eaters*. New York: William Morrow, 2012. Print.

Mannur, Anita. *Culinary Fictions: Food in South Asian Diasporic Culture*. Philadelphia: Temple University Press, 2009. Print.

Seinfeld, Jessica. *Deceptively Delicious: Simple Secrets to Get Your Kids Eating Good Food*. New York: HarperCollins, 2007. Print.

Yach, Derek, Zoë Feldman, Dondeena Bradley, and Robert Brown. "Preventive Nutrition and the Food Industry: Perspectives on History, Present, and Future Directions." *Preventive Nutrition*. Eds. Adrienne Bendich and Richard J. Deckelbaum. Totowa, NJ: Humana Press, 2010. 769-792. Print.

16.
What Are We Feeding Our Children When We Read Them a Book?

Depictions of Mothers and Food in Contemporary Australian Picture Books

LAUREL COHN

WHAT IT MEANS TO BE A MOTHER is largely defined by what a mother *does*, particularly in relation to her children and immediate family, and among the most fundamental aspects of *doing* mothering are those related to food. From breastfeeding to preparing and serving meals and snacks to children, mothers in most cultures are the primary food givers to their young. This chapter explores how Australian writers and illustrators in the twenty-first century depict the act of mothering in picture books for young children in relation to cooking and serving food. Moreover, it draws on the idea that children's texts can be understood as sites of cultural production and reproduction (Anstey and Bull 206), with social conventions and ideologies embedded in their narrative representations (Allan 56). The textual and illustrative references to food preparation and provision in the books examined reveal a strong correlation between the types of foods depicted and the ethnicity of the maternal figures involved. Although these picture books generally have benign liberal agendas and offer positive images of Aboriginal Australians or non-Anglo-Australian characters,[1] when it comes to the relationship between mothers and food, there are clear differences in the ways in which non-marked or normative ethnicities are represented in contrast to marked or non-normative ethnicities.

My analysis of depictions of food and food practices in recent Australian picture books for younger readers is based on a survey of 124 books that were shortlisted for, or won, Children's Book Council of Australia awards between 2001 and 2013. Of the eighty-seven titles that contain food and have human or anthropomorphised characters, twenty-six (30 percent) contain textual or illustrative references to maternal figures involved in food preparation or provision. Most of these depictions are incidental (where food references provide context or background but do not play a major role in the story line), as opposed to featured (where food or food events are significant in the story line). Incidental depictions are particularly interesting in that they are not determined by the plot; their inclusion as "background" or "context" indicates the food practices and types of foods that are considered a "normal" part of life. Interviews with writers and illustrators have revealed that they are often unaware of the frequency of incidental portrayals of food in their works (Blackwood, Personal interview; Graham, Personal email), which supports the notion that such depictions provide access to hidden assumptions.

Examination of this data set reveals that there is a strong correlation between non-Anglo-Australian maternal figures and home-cooked meals, and a clear link between Anglo-Australian mothers and sugar-rich snacks. The alignment of food type and ethnicity draws attention to the role food plays in establishing cultural identity. As Fischler notes, "Human beings mark their membership of a culture or a group by asserting the specificity of what they eat, or more precisely ... by defining the otherness, the difference of others" (Fischler 280). It is important to note that the writers and illustrators of the books surveyed operate within an industry that is largely a product of a white, middle-class culture (Bradford 166) and are creating cultural artefacts for a predominantly Anglo-Australian audience.[2] Overall representation of non-Anglo characters in the full survey set is low, less than 10 percent. However, this rises dramatically in the data set of twenty-six books: nine of these titles (34 percent) feature non-Anglo characters. In all of them, the foods referred to are particular to the ethnicity of the characters, who are clearly positioned by the narrative structures as "other." It can be argued, therefore, that the surveyed books reveal an unintended coupling of home-cooked meals with "otherness" and sweet treats with a normative self.

The act of "othering"—identifying someone or something as significantly different or opposite—implies that there is a homogenous group to which the "self" belongs and a border that separates "self" and "other." The term "othering" has negative connotations of control and conquest (Huggan 14), but I would suggest that in these books othering is best understood as a way of constructing a cultural identity distinctive from the middle-class, Anglo-Australian norm, a process that domesticates "alienness" through textual and illustrative storytelling devices. This is a more neutral reading of the idea of otherness than is recognized in postcolonial discourses, rendering the concept applicable to stories where difference is celebrated. Although the extent and nature of othering differs in the books discussed here, in contemporary Australian picture books, there is, generally speaking, a stable notion of the normalized self. By far the majority of characters in the picture books in the survey set are fair-skinned, have two parents, live in comfortable suburban homes, and have possessions and lifestyles that could non-controversially categorize them as middle-class Anglo-Australians. Even texts with anthropomorphized animal characters conform to this normative self, as shown in their physical and social settings, language usage, appearance and activities, and alignment with Anglo-Australian characters. Fair-skinned characters may or may not be of Anglo-Celtic or Anglo-Saxon origin; however, Giselle Liza Anatol's comments on white characters as the dominant social group in the Harry Potter books could just as easily apply to the books in the survey set: "whiteness becomes the 'default' for unmentioned race; it is interpreted as the norm and assumed when unstated" (173). Certainly contemporary Australian picture books use white, middle-class characters as a standardized, unmarked version of the self.

Each of the stories featuring non-Anglo-Australian characters use food and food practices to help define ethnic distinctiveness. There are five stories set in Aboriginal communities, two refugee stories (one set in the Balkans, one in Afghanistan), an immigrant story that begins in China, and a wordless picture book comparing an Australian family with a Moroccan family. The texts set in Aboriginal communities all contain references to bush tucker—native plants and animals used by Aboriginal Australians for culinary and medicinal purposes—with the associated food practices playing an integral role in defining cultural identity. In

Collecting Colour[3] the Aboriginal mother and aunt provide a picnic lunch of magpie goose sandwiches and icy water, and later cook a freshly caught barramundi on the campfire. In *You and Me: Our Place*, Auntie Ruby shows the two boys at the centre of the narrative how to find pipis and longbums in the sand and mangrove worms in the mangrove tree bark. Later, she cooks fish on an open fire for a small gathered crowd. A maternal figure by an outdoor cooking fire is a repeated motif through *A is for Aunty*, which contains many textual and visual references to food, including how to find and prepare bush tucker such as quandongs, witchetty grubs, and yabbies. The non-fiction title *The Papunya School Book of Country and History* positions bush tucker as central to the changing social and political circumstances of the A<u>n</u>angu over many decades and includes an illustration of women and children gathering bush tucker in the low desert scrub. In *Tom Tom*, the references to Granny Annie and Granny May preparing meals for the title character are textual only. However, at preschool Tom Tom is shown pretending to cook damper (Australian bush bread) that he has made out of play dough on an open fire, "just like Granny May." This image reinforces the idea of the maternal figure as bush tucker provider. In all these books, the specificity of bush tucker marks the characters' cultural identity.

Although the link between mothering and food provision is strong across cultures, the citation of "Auntie" and "Granny" draws attention to the notion of "maternal figure," as opposed to "mother" in these books. The Aboriginal characters in all the texts mentioned above are depicted as living in extended family groupings, as is the norm in Aboriginal communities and, indeed, in some other non-Anglo communities, with mothering being the province of a range of female figures, not just the biological, female progenitor. In addition, it should be noted that Aboriginal Australian kinship systems employ a different and often more abstract naming and labelling protocol to kinship systems based on the Anglo-Celtic nuclear family, and translations of terms, such as "mother," apply in some cases to numerous female kin across generations (Morphy 26). Although this may problematize who is "mother," the act of preparing and serving bush tucker (and other foods) by female adults labelled as mother, aunt, and granny are all clearly positioned in the books as part of a "mothering" role.

It is not only the types of foods that can indicate a marked ethnicity but also the relationships to food. Home-cooked meals in three other stories featuring non-Anglo characters are linked to a lost and longed for sense of home. In *Ziba Came on a Boat*, the young protagonist recalls her former life in Afghanistan as a way of escaping the grim reality of the trip that she and her mother are undertaking on an overcrowded boat. One double-page illustration shows a traditional Afghani kitchen scene with Ziba, her mother, and two aunties preparing flat bread, meat, and yoghurt over a three-chambered, wood-fired stove. Li Cunxin's autobiographical *The Peasant Prince*, also includes scenes of food preparation and provision as a memory of the past, in this case Li's poverty-stricken boyhood in a remote Chinese village. Li can be seen fanning the fire, while his mother attends to a pot on the wood-fuelled stove. On the opposite page, the mother, with a smile on her face, serves out portions from a central dish to the father and seven boys. The image is sentimentally nostalgic and notably devoid of the anxiety referenced in the text, which draws attention to the mother's concerns about the threat of her children dying from starvation. Food as a symbol of survival, comfort, and family is also evident in *My Dog*. Set in the war-torn Balkans, the story follows the experiences of a young boy displaced by ethnic cleansing. After being separated from his parents, he falls in with an old man, who eventually takes him to a safe haven, his daughter's house. This is illustrated as a kitchen scene, the three smiling characters sitting at a table shelling peas, with the boy nestled into the woman's lap as if he were the woman's son. Although not completely absent in contemporary Australia, hunger (and death) due to poverty or refugee status is not a known experience to most young children in the first-world economy. In this way, these stories position the characters as differentiated from the unmarked, normalized self, and by association, their relationships with food take on a quality of "otherness." Food is seen to nourish not only their bodies but also their sense of safety, family, and home. The act of cooking in these texts also signifies a lost and longed for mothering: meal preparation is represented as involving a loving interaction between the central characters and their mothers or in the case of the boy in *My Dog*, a mother substitute.

The alignment of home-cooked meals with "otherness" is most explicit in the wordless picture book *Mirror*. Binary oppositions lie at the conceptual heart of this book, paralleling the similarities and differences in a day-in-the life scenario of a family in a major Australian city and a family from a remote village in southern Morocco. Many aspects of the two ways of life are contrasted, including food acquisition, preparation and, consumption, with one spread devoted to breakfast and one to dinner. The Australian dinner scene shows the mother "preparing" the meal by dialling the phone with a take-away fish and chips menu at hand. In contrast, the Moroccan dinner scenes portray the mother drawing water from the well, peeling potatoes, stirring a pot on a clay oven and mixing grain. The contrasts between the evening meals serve a narrative function to draw attention to the differences between the two families. Although ordering home-delivered fish and chips may not be considered *usual* in terms of dinner preparation in Australia, it does represent a recognizable particularity. By extension, the reader can assume that the labour-intensive, home-prepared Moroccan meal is typical or particular to that culture. This is the only book in the data set, one could argue, that "ethnicizes" the Australian family by inviting the reader to examine the recognizable scenario in the same way as the unfamiliar one. This can be understood as part of a process whereby foreign phenomena can be comprehended within a frame of familiarity, a particular mode of othering (Huggan 13).

Setting the narrative in the past is another kind of othering. *Lizzie Nonsense* is the story of a family living in a remote Australian bush hut in the late nineteenth century. Mama's days are filled with laborious domestic chores. Lizzie helps with dinner and dreams of peaches and cream and little sweet cakes, but Mama says they are having "turnips as usual." Mama is seated at a rustic table peeling turnips with Lizzie looking over her shoulder; both are wearing long dresses and white aprons. Here, the characters involved in food preparation, although Anglo-Australian, are positioned as "other" through historical distance.

The remaining sixteen titles contain depictions of Anglo-Australian maternal figures preparing and serving food in contemporary settings that could be considered familiar to the normalized, middle-class, Anglo-Australian reader. The majority (twelve titles) contain portrayals of ethnically unmarked mothers making or offering sugar-rich snacks and treats. Six of these texts reference mothers, aunts, or grandmothers making or serving cakes, cupcakes, or sweet drinks for a festive occasion, such as a birthday party, social gathering, or special celebration;[4] five books depict sugar-rich foods being offered directly to children in the maternal figure's care;[5] and one portrays a mother carrying a tray laden with teapot, cupcakes, and biscuits into a busy shearing shed.[6] The different contexts in which the act of preparing and providing sugar-rich snacks is positioned in these titles conform to the social conventions of a middle-class, Anglo-Australian society, in which sweet foods are widely understood to be a "normal" inclusion at a party or social gathering, a given as dessert, and a standard item of between-meal rituals, such as morning or afternoon tea. The frequency of such depictions, together with the lack of sugar-rich foods in the books featuring non-Anglo characters, appears to inadvertently promote the Anglo-Australian mother as maker and provider of sweet foods as an exemplar of "normal" motherhood behaviour. To return to Fischler's notion of food and cultural identity, these characters can be seen to assert the specificity of sugar-rich snacks as a mark of Anglo-Australian identity.

Only five books make reference to Anglo-Australian mothers preparing or serving meals. Aside from *Mirror*, mentioned earlier, where the Australian mother orders take-away fish and chips, these depictions are all incidental, found in scenes with a non-food focus. In *Chatterbox*, Daisy erupts with words after an extended, unexplainable silence and, among other things, she tells her Nana she does not like her porridge lumpy, a passing allusion to Nana's role as breakfast cook. In *Diary of a Wombat*, the bemused family stand around the backyard barbeque watching the wombat make itself at home with a dust bath; it is the father in the cooking role behind the hot plate, with the mother alongside holding a platter of sausages and kebabs. In *The Big Little Book of Happy Sadness*, George's grandmother clutches a baking tray with a roast chicken while listening to George excitedly ask if they can get a dog. In *Eight*, the central character takes his beloved stuffed toy on a family outing in the bush; the picnic lunch consists of cold chicken, salad and "sticky" chocolate cake, with the accompanying image showing the mother passing a slice of layered cake to the father. Although textual and illustrative references to home-cooked meals can be found in other titles with Anglo-Australian characters, mothers are not shown to be actively preparing or serving these meals. The relative paucity of depictions of ethnically unmarked mothers offering more nutritious foods is notable given the cultural expectations of mothers as caretakers of their children's well-being. At the same time, the linking of non-Anglo-Australian mothers with home-cooked meals can be seen as a means of signifying a cultural authenticity, a closeness to the earth that is differentiated from the normalized Australian culture represented in picture books. This suggests an unintended alignment of mothers preparing and serving meals with "otherness," which creates a distancing effect between meals that may generally be considered nutritious and the normalized self.

These findings are noteworthy in terms of the way picture books enculturate their audiences. Children's literature is widely understood to play a significant part in a children's developing understanding of the world around them and their place in it (Anstey and Bull; Nodelman; Stephens; Weitzman et al.). The versions of the world presented in these books are necessarily informed not only by book creators' imaginations, personal values, and ideologies but also by the social, cultural, and historical contexts in which the books are created and read. Although older readers are increasingly engaging with picture books of conceptual and textual complexity, all the books discussed here are intended for an inexperienced audience, young children "in need of learning how to think about their world, how to see and understand themselves and others" (Nodelman 131). As such, they play an important role in enculturation: "picture books are a significant means by which we integrate young children into the ideology of our culture" (Nodelman 131).

Societal norms conveyed by picture books regarding gender have been the focus of numerous studies over the decades concerned about the impact of particular types of role modelling on young children (Adams, Walker and O'Connell; Anderson and Hamilton; DeWitt et al.; Gooden and Gooden; Hamilton et al.; Weitzman et al.). Some researchers also point to the impact on the adult who reads the book aloud, usually a parent (Anderson and Hamilton; Fraustino; Papazian). These adults, Papazian argues, "are constructed, just as children are, in and by children's picture books" (135). Thus, in presenting images of and ideas about motherhood and food, for example, picture books not only shape a child's notion of what it means to be a mother but also a parent's understanding of what that role entails (Papazian 124).

Given the robust debate across Australia and other Western societies about what we eat and the frequent references in the news media to diet-related illnesses, I would suggest there is a tension between the normalized mother paradigm relating to food in the picture book discourse and the "good" mother paradigm advocated by public health nutrition discourses that recommend healthy eating patterns be established in early childhood (such as the Australian Dietary Guidelines), including the limiting of high-sugar foods. Notions of what constitutes a healthy diet change over time, and it is not my intention to suggest that book creators should be adhering to certain codes of food consumption promoted by certain sectors of society; children's literature often challenges notions of correct ways of being and celebrates the flouting of rules. Rather, I wish to draw attention to what I consider an unexamined ideology embedded in picture books about mothers as food providers. It is interesting to note, for example, that children's consumption of sweets in fiction for the young has been seen as a form of resistance to adult culture (Daniel 83-85). Yet in the picture books discussed here, it is the adult who is supplying the sweets, and there is no dynamic of resistance at play either in terms of the food offered or the social conventions of the mothering role.

I would argue that children's books are a vehicle for communicating cultural rules and attitudes about how motherhood is enacted, and I concur with Kerry Mallan's proposition that "In reading literature we need to be mindful that representation risks promoting a specific mode of being as its ideal" (5). The findings considered here remind us that what is taken for granted in a culture—what may be interpreted as the ideal—can be rendered invisible by being linked to societal presuppositions that the book creators and audience both subscribe to (Stephens 50). I contend there are unexamined, and perhaps unexpected, cultural assumptions about ethnicity, motherhood, and food embedded in contemporary Australian picture books. These have the potential to inscribe a system of beliefs about gender, cultural identity, and food that contributes to readers' understanding of the world and themselves.

NOTES

[1]The cultural identifier "Anglo" (a shortened form of "Anglo-Celtic" or "Anglo-Saxon"), although technically referring to those of British descent, has become a short-hand signifier of white, English-speaking people in Australia as well as in Canada, New Zealand, and the U.S. I use the term Anglo-Australian to broadly indicate members of the dominant culture in Australia (white, English-speaking).

[2]Less than 15 percent of the data set is published internationally.

[3]Author and illustrator names are listed in the reference section.

[4]*A Bus Called Heaven*, *Irving the Magician*, *No Bears*, *Seven More Sleeps*, *Special Kev,* and *Tales from the Waterhole.*

[5]*Jethro Byrde Fairy Child*, *Maudie and Bear, The Potato People*, *The Terrible Suitcase,* and *You'll Wake The Baby!*. Although the character "Bear" in *Maudie and Bear* is fleetingly referenced as "he," Bear undertakes activities traditionally aligned with mothers: primary carer, cook, cleaner, comforter, and general playmate to Maudie. As there are no other parental or adult figures, I have counted Bear as a maternal figure.

[6]*A Year on Our Farm.*

WORKS CITED

Adams, Matthew, Carl Walker and Paul O'Connell. "Invisible or Involved Fathers? A Content Analysis of Representations of Parenting in Young Children's Picturebooks in the UK." *Sex Roles* 65.3/4 (2011): 259-70. Web. 17 Jul. 2013.

Allan, Cherie. *Playing with Picturebooks: Postmodernism and the Postmodernesque*. Basingstoke: Palgrave Macmillan, 2012. Print.

Allen, Emma, and Freya Blackwood. *The Terrible Suitcase*. Adelaide: Omnibus Books, 2012. Print.

Allen, Pamela. *The Potato People*. Melbourne: Viking, 2002. Print.

Anderson, David A., and Mykol Hamilton. "Gender Role Stereotyping of Parents in Children's Picture Books: The Invisible Father." *Sex Roles* 52.3/4 (2005): 145-51. Web. 13 May 2013.

Anatol, Giselle Liza. "The Fallen Empire: Exploring Ethnic Otherness in the World of Harry Potter." *Reading Harry Potter: Critical Essays*. Ed. Giselle Liza Anatol. Westport: Praeger Publishers, 2003. 163-78. Print.

Anstey, Michèle, and Geoff Bull. *Reading the Visual: Written and Illustrated Children's Literature*. Sydney: Harcourt, 2000. Print.

Australia. National Health and Medical Research Council. "Eat for Health: Australian Dietary Guidelines: Summary." *Eat for Health*. National Health and Medical Research Council, 2013. Web.15 May 2013.

Baker, Jeannie. *Mirror.* Sydney: Walker Books, 2010. Print.

Blackwood, Freya. Personal interview. 5 November 2013.

Bradford, Clare. *Reading Race: Aboriginality in Australian Children's Literature*. Melbourne: Melbourne University Press, 2001. Print.

Cunxin, Li, and Anne Spudvilas. *The Peasant Prince*. Melbourne: Viking, 2007. Print.

DeWitt, Amy, Cynthia M. Cready, and Rudy Ray Seward. "Parental Role Portrayals in Twentieth Century Children's Picture Books: More Egalitarian or Ongoing Stereotyping?" *Sex Roles* 69.1/2 (2013): 89-106. Web. 17 July 2013.

Daniel, Carolyn. *Voracious Children: Who Eats Whom in Children's Literature*. London: Routledge, 2006. Print.

Dunstan, Kylie. *Collecting Colour*. Sydney: Lothian Books, 2008. Print.

Fischler, Claude. "Food, Self and Identity." *Social Science Information* 27.2 (1988): 275-92. Web. 17 July 2013.

Fraustino, Lisa Rowe. "The Apple of Her Eye: The Mothering Ideology Fed by Best-Selling Trade Picture Books." *Critical Approaches to Food in Children's Literature*. Eds. Kara Keeling and Scott Pollard. New York: Routledge, 2009. 57-72. Print.

French, Jackie, and Bruce Whatley. *Diary of a Wombat*. Sydney: Angus & Robertson, 2002. Print.

Gooden, Angela M., and Mark A. Gooden. "Gender Representation in Notable Children's Picture Books: 1995-1999." *Sex Roles* 45.1/2 (2001): 89-101. Web. 23 July 2013.

Graham, Bob. *A Bus Called Heaven*. Sydney: Walker Books, 2011. Print.

Graham, Bob. *Jethro Byrde, Fairy Child*. Sydney: Walker Books, 2002. Print.

Graham, Bob. "Re: depiction of food and eating." Message to the author. 9 June 2014. Email.

Graham, Bob. *Tales from the Waterhole*. Sydney: Walker Books, 2004. Print.

Hamilton, Mykol C., et al. "Gender Stereotyping and Under-Representation of Female Characters in 200 Popular Children's Picture Books: A Twenty-First Century Update." *Sex Roles* 55.11/12 (2006): 757-65. Web. 23 July 2013

Heffernan, John, and Andrew McLean. *My Dog*. Gosford: Scholastic 2001. Print.

Huggan, Graham. *The Post-Colonial Exotic: Marketing the Margins*. London: Routledge, 2001. Print.

Jinks, Catherine, and Andrew McLean. *You'll Wake the Baby!* Melbourne: Penguin, 2000. Print.

Lee, Lyn, and Kim Gamble. *Eight*. Adelaide: Omnibus Books, 2006. Print.

Lofthouse, Liz, and Robert Ingpen. *Ziba Came on a Boat*. Melbourne: Viking, 2007. Print.

Mallan, Kerry. *Gender Dilemmas in Children's Fiction*. Basingstoke: Palgrave Macmillan, 2009. Print.

Matthews, Penny, and Andrew McLean. *A Year on Our Farm*. Adelaide: Omnibus Books, 2002. Print.

McKimmie, Chris. *Special Kev*. Sydney: Allen & Unwin, 2008. Print.

McKinlay, Meg, and Leila Rudge. *No Bears*. Sydney: Walker Books, 2011. Print.

Morphy, Frances. "Lost in Translation? Remote Indigenous Households and Definitions of the Family." *Family Matters* 73 (July 2006): 23-31. Web. 6 April 2015.

Nodelman, Perry. "Decoding the Images: How Picture Books Work." *Understanding Children's Literature*. 2nd Edition. Ed. Peter Hunt. London: Routledge, 2005. 128-39. Print.

Norrington, Leonie, and Dee Huxley. *You and Me: Our Place*. Adelaide: Working Title Press, 2007. Print.

Omerod, Jan. *Lizzie Nonsense*. Sydney: Little Hare Books, 2004. Print.

Omerod, Jan, and Freya Blackwood. *Maudie and Bear*. Sydney: Little Hare Books, 2010. Print.

Papazian, Gretchen. "Picturing Mom: Mythic and Real Mothers in Children's Picture Books." *Mothers Who Deliver: Feminist Interventions in Public and Interpersonal Discourse*. Eds. Jocelyn Fenton Stitt and Pegeen Reichart Powell. Albany: SUNY Press, 2010. Print.

Papunya School Publishing Committee. *Papunya School Book of Country and History*. Sydney: Allen & Unwin, 2001. Print.

Riddle, Tohby. *Irving the Magician*. Melbourne: Viking, 2005. Print.

Russell, Elaine. *A is for Aunty*. Sydney: ABC Books, 2001. Print.

Stephens, John. *Language and Ideology in Children's Fiction*. London: Longman, 1992. Print.

Sullivan, Rosemary. *Tom Tom*. Adelaide: Working Title Press, 2008. Print.

Thompson, Colin. *The Big Little Book of Happy Sadness*. Sydney: Random House, 2008. Print.

Weitzman, L. J. et al. "Sex-Role Socialization in Picture Books for Preschool Children." *American Journal of Sociology* 77.6 (1972): 1125-50. Web. 13 May 2013.

Wild, Margaret, and Deborah Niland. *Chatterbox*. Melbourne: Penguin, 2006. Print.

Wild, Margaret, and Donna Rawlins. *Seven More Sleeps*. Adelaide: Working Title Press, 2004. Print.

17.
Gluten-Free Casein-Free

Food, Autism, and Challenges to Scientific Motherhood and Neoliberalism

EMILIE ZASLOW

SHORTLY AFTER DECIDING TO PUT HER daughter on a gluten-free/casein-free/soy-free (GFCFSF) diet, Lorena asked the online Dietary Intervention (DI) community for help "navigating this strange new world." In particular, she was having trouble finding a source of protein that her daughter, Rachel, was willing to eat and was frustrated that even on the GFCFSF diet, Rachel was continuing to exhibit behaviours associated with autism.[1]

> Rachel will not eat meat or beans so I am supplementing with brown rice protein powder but now I am worried about arsenic! Also, are there any safe yogurts? We had a coconut milk yogurt but I have discovered that the yogurt has carrageenan [which has been linked to inflammation, diabetes, and cancer]. So now the only meal she will actually eat is gf pasta that is made from rice (arsenic!) or corn (GMOs and pesticides!).

Lorena received nearly thirty responses, including some of the comments below, with details on how to approach the protein issue:

> You could buy gelatin from Great Lakes. 1 tbsp. has 6 grams of protein. You can mix this into any cold drink and you can't tell it's there. 365 organic almond milk from WFs [Whole Foods] doesn't have carrageenan. Of course you can make your own almond milk; it's the best. But I have a full time job so that is out of the question.

> The protein powder likely has glutamines in it or something similar (look for anything that starts with gluta- or aspart- on the label). That could account for the increased behaviors. You can also get protein from quinoa and/or amaranth. These are fantastic gf 'grains' (quinoa isn't technically a grain) that are WHOLE protein food sources.
>
> We love chia seeds and hemp seed for protein. Spaghetti squash makes a great sub for noodles.
>
> Are you sure you are 100% GFCFSF? If not, that could be why she is still stimming.[2] We all make mistakes at first because there is SO much to learn ... like d-alpha-tocopherols is made from soy.

Scholars have argued that when mothers of children with special needs spend their time, energy, and money on alternative care for their children, such as those involved in feeding practices, such as the GFCF diet, the politics of motherhood becomes individualized and ineffective. Rather than fighting for policy change, funding redistribution, consumer boycotts, equal rights, or other structural social changes, mothers largely focus their resources on individual children (Douglas; Sousa; Yochim and Silva). From this lens, the practice of implementing the diet and the discursive world of the online communities that support the diet serve to reproduce the kind of individualized, intensive mothering valued in a neoliberal economy (Vandenbeld Giles 9).

However, as this virtual ethnography demonstrates, analyzing the actual communities of care allows for a shift in perspective. The social practices of mothers in online GFCF communities—revolving around the everyday sharing of recipes, observations about food reactions, and tips related to food selection and preparation—challenge aspects of medical-scientific epistemology as well as the deregulation and corporatization of food production in the United States. Through these seemingly commonplace communicative acts and the practice of implementing the diet, mothers position themselves as authoritative experts, whose knowledge is founded on shared experience. In the acts of knowing and sharing, mothers engage in a maternal politics that in many ways challenges normative medical and capitalist discourses as well as the neoliberal push to individualize motherhood. This essay employs qualitative textual analysis to explore the complex and contradictory politics of mothers' implementation of the GFCF diet and their participation in online community discussions of the diet. Furthermore, it examines how the mothers' work serves to disrupt traditional power relations between food producers and consumers, between doctors and patients, and between evidence-based and experiential knowledge.

ETIOLOGY OF AUTISM, THE ROLE OF MOTHERS, AND THE GFCF DIET

As early as the 1970s, Dr. Benjamin Feingold proposed an additive-free and salicylate-free diet as a behavioural intervention for hyperactive children, and in the mid-1990s some in the autism community began focusing on diet as a key treatment tool (Eyal 21). Although it is unknown how many children are being fed a GFCF diet, currently between a third and one half of all children diagnosed with autism will participate in complementary or alternative interventions, the most popular of which are special diets (Adams; Perrin et al.). Even though not every mother who participates in the two online communities analyzed in this essay has a child diagnosed with autism, many do, and those whose children have other disorders rely on the experiential knowledge of the autism community. Thus, a brief history of autism etiology and interventions is instructive in situating the GFCF diet and the role of mothers in shaping knowledge.

In 1943, Leo Kanner identified autism as a congenital disorder. At the same time, he was influenced by contemporary psychological theories of the day and in subsequent publications, both medical and popular, he began engaging in mother blaming by suggesting psychodynamic factors were causing autism (Raz 78-79). In 1960, Kanner told *Time* magazine that parents of children with autism were "cold and rational" individuals who "happened to defrost long enough to produce a child" (qtd. in Raz 79). Later, in a continuation of holding mothers responsible for their children's disorder, Bruno Bettelheim popularized the term "refrigerator mothers" and compared the behaviours of those who had undergone neglect and trauma in the concentration camps at the hands of SS guards with the behaviours of children with autism whom, he believed, had undergone a similar neglect and trauma living with their unaffectionate mothers (Sousa 222).

Theories of maternal deprivation lost ground in the 1970s as gender relations and maternal work patterns shifted (Raz 91) and with an active coalition of parents and researchers, spearheaded by Bernard Rimland, a genetic neurological etiology became commonly accepted (Douglas 171). As with Kanner, who had gotten most of his data from parental reports, Rimland used a checklist, in his 1964 *Infantile Autism,* that parents could fill out and send back to him. Through these checklists and subsequent conversations with parents, Rimland formulated the biogenetic theory of autism that is commonly accepted today. In addition, from the onset of his work on applied behaviour analysis (ABA), with behavioural psychologist Ivar Lovaas, parents were included as integral elements in the study of the disorder and interventions. In a 2006 history of his research on autism, Rimland wrote, "As the years went on, I continued to find, repeatedly, that parents, especially the mothers, were remarkably effective at identifying treatments" (qtd. in Eyal 22).

Rimland also increasingly began to rely on parents rather than doctors or scientists to identify environmental factors—vaccinations, milk, wheat, and polluted ecosystems—that they believed to exacerbate autistic behaviours in their children (Douglas 171; Eyal).[3] In 1995, he helped form Defeat Autism Now! (DAN!), a research and training project focused on biomedical treatments for autism, including diet, supplements, and heavy metal detoxification.[4] Rather than embracing neurodiversity (the *acceptance* of all neurological variations) or focusing on the *management* of autism through behavioural interventions, those who implement biomedical interventions seek *recovery* from autism. Those who follow the GFCF diet, a cornerstone of the biomedical approach, believe that children with autism often have abnormal digestive systems, resulting in the inability to fully absorb certain sugars, carbohydrates, and proteins as well as in increased intestinal permeability. This allows opioids formed in the breakdown of gluten (the protein found in wheat) and casein (the protein found in milk) to enter the brain, causing "brain fog" and other autistic behaviours (Adams 12-13; Karnik 5). Mothers' experiential knowledge was instrumental in changing the conceptualization of autism and in identifying both therapeutic and biomedical interventions.

Mothers of children with autism raise their children in a society with competing discourses surrounding disability; there is a medical model that "presents disability as a problem residing within the body or mind of an individual" as well as a social model that identifies the problem as a society unwilling to accept difference (Landsman). Although the mothers in this study challenge some aspects of medical epistemology, they largely embrace a medical model of autism as a disorder. And even though some may embrace neurodiversity and celebrate their child's different ways of thinking, the mothers' focus on dietary interventions is aimed at alleviating what they perceive to be behaviours that interfere with their children's social, emotional, and/or academic well-being.

NEOLIBERALISM, INTENSIVE MOTHERING, AND MOTHERS OF CHILDREN WITH SPECIAL NEEDS

Neoliberalism offers a productive frame of analysis that has frequently been used to make sense of motherhood (Vandenbeld Giles) and the practices of mothers with children who have special needs (Douglas; Yochim and Silva). These authors suggest that in our neoliberal era, as governments have reduced social and community services, such as funding for health and education, and deregulated food and pharmacological production and marketing, mothers have been called on to pick up the slack. Indeed, as MacKendrick argues, government has failed "to properly evaluate the safety of synthetic chemicals and implement stringent regulations and legislative frameworks to govern chemical innovation, manufacture, and release" leaving mothers responsible for eliminating their children's health risks (706). Moreover, neoliberalism— fundamentally in support of a free market and, therefore, in service of the production of qualified labourers for the market—requires the ideal neoliberal mother to "maximize [her children's] bodily and mental health potential" (Yochim and Silva 409) and raise children who will ultimately become human capital, even as they are growing up in chemically compromised environments. Since neoliberalism functions as an ideology, it stands to reason that the value of child care and wellness would be leveraged so that mothers would accept the government's off-loading of labour and co-operate in the raising of healthy consumer-citizen employees. From this perspective, mothers come to believe that the provision of educational, health, and therapeutic services for their children with special needs is their personal moral obligation rather than a fundamental element of social welfare (Vandenbeld Giles 10).

Yet the ideology of neoliberalism does not operate in isolation; it is augmented and amplified by the perpetuation of gendered-based divisions of labour and the ideology of intensive mothering (Hays). Intensive mothering is a child-centric mode of care that relegates a mother's interests, desires, and personal development to be of less importance than those of her children. In this scenario, the good mother spends her time, energy, and income on children's activities, consumer goods, education, and enrichment rather than on those that would contribute to her self-actualization.

The growing body of research on mothering children with special needs identifies neoliberal intensive mothering as a profoundly pressure-filled position where mothers are encouraged to embrace the role of "warrior-heroes," in which they must wage battle "against social and political forces to gain medical and educational interventions for their children despite the high personal and financial costs to themselves and their families" (Sousa 220). These warrior-heroes face enormous pressure because they feel responsible for mastering medical knowledge and, simultaneously, for relying on instinctual knowledge of their children to dismiss evidence-based research (Yochim and Silva 409). Supported by celebrity mom and activist Jenny McCarthy, neoliberal intensive mothering discourses are said to place mothering "in opposition to science and medicine" so that mothers must "feverishly negotiate" between maternal instinct and controlled studies (Yochim and Silva 407-410). From a neoliberal perspective, this process further privatizes the experience of mothering because a mother's focus is on wading through a myriad of choices and making decisions about her own child's interventions rather than focusing her resources on advocating for social equality, neurodiversity or structural changes in policy, funding allocations, social welfare practices, and research streams.

Indeed, mothers of children with special needs are asked to engage in an intensive mothering in which success is only possible for those with money, time, and advanced education (MacKendrick 722; Sousa 238). Yet the active and involved mothers of children with special needs exist within a complex and contradictory web of power relations. An alternative political agency, activism, and meaning can develop even as mothers engage in the decidedly gendered and intensive practices of cooking, creating recipes, and negotiating over food (Cook; West). As the mothers in the online communities in this study implement and discuss the GFCF diet, they are critically interacting with, and challenging, dominant ideologies of motherhood and neoliberal capitalism.

CASE STUDY OF TWO ONLINE COMMUNITIES

These complex power relations are explored through a virtual ethnography (Hine) of member postings between 2001 and 2013 in two online communities. The Dietary Intervention (DI) community is explicitly devoted to parents of children on the autism spectrum who are interested in a GFCF diet, and the Sensory List is a community for parents whose children suffer from difficulties with sensory processing.[5] The DI community has over fifteen thousand members, and since 2000, has averaged three thousand messages per month, whereas the Sensory List, though much smaller, has over four thousand members with an average of seven hundred messages per month. As with most online communities, gathering demographic information on the women who participate in these communities is difficult. However, based on discussions of the financial burdens involved in implementing a GFCF diet, including discussion of how one might use welfare benefits to pay for the foods that are on the diet, it can be determined that a range of mothers along the socio-economic spectrum, with the largest concentration being in the middle classes, participate in these communities. This research is explicitly feminist in its value of women's everyday experience and knowledge (Code).

CHALLENGING SCIENTIFIC MOTHERHOOD AND DEREGULATION OF FOOD OVERSIGHT

Whereas mothering was once a skill passed down through generations of women, scientific mothering is an ideology that, like intensive motherhood, structures family and social relationships. Scientific motherhood emerged as a result of mid-nineteenth-century medical advancement, urbanization, professionalization, and changes to extended family structures that demanded women learn mothering from male scientific and medical experts who, in turn, profited from imparting parenting advice (Apple 16). Today, scientific motherhood is materialized in the parenting advice book market as well as in prenatal and postnatal classes on how to care for newborns. For mothers with children who have special needs, this often translates into medical professionals who dismiss, patronize, or resist their efforts to participate in treatment plans (Schaffer, Kuczynski, and Skinner). In the case of autism, mothers who have questioned genetic etiology of autism and sought to direct the medical community to explore environmental causes have been ridiculed in media and the scientific community (Bumiller 884-885). By employing the GFCF diet as a treatment for "recovering" their children from autism and other neurological disorders, the mothers in this study directly challenge scientific motherhood and the mainstream medical community who do not believe that autism is curable. Routinely, mothers in these communities turn to one another rather than medical professionals, and to experience-based evidence rather than empirical and controlled studies, in order to make treatment decisions for their children. Because the GFCF diet is not a recognized treatment option within the medical community and because research funding has not supported the study of biomedical interventions, mothers must rely on one another and their own evidence as proof that the diet is an effective treatment.

The mothers' practice of sharing stories and recipes and of raising GFCF children insists on the validity of what I have previously called "feminine epistemology," a (learned, non-essentialist) form of knowledge, culturally associated with women, which privileges experience, anecdotal evidence, and collaborative knowledge production (Zaslow 5-6). Feminine epistemology need not always be in opposition to science; in the case of the GFCF diet, it aims to fill in where the institutional, political, and economic structure of the medical establishment has stymied research. Although the mothers in this study are focused on treatment plans for their own children, their discourse is neither individualizing nor accepting of the power relations that govern medical, food industry, and pharmacological superiority. Thus, although their communication can be empathic or practical (recipes, lists of foods that are "legal" within the diets regulations, and strategies for getting children to eat), it also often decidedly challenges scientific and neoliberal motherhood.

When a new community member wrote to the DI community asking how she might convince her husband that going GFCF would be good for their son, Annette shared links to several of the few inconclusive studies of the diet. Most responders, however, agreed with Saskia, who declared "nothing [is] more powerful than testimonials," and Lisa shared a story about the power of connected knowing:

> I found it nearly impossible because there were few resources. I didn't understand cross-contamination. I didn't know that I couldn't give him small bites here and there. I also didn't realize that for our son we also had to rid the body of corn and soy. Once I found this group ten years later, we tried it again—the right way. Our son was non-verbal, aggressive, had seizures and sleeping issues. Today he speaks, he is not aggressive or self-abusive. He no longer has seizures. He sleeps through the night! Any question that it helped our son? This week his neurologist asked me if I thought that perhaps he has been misdiagnosed! I laughed. He was correctly diagnosed. He has just been improved due to years of work.

The privileging of food rather than pharmaceuticals as a primary treatment, when pharmaceuticals are an option, is also a challenge to normative medical approaches and to corporate-capitalist power. In one instance, Gloria reminds another mother that she must follow through with the diet because

> You will never get back the lost time in your child's life. I did not hear the word "mommy" out of my daughter's mouth until she was 4 and it wasn't because she was on Ritalin or Prozac or Haldol, it was because the source of toxins were removed from her body. It was because her gut was healing and it was because we started intense therapy. We are not powerless even when the medical professionals fail us.

It is not only the medical profession that they see as failing them but also the consumer food market. Both Lisa's choice to cut corn and soy from her son's diet, which are hidden additives in many processed foods, and Lorena's attempt to remove arsenic, pesticides and genetically modified foods from her daughter's diet demonstrate mothers rejection of conventional, corporatized feeding practices. Though not always overtly activist, the mothers in these communities do address the lack of government oversight on food production. In one example, Silvia writes,

> For instance, there is actually blue dye in the nitrate portion of lunchmeat and bacon; the FDA does not require that disclosure on packaging. Another one: while there may not be any preservatives in string cheese, it is common practice to line the inside plastic with preservatives.

At other times, particularly in the DI community, discussions can be more directly critical of specific corporations that produce foods with genetically modified organisms, hidden preservatives, or unnecessary additives.

Many mothers on these sites discuss how difficult it is to start the diet, although they commonly note that "once you get the hang of it, it's not so bad." Still, even as they are "hanging in there," their discourse does not suggest that they are overwhelmed by pressure or struggling to navigate through a labyrinth of competing fields of knowledge, none of which they can master. There is a great deal of expertise on food preparation and how to take back the family's (or child's) diet from corporate food producers. Instead of pain, mothers often express joy that they have been able to use the GFCF diet to sustain social connection and family life and to empower themselves and their children (DeVault 230).

Moreover, as members of this community of connected knowing, they are not experiencing this intensive mothering as individualized. Amanda captures the sentiment when she writes, "Being able to read and interact with people who speak the same language as I do, who understand what is happening in my household, who so generously give advice and share experiences, is nothing short of amazing." In their private and shared implementation of the GFCF diet as a form of recovery for their children, the mothers in these communities affirm their ability to participate in the production of knowledge and to challenge the privatization of motherhood and the corporatization of food production.

CONCLUSION

Much of the research on mothers and health-related care has focused on the negative (Corman 439). Following this tradition, Douglas argues that mothers of children with autism are "self-governing and instrumental;" she implies that mothers are complicit in sustaining neoliberal ideology and economy as they intensively mother, filling in where a free market economy has failed to provide adequate social welfare and government regulation (Douglas 17). Although the mothers in this community *are* participating in intensive mothering—which is certainly easier and less oppressive for women who have the economic, educational, and cultural resources to actualize their intensity—this study of selected but representative conversations among mothers who participate in two online communities leads to a more nuanced analysis.

As we saw with Lisa and Gloria whose children now speak and sleep, an intensive focus on feeding sometimes alleviates daily challenges and makes living easier and more pleasurable for both child and parent. Additionally, as I have demonstrated in this chapter, the very act of participation in the community can be seen as an activist challenge to market-driven medical and food industries rather than an acceptance of normative medical views on autism as a genetic rather than environmental disorder, as well as a challenge to food production that privileges cost over health risk. Just as one mother tells another that she must learn to "separate food from love" if she is to be successful on the GFCF diet, scholars must learn to separate mothering from patriarchal and consumerist ideologies if they are to critically analyze the complex and contradictory positions of mothers, as they feed their children with special needs.

NOTES

[1]Gluten-free/Casein-free (GFCF) is standard for the diet. Many others add soy-free and corn-free, making it the GFCFSFCF diet.
[2]Stimming is a colloquialism for self-stimulating behaviours, such as hand flapping, rocking, and spinning in circles.
[3]The Centers for Disease Control and Prevention, and all other recognized medial institutions, currently argue that research definitively shows that there is no link between vaccinations and autism. Despite this, many individuals, including some of the mothers in the online communities discussed in this chapter, continue to believe that the ingredients in vaccinations may be responsible for their children's autism. Research on environmental factors, including food-related factors such as pesticides and water pollution, is still developing (Hamblin).
[4]Defeat Autism Now! became the Autism Research Institute in 2011.
[5]Both are email listservs; one is open to the public and the other requires acceptance by the moderator. To protect the participants' identities and the identities of their children, pseudonyms have been given to the name of the groups, the mothers, and the children. In addition, where a direct quote is used, minor changes may be made, but the original intent has been maintained. For additional details, see Zaslow.

WORKS CITED

Adams, James. "Summary of Dietary, Nutritional, and Medical Treatments for Autism-Based on Over 150 Published Research

Studies" *ARI Publication* 40 (2013): 1-53. Print.

Apple, Rima. "Constructing Mothers: Scientific Motherhood in the Nineteenth and Twentieth Centuries." *Social History of Medicine: The Journal of the Society for the Social History of Medicine* 8.2 (1995):161–78. Print.

Bumiller, Kristin. "The Geneticization of Autism: From New Reproductive Technologies to the Conception of Genetic Normalcy." *Signs: Journal of Women in Culture and Society* 34.4 (2009): 875-99. Print.

Code, Lorraine. *What Can She Know? Feminist Theory and the Construction of Knowledge*. Ithaca, NY: Cornell University Press, 1991. Print.

Cook, Daniel T. "Semantic Provisioning of Children's Food: Commerce, Care and Maternal Practice." *Childhood* 16.3 (2009): 317-34. Print.

Corman, Michael K. "The Positives of Caregiving: Mothers' Experiences Caregiving for a Child With Autism." *Families in Society: The Journal of Contemporary Social Services* 90.4 (2009): 439-45. Print.

DeVault, Marjorie L. *Feeding the Family: The Social Organization of Caring as Gendered Work*. Chicago: University of Chicago Press, 1991. Print.

Douglas, P. N. "As If You Have a Choice: Autism Mothers and the Remaking of the Human." *Health, Culture and Society* 5.1 (2013): 167-81. Web. 25 June 2014.

Eyal, Gil. "[Keynote Address, 2010 BJS Annual Conference:] How Parents of Autistic Children Became Experts on Their Own Children: Notes toward a Sociology of Expertise." *Berkeley Journal of Sociology* (2010): 3-17. Web. 25 June 2014.

Hamblin, James. "The Toxins That Threaten Our Brains" *The Atlantic*. The Atlantic Monthly Group, 18 March 2014. Web. 25 June, 2014.

Hays, Sharon. *The Cultural Contradictions Of Motherhood*. New Haven, CT: Yale University Press, 1996. Print.

Hine, Christine. *Virtual Ethnography*. London: Sage, 2000. Print.

Karnik, Jenika. "Effect of Celebrity Endorsements on Treatment Choices Made by Professionals and Parent with Children Diagnosed with ASD." Thesis. Southern Illinois University Carbondale,

1 Aug. 2013. Web. 6 Aug. 2014.

Landsman, Gail. "Mothers and Models of Disability." *Journal of Medical Humanities* 26.2-3 (2005): 121-139. Print.

MacKendrick, Norah. "More Work for Mother: Chemical Body Burdens as a Maternal Responsibility." *Gender & Society* 28.5 (2014): 705-728. Web. 25 June 2014.

Perrin, James, et al. "Complementary and Alternative Medicine Use in a Large Pediatric Autism Sample." *Pediatrics* 130.2 (2012). n.pag. Web. 25 June 2014.

Raz, Mical. "Deprived of Touch: How Maternal and Sensory Deprivation Theory Converged in Shaping Early Debates over Autism." *History of the Human Sciences* 27.2 (2014): 75-96. Print.

Schaffer, Rebecca, Kristine Kuczynski, and Debra Skinner. "Producing Genetic Knowledge and Citizenship through the Internet: Mothers, Pediatric genetics, and Cybermedicine." *Sociology of Health & Illness* 30.1 (2008): 145–159 Print.

Sousa, Amy C. "From Refrigerator Mothers to Warrior-Heroes: The Cultural Identity Transformation of Mothers Raising Children with Intellectual Disabilities." *Symbolic Interaction* 34.2 (2011): 220-43. Print.

Vandenbeld Giles, Melinda, ed. *Mothering in the Age of Neoliberalism*. Bradford, ON: Demeter Press, 2014. Print.

West, Isaac. "Performing Resistance In/from the Kitchen: The Practice of Maternal Pacifist Politics and La WISP's Cookbooks." *Women's Studies in Communication* 30.3 (2007): 358-83. Print.

Yochim, Emily Chivers, and Vesta T. Silva. "Everyday Expertise, Autism, and "Good" Mothering in the Media Discourse of Jenny McCarthy." *Communication and Critical/Cultural Studies* 10.4 (2013): 406-26. Print.

Zaslow, Emilie. "Revalorizing Feminine Ways of Knowing: The Challenge to Biomedical Epistemology in an Online Mothers' Health Community." *Information, Communication & Society* 15.9 (2012): 1352-72. Print.

18. I Feed Therefore I Am

Mothers, Pasta, and Advertisements

SIMONA STANO

MOTHERHOOD HAS ALWAYS BEEN ASSOCIATED with feeding and nurturing (Muzzarelli and Re). Common iconography features several representations of women harvesting, cooking, salting and drying various food products. The medieval handbook *Tacuinum sanitatis* (fourteenth century), for instance, depicts two women in the act of preparing pasta: one of them, with her head covered and an apron wrapping her hips, kneads the dough, while the other carefully places it on a staircase in order to dry it.

Beyond the peculiarities of each representation, feeding and serving foods are some of the main functions generally associated with the female sphere. Several authors (Cline; Counihan; Probyn; Inness; Colella; Muzzarelli and Tarozzi; Neuhaus; Procida; Muzzarelli and Re) have explored this topic both in the scientific field and in the humanities. The following paragraphs will explore the role of motherhood in food advertising—representing both the mirror and the generator of present-day socio-cultural values—from a semiotic point of view, paying particular attention to pasta, which emblematically recalls home cooking in both Italy and abroad.

PASTA, "ITALIAN IDENTITY," AND DOMESTICITY

Pasta is generally recognized as the Italian food *par excellence* by both nationals and foreigners. However, it was only between the seventeenth and eighteen century that its consumption began to spread widely. Moreover, only in the post-unification period

(1880–1920), after the Italian mass emigration to the United States of America, did this food product become a symbol of Italian identity and "domesticity" (Capatti and Montanari; Gabaccia; La Cecla). This is why the collective representations of pasta generally stress the role of the family (Stano) and, particularly, the figure of the mother.

Barilla Group, which is the world leader in the pasta market, has always emphasized the link between food and motherhood in its commercials. The following paragraphs, which will deal with the analysis of some relevant examples, will reflect on how motherhood has taken on different forms in Barilla's advertisements with the passage of time and the variation of *habitī* (Bourdieu) and sociocultural codes.

BARILLA: HOME, MOMS, AND PASTA

Barilla was created in 1877, when Pietro Barilla opened a bakery in Parma, Italy. After initial difficulties, his enterprise started to grow, and in 1910, it became the first factory equipped with a continuous furnace, employing eighty workers. Immediately realizing the importance of advertising, Pietro's sons, Gualtiero and Riccardo, gave rise to a trend that over the years has led the Parmesan company to collaborate with leading Italian and international artists to create calendars, posters, and eye-catching advertisements.

In *The Invention of Tradition: The Case of Pasta, a Symbol of Italian Identity* (Stano) I point out that Barilla pasta is commonly celebrated according to certain values, such as conviviality, sharing, and joy of staying together. In this sense, the figure of the house and the family prove to be crucial: their concrete manifestations (e.g., the domestic space, the wedding rings, the table, and the family gathered around it) are recurrent, and there are also several references to various concepts, such as domesticity, simplicity, and tradition. Furthermore, as I will describe in the following paragraphs, the figure of the *mother* plays a crucial role by assuming different forms and connotations.

Erberto Carboni's Advertisements (1952)

In 1952, Barilla's commercial communication was entrusted to the

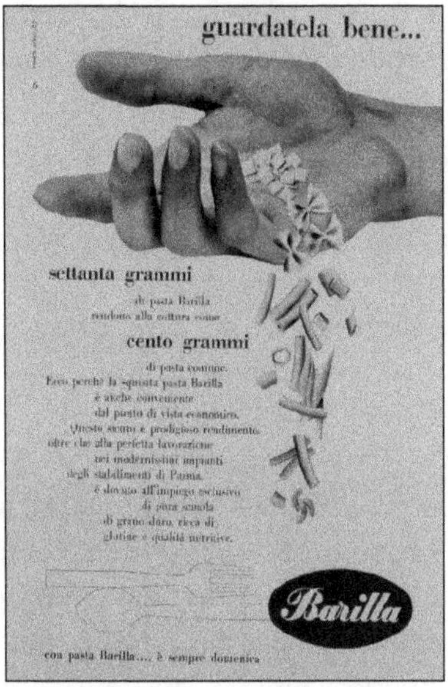

Figures 1, 2, and Figure 3:
Erberto Carboni's posters of Barilla,
© Archivio Storico Barilla, Parma, Italy.

Italian architect and advertiser Erberto Carboni, who designed three advertisements that are very significant with respect to the representation of motherhood. Figures 1, 2, and 3 show a progressive objectification of the female figure: referred to as *signora* (an Italian term denoting her status as a married woman and, presumably, mother), the woman in the first image is not represented in her entirety, with a pot metaphorically substituting for her belly (and womb). The visual configuration of the page draws attention to the logo, whose crucial role is stated by the verbal text: the lady "has no worries" (è *tranquilla*)[1] because the "superior quality" of the ingredients used to produce Barilla pasta ensures a successful cooking performance; she is simply required to put the food product into a pot. This message is reiterated in the second image, where the female figure is represented by a synecdoche (the hand), further objectifying the woman and subjectifying Barilla pasta, whose good qualities are stated by the verbal text. Furthermore, the headline (*guardatela bene...*) invites observers to focus their attention on the product, reducing the hand (and, therefore, the female figure) to a mere "tool" needed to hold it. Finally, in the third image, the woman completely disappears: the four polychromatic bowls dominating the visual scene create a metonymy (i.e., container for contents) recalling pasta, which is identified by the logo occupying the oval shallow bowl at the end of the handle of the spoon, located at the bottom of the image. Such a utensil represents the only reference to the human subject, since it recalls the practices of preparation and consumption of the advertised product. Nonetheless, the slogan and the logo clearly sanction who is the real subject of the depicted scene: Barilla pasta, which is said to be able to stimulate anyone's appetite (*la pasta del buon appetito*).

Barilla's First Carosello (1958)

Moving on to audiovisual commercials, it is essential to consider Barillo's first *Carosello*,[2] produced in 1958. After reciting the famous sonnet from Dante Alighieri's *Vita Nova*, "*Tanto gentile e tanto onesta pare*" ("So gentle and so honest she appears"), the young journalist Giorgio Albertazzi presents Barilla's new gluten pasta, introduced by a cheerful group of children of different ages dancing around a huge box of pasta. The decision to have a sonnet by Dante Alighieri, the "father of the Italian language," thereby suggests that Barilla pasta is also to be understood as representing quintessential Italian spirit.

Although not directly represented on the screen, the mother plays here a crucial role, which is clearly expressed by the children's choir: "We are healthy babies, do you know why? / Our mom found it! / She gives us the new Barilla pasta / which is gluten pasta." This points to the strong *practical* valorization (Floch, "Le Carré Sémiotique" and "Sémiotique, Marketing et Communication") of the product: Barilla pasta is praised for its nutritive qualities (as it can provide the body with the energy it needs to grow in a healthy way)—that is, in accordance with those *use values* (Floch "Le Carré Sémiotique" and "Sémiotique, Marketing et Communication") that make it a "safe food product for all stages of life." Motherhood, therefore, acquires particular visibility: as mothers understand the potential of Barilla pasta, they give it to their children, who can consequently grow healthy and strong.

The Little Girl with the Yellow Raincoat (1987)

In the late 1980s and early 1990s, Barilla released a series of commercials called *Dove c'è Barilla c'è casa* ("Where there is Barilla there is a home"). In the first video of this series (1987), a little girl in a yellow raincoat, having missed her bus after leaving school, starts walking towards her house. Meanwhile, a woman (presumably her mother), while waiting for her husband (who will appear on the screen shortly afterwards) and her daughter, is cooking pasta. The camera then moves to the clock and the worried expressions of the two parents: it is almost one o'clock in the afternoon (Italian lunch time), and their daughter has not returned home from school yet. Along the way, in fact, the child found a lost kitten and stopped a while to put it under her raincoat and take it home with her. Suddenly, the father sees his daughter from the kitchen window and goes with his wife to the door. Here, their worried and almost reproachful expression immediately gives way to a moment of hilarity: the little girl takes the kitten from her raincoat and smiles looking at her mother, who, returning the smile, invites them to enter. The commercial then ends with the woman placing a bowl of milk on the ground to feed the kitten and then hugging her daughter, while in the background, the man brings to the table a dish full of the pasta previously cooked by the woman. Finally the tagline "Where there is Barilla there is a home," spoken by the voice over, appears on the screen, followed by the Barilla logo (Stano).

We have in this case a *utopian* (Floch "Le Carré Sémiotique" and "Sémiotique, Marketing et Communication") valorization of pasta, since the commercial refers to the *basic values* of conviviality, family, and hospitality. Barilla pasta is presented as the incarnation of the house, as it is generally conceived in the Italian culture: home, protection, and love. In this sense, the mother plays a crucial role: feeding both her family and the kitten, she is inseparably tied to the advertised food product.[3] Such a conjunction finds visual expression in the moment when the woman's hand, which embodies a specific expertise, picks a package of pasta out of a series of different types and pours its content into a pot containing boiling water.

PASTA, MOMS, AND "DISCURSIVE REGIMES"

In a series of commercials released in 1993, a young boy invites his American basketball coach to have lunch at his house without giving notice to his family. The commercials show a different perception of the same event, depending on the specific point of view of the characters appearing on the screen: the boy's younger brother, his older sister, his coach, and his mom. Building on a research by Daniela Losito and Emanuela Zerbinati, Guido Ferraro described their different perspectives in terms of *discursive regimes*.[4] The younger brother fears that the arrival of the foreign guest might disturb his habits, forcing him to resign to his daily plate of pasta (*positional* regime). The young American is mainly interested in physical efficiency, that is, in the nutritive qualities of pasta (*causal* regime). The older sister, who is attracted to the young man, wants to assert her identity through cooking, although she does not actually perform such an action (*perspective* regime). Finally, the mother is able to combine all these perspectives together, responding to everyone's needs (*multiperspective* regime): she does not disappoint her youngest son, providing him with his favourite and usual food; she satisfies the athlete's energetic needs, thanks to the nutritive qualities of the advertised product; and she lets her daughter take credit for the cooking performance, although she is the actual cook.

"A Sea of Love" (1999) and "Gathering Family" (2000)

The relation between pasta and motherhood is further enhanced in the commercial *Un mare d'amore* ("A sea of love"). While driving to the sea, a young couple discovers an abandoned building facing the sea. They enter it, and whereas the young man directly goes to the sea, the woman looks around and finally extracts a

Figure 4—Commercial Barilla: Snapshots (1999)

box of pasta from her beach bag and places it in a small windowpane in which it perfectly fits. By doing so, she makes such a space become a *domestic* space. This, moreover, has a strong impact on the female figure herself, who is subjected to a visible transformation: the young unmarried lady appearing on the screen at the beginning of the commercial (Figure. 4, the top) turns into an older woman (Figure. 4, the bottom), who is connoted as a "mother" in the final scenes. The joining link between these states is precisely Barilla pasta, which is represented as the emblem of such a transformation—whose "naturality" finds expression in the female hand (Figure 4, the middle) that marks continuity between the initial and the final part of this short story.

In the commercial *Riunione di famiglia* ("Gathering Family"), pasta represents a direct metaphor of motherhood: different characters, appearing in separate scenes, receive a letter only containing a piece of pasta. In fact, no word is needed to understand such a message: their mom (who will appear shortly afterwards) is waiting for them. The commercial, therefore, ends with all the family gathering at the mom's house and with the woman welcoming her sons and daughters with her husband, before bringing to the table a dish full of pasta.

BARILLA ABROAD: MOMS COOK AT HOME, AND DADS COOK AT RESTAURANTS

Commercials shown in foreign countries generally feature the same themes described above. In a U.S. commercial released in 2000, for instance, an Italian man is married with an American woman, and they live in the United States with their two kids. When the woman's sister visits them, the two women move to the kitchen. Here is where the younger lady, pointing at the box of spaghetti leaning on the counter, sanctions her sister's motherhood by saying "Barilla Plus. You're such a good mom."

By contrast, in the commercial *Piccolini Barilla* pasta is eaten at a restaurant, as it is often the case in the United States (Stano). However, the video is set in Italy, where a young woman walks down the street with her daughter. They stop at a restaurant, where they are served some pasta cooked by a young chef, whose identity is revealed at the end of the commercial by the Italian-speaking kid: "Papà! Ciao!" ("Hello dad!").

CONCLUSION

As I outlined in the previous paragraphs, motherhood plays a crucial role in Barilla's commercials. The representations of mothers and motherhood have changed over time and so have the meanings associated with them. In the advertisements by Carboni, as well as in the 1958 *Carosello*, the female figure mainly corresponds to the prototypical housewife, according to common models for advertising communication in the 1950s and 1960s. Images, texts, and/or vocal elements depict a portrait of a de-subjectified woman, completely devoted to housework and to the care of her family. This finds expression in the progressive objectification of the female figure, which is segmented, reduced to functional components of her body, and even substituted either by the means or the addressees of her care. Wife and mother *par excellence*, such a woman does not exist per se, but rather is only there to satisfy her family's needs. Her subjectivity is reduced to the ability of making the right choice to feed her children and family, although the advertisements promptly remind the viewer that the real subject is Barilla pasta itself, whose excellent qualities eliminate any worry for the so-called "signora."

Over time the image of mothers promoted by Barilla's advertising has partially changed. As pasta was no more valorized for its practical qualities (e.g., nutritive capacity, cooking times, hardness, water absorption, etc.) but rather for its relationship to basic values, such as love, protection, and joy of staying together (Stano), the role of mothers changed accordingly. The maternal figure became the incarnation of such values and, as such, progressively acquired visibility in advertising.

Despite the shift from the practical to the utopian level, however, such a figure has remained indissolubly related to other people's needs or desires, which stresses the opposition between the female and the male spheres, since men, together with children, are the receivers of maternal (that is, feminine) care. The only case overturning this condition is the commercial *Piccolini Barilla*, where cooking is performed by the young girl's dad. Nonetheless, this example points out another fundamental opposition characterizing the contrast between the male domain and the female sphere: the public versus private dimension. According to the Western *imaginarium*[5]—which tends to naturalize the accomplished male chef, trained in established and prestigious food traditions, as the culinary ideal (Parasecoli)—the only case representing a male cook identifies it with the chef of a restaurant, that is, a man working in a public space. By contrast, women have generally been relegated to the private sphere of the domestic kitchen, highlighting their doing for others. Whether considering the independent (and apparently not married) mom of the 1993 commercial or the lady welcoming the little kitten with a bowl of milk, the maternal figure is always defined by what she does for other people—namely feeding them and responding to their expectations and desires. What is more, pasta is precisely what makes women "good" mothers in these commercials: this is the case of the U.S. commercial *Sisters*, where the American woman is described as a "good mom" because she cooks Barilla Plus pasta, or that of the commercial *Un mare d'amore*, where pasta marks the passage from youth to maturity and motherhood. Finally, in *Riunione di famiglia*, Barilla pasta even substitutes for motherhood, metaphorically recalling it.

In summary, the analysed case studies suggest that, regardless of the different forms and connotations assumed by the female figure in Barilla's advertising over time, the collective representations of motherhood generally tend to identify it with feeding and nurturing, recalling an association that date long back in time. In other words, it is as if—irrespective of their age, marital status, origin, or emancipation from old-style stereotypes—all these moms, either looking at the camera or through hushed-up voices, tell the viewer: *I feed therefore I am.*

NOTES

[1]All translations are the author's.

[2]*Carosello* (Italian for "carousel") was an Italian television advertising show, broadcast on RAI, Italy's national public TV, from 1957 to 1977. It generally included short sketch comedy films or other entertainment shows, followed by commercials.

[3]It is precisely the preparation of the meal that highlights her crucial role: the child is independent, can walk alone toward her house, and take initiative (i.e., save the kitten), but she still depends on her mother for food.

[4]On the base of the opposition between the *subjective* level, which is related to the subject, and the *objective* level, which stresses socially and inter-subjectively recognized values, as well as on the contrast between the *relative* and *absolute* axis, Ferraro identifies four *discursive regimes*. In the *causal* regime, the emphasis is put on objective facts, and what one does defines what one is. The *positional* regime is based on the subject, whose actions are defined by his same essence; this is within the realm of tradition and socially recognized roles. The third discursive regime is the *perspective* regime: the "perspective hero" is someone who does not accept any external definition and goes against socially established roles and values, and acts according to his own feelings and nature. Finally, the *multiperspective* regime identifies the "seducer," namely the one who is able to be for others what they want him to be. In Ferraro's view, in fact, seduction is essentially an interpretative process, which consists of grasping other people's desires and breaking into their narrative programs as a value-object.

[5]The term *imaginarium* is here used to refer to the socially shared depository of images or, more generally, of *figures*, which comprise part of a cultural *encyclopaedia* (Eco, "A Theory of Semiotics," "Lector in Fabula," and "Semiotics and the Philosophy of Language") that directs and regulates its imaginative paths. More specifically, Ugo Volli distinguishes between an "internal imaginarium" (intended as a "cultural pattern for the production of images and figures," [Volli 35]) and an "external imaginarium" (conceived as a "material system of production and storage of [these] images" [Volli 35]). Several works have investigated the term and its meanings, which are not easy to define (Leone).

WORKS CITED

Alighieri, Dante. *Vita Nova*. Evanston, IL: Northwestern University Press, 2012. Print.

Barilla. *L'allenatore di basket I, II, III and IV*. 1993. Commercial. Barilla media archive, Parma, Italy.

Barilla. *Carosello* (commercial). YouTube, 1958. Web. 7 Mar. 2015.

Barilla. *La bambina con il keeway giallo* (commercial). YouTube, 1987. Web. 7 Mar. 2015.

Barilla. *Un mare d'amore* (commercial). YouTube, 1999. Web. 7 Mar. 2015.

Barilla. *Riunione di famiglia* (commercial). YouTube, 2000. Web. 7 Mar. 2015.

Barilla. *Sisters* (U.S. commercial). YouTube, 2000. Web. 7 Mar. 2015.

Barilla. *Piccolini Barilla* (U.S. commercial).YouTube, 2004. Web. 7 Mar. 2015.

Bourdieu, Pierre. *Distinction: A Social Critique of the Judgement of Taste*. London and New York: Routledge, 1984. Print.

Capatti, Alberto and Massimo Montanari. *La Cucina Italiana: Storia di una Cultura*. Rome: Laterza, 1999. Print.

Cline, Sally. *Just Desserts: Women and Food*. London: Deutsch, 1990. Print.

Colella, Anna. *Figura di Vespa e Leggerezza di Farfalla: Donne e Cibo nell'Italia Borghese di Fine Ottocento*. Florence: Giunti Editore, 2003. Print.

Counihan, Carole. *The Anthropology of Food and Body: Gender, Meaning, and Power*. Routledge: New York, 1999. Print.

Eco, Umberto. *A Theory of Semiotics*. Bloomington: Indiana University Press, 1976. Print.

Eco, Umberto. *Lector in Fabula*. Milan: Bompiani, 1979. Print.

Eco, Umberto. *Semiotics and the Philosophy of Language*. Bloomington: Indiana University Press, 1986. Print.

Ferraro, Guido. *L'Emporio dei Segni*. Rome: Meltemi, 1998. Print.

Floch, Jean–Marie. 1983. "Le Carré Sémiotique. Pour une Topographie du Sens." *Sémiotique & Publicité* II (1983): 57-79. Print.

Floch, Jean–Marie. *Sémiotique, Marketing et Communication*. Paris: Presses Universitaires de France, 1990. Print.

Gabaccia, Donna. *From Sicily to Elizabeth Street: Housing and Social Change Among Italian Immigrants, 1880-1930*. Albany: State University of New York Press, 1984. Print.

Inness, Sherrie. *Cooking Lessons: The Politics of Gender and Food*. Lanham: Rowman and Littlefield, 2001. Print.

La Cecla, Franco. *La Pasta e la Pizza*. Bologna: Il Mulino, 1998. Print.

Leone, Massimo. *Immaginario / Imaginary – Lexia* 7-8. Turin: Aracne, 2011. Print.

Losito, Daniela, and Emanuela Zerbinati. "Lungo il Filo degli Spaghetti." *Lexia (Old Series)* 3 (1994): 3-10. Print.

Montanari, Massimo. *L'Identità Italiana in Cucina*. Rome-Bari: Laterza, 2010. Print.

Muzzarelli, Maria Giuseppina, and Fiorenza Tarozzi. *Donne e Cibo. Una Relazione della Storia*. Milan: Mondadori, 2003. Print.

Muzzarelli, Maria Giuseppina, and Lucia Re. *Il Cibo e le Donne nella Cultura e nella Storia*. Bologna: Clueb, 2005. Print.

Neuhaus, Jessamyn. *Mainly Meals and Mom's Home Cooking: Cookbooks and Gender in Modern America*. Baltimore: Johns Hopkins University Press, 2003. Print.

Parasecoli, Fabio. "Starred Cosmopolitanism: Celebrity Chefs, Documentaries, and the Circulation of Global Desire." *Semiotics of Food—Special Issue of Semiotica* 211.1/4, In Press.

Probyin, Elspeth. *Carnal Appetites. Food Sex Identities*. New York: Routledge, 2000. Print.

Procida, Mary A. "No Longer Half-Baked. Food Studies and

Women's History." *Journal of Women's History* 7.3 (2004): 197-205. Print.

Stano, Simona. "The Invention of Tradition. The Case of Pasta, a Symbol of Italian Identity." *Signs & Media* 8 (2014): 136-152. Print.

Volli, Ugo. "L'Immaginario delle Origini." *Immaginario/Imaginary—Lexia* 7-8 (2011): 31-61. Print.

V.

SPACES, BORDERS, ENVIRONMENTS AND MATERIALITY

19. Mothering and Food Work in Nuclear Family Home Design

A Spatial Analysis of Feeding Children

JENNIFER L. JOHNSON

CHOCOLATE FINGER PRINTS ON THE FRIDGE, cereal swept into a corner, perhaps some pumped breastmilk or baby formula dripped over the arm of the nursing chair in the eat-in kitchen … these adornments are not included in the show-home version of my house. Evidence of the food negotiations, preparations, consumption (and clearing up) that are at the core of daily life with small children are invisible in the mock-ups for new home design. No one remembers what the architect promised my lived-in home would look like, but not much consideration was given as to how the design would facilitate the raising and feeding of children within its walls. I have evidence of this in the numerous kitchen renovations previous owners have undertaken to make the space easier to work in. I did not have a choice in the design of my kitchen. But do those with the means to build entirely new homes have a choice of designs that can facilitate the very basic function of feeding children?

This chapter considers the practice of child-infant feeding and mothering in relation to the spaces that (fail to) contain them. How does the organization of space help or hinder the feeding of children? How do spaces or home designs shape the way children are fed, and what do they say about the gendered relations of power enacted within them?

Feminist geographers and others have produced a rich body of literature on the gendering of the home as a space in which relations of power between men and women play out (Johnson, "Browsing the Modern Kitchen," "Hybrid and Global Kitchens").

They call attention to the kitchen as a gendered place that is otherwise ignored or only referenced as a backdrop to popular culture and architectural design literature (Hayden; England). The home is gendered as feminine in opposition to a masculinized public world of paid work, while specific spaces within the home, such as the kitchen, are also feminized, classed, and, sometimes, racialized because of their association with (un)paid domestic labour and childrearing. Unfortunately, not many scholars examine what it is actually like to raise children in these spaces. It is possible that the lack of discussion about feeding children is symptomatic of that false dichotomy in the debates between stay-at-home mothers and mothers who engage in paid work (Dillaway and Paré) where mothers caring for children at home full time are thought to embrace female essentialism and 'working' mothers must completely reject all notions of maternalism in order to maintain a hold on paid work. It is as though by discussing the intimate and affective labour involved in child feeding, feminists might be led dangerously towards asserting an essentialist view of women's role in the home, even though it might also lead to a better understanding of this form of (un)paid work. Simultaneously, the literature on mothering often focuses on discursive practices of child feeding rather than the spatial or material context in which it takes place (O'Key and Hugh-Jones; Monterrosa et al.). Locating mothers as mere food "workers" in the home is currently out of step with efforts to recuperate mothers as subjects in this literature. Taking these absences and gaps into account I argue that the affective imperative to engage in motherhood by acting as a selfless provider of food can still be challenged without diminishing the material significance of mothering's relationship to food work and the places in which this work is practised. First, I discuss select historical turning points in Western home and kitchen design provided by feminist geographers, as it intersects with scholarship on mothering. As a contemporary illustration of the spatial practice of food provision in mothering, I use the example of new home design to demonstrate the invisibility of this everyday practice in the consumer citizen's imagination as he or she contemplates the purchase of a new home.

KITCHENS, CHILDREN, AND FOOD WORK

Following Floyd's approach to the critical interpretation of everyday objects I suggest that the kitchen and, indeed, the design of the entire home be read as a text, and that from this practice, a great deal can be learned about gender, class, race, and sexual relations of power simply by looking at the organization of space. The placement of kitchens at the rear of many nineteenth-century European home designs, later carried over to North American domestic architecture, corresponds to the desire to hide domestic labour and children from view. Scholars such as Cierrad, Parr, and Hayden as well as others have discussed how the location of kitchens at the back of the house maintained gendered relations of power within the hetero-nuclear family in a number of ways.

First, the rear placement of kitchens consolidated activities associated with mothering and food in a space meant for only one family to access. Although scholars of culinary practice note the important cultural and intergenerational learning that takes place between grandparents, mothers, and daughters in this space (Deutsch; Sutton), it was still meant to be a domain ultimately owned by a male head of household in a nuclear family. Important exceptions to this rule are the kitchens of some farm women who frequently placed this important room wherever they could best observe and direct the paid farm labourers they were also in charge of feeding alongside their own families (McMurray). Second, the location of kitchens at the rear of the home facilitated domestic labour in the wealthiest homes but was primarily organized to maintain racial and ethnic or class hierarchies between servants and masters, so feminists also understand the kitchen as a space that has historically functioned to racialize and class (un)paid food work. Third, the kitchen-at-rear design was frequently translated for the middle and working classes and exacerbated women's domestic labour at a time when most women either shopped daily for fresh food or had things delivered to the front door (Cierrad). Child minding and feeding often had to be simultaneous to other domestic or paid work rendering the kitchen a combined: nursery; dining; clothes-washing; piece-work space. In the twentieth century, the introduction of large appliances shifted women's control over the organization of this space to a streamlined food work space that did not necessarily facilitate child feeding (Land), as women relinquished some control over domestic organization in exchange for electricity and indoor plumbing. Finally, the rear placement of the kitchen rendered most of women's child and food work completely invisible to the public, even to other women. The privatization and individualization of this work was compounded by the emergent science of child feeding honed by home economists, nutritional science, and direct government involvement in public health, which emerged contemporaneously to the streamlining of the North American kitchen (Land).

Some arguably revolutionary changes to European kitchen design in the 1930s included smaller, narrow, specific function spaces that were clearly delineated as work-only spaces. Margarete Schutte-Lihotzky is credited with the modern "galley" style kitchen, which was taken up by German architects after World War I (Parr 661). The Frankfurt model, as it came to be known, was meant for dense urban housing developments, as was a later Swedish modelled kitchen made famous by Alva and Gunnar Myrdal (Parr). Although the minimalist and functional galley style kitchen has been modified many times for different cultural contexts, its original purpose was subversive. These kitchens, inspired by the social democratic politics of Northern Europe at the time, rejected any flourish of a bourgeois aesthetic. Reduced to its bare functions, these kitchens were premised on the construction of much larger community style kitchens and dining areas on the main floors of highly populated apartment buildings. Their invention did not promise the end of kitchen-related domestic labour but rather experimented with the socialization of food work and (sometimes) child care in urban areas. These designs came about partly in response to urban population growth, although in some communist countries, it also embedded low-level state surveillance in everyday foodways (Von Bremzen).

Whether these tiny but functional kitchens actually facilitated the feeding of children is worth pondering, particularly as later versions of these buildings eliminated the multi-family communal dining areas. One was not meant to "mother" in the functionalist galley kitchen. Although socialized dining arrangements could possibly allow for the sharing of some types of child-food work, it is unlikely that they could accommodate the full range of needs that small children have. Here, children were presumably removed from the nuclear family kitchen space altogether, with a mother now running back and forth between a makeshift dining area for children and the kitchen, in addition to supervising them in a communal dining area and providing her share of the cooking and cleaning up there as well (Von Bremzen). The streamlined North American kitchen referenced by Land bridges the functionality of the Frankfurt kitchen and the necessarily maternalist organization of earlier kitchens dedicated to domestic labour and childrearing, but none seem sufficient for the complexity of child-food work.

CAN NEW HOME DESIGNS SIMPLIFY CHILD FEEDING?

Contemporary marketing materials on new home building can be understood as cultural texts that require interpretation beyond their immediate use as building plans. New home designs are significant not because they are exemplary of how all people live but because in new home design, there is the opportunity to simplify many tasks associated with domestic labour, including the task of feeding children. A select few designers have market research proving that consumers are explicitly interested in more caregiver-child friendly designs (King et al.). But in the vast majority of contemporary blue prints, floor plans, and home-builder websites that I consulted between 2010 and 2014 from the North American market for the nuclear family home, I found little evidence of either consumer or builder interest in designs that simplify child feeding.

Elements that proliferate in new home design include some predictable as well as surprising themes. Like many products designed for use by families, new home design marketing materials suggest, even to the point of deception, a range of fantasies about the spaces in which one will pay handsomely to live. One example of this includes idyllic and romantic imagery of (usually white) children playing in a pastoral field for a home design that was clearly intended as triplex in-fill for dense suburban American neighbourhoods. As a material product subject to neoliberal market forces, new home design is an important barometer of what people desire and what they are willing to pay for and, thus, is a partial indicator of what is important to consumers in housing construction. The fantasy of living in a home styled after aristocratic English country living may be the window dressing that makes living near a major highway palatable. New home design is, thus, a material and affective barometer of what is important to consumers in housing construction.

In new home design two important things happen to the kitchen; first, it moves forward to a central area or to garage-linked entrance (in the case of suburban neighbourhoods) and second, it becomes open plan. The proximity of kitchen to garage is a partial gesture towards making child care and food work easier. But the elimination of walls between dining and living rooms that is characteristic of late-modern architecture revolutionizes the kitchen as a main, if not *the* main, feature of a home, and this bears further scrutiny. In form, the open-plan kitchen apparently flattens metaphorical relations of power between men and women as either "kitchen dwellers" or "masters at the head of the dining table" by eliminating material barriers between these spaces. Spatially, this move suggests that food work and other domestic labour can be accomplished while children can be attended to by a caregiver of any gender, but the overwhelming absence of children and babies in these materialsleaves the consumer with a lot of imagining to do.

DO "OPEN-PLAN" AND PUBLIC EATING EQUAL BETTER CHILD FEEDING?

In new home designs, the open-plan kitchen is a central staging area for culinary creations and fantasy, and it also has significant implications for the work of mothering through child feeding. The offering of food is facilitated in the open-plan kitchen design through the full visibility of a refrigerator and countertops, along with the possibility of social entertainment. But whereas once the dining room door could be closed to the kitchen area, the open-plan kitchen leaves the cook, still often the mother, subject to more surveillance by guests as well as to being the regulator of accessible food for children via "island" pantries and refrigerators. Additionally, strangers who happen by the front door or who are entertained briefly can make their appraisals of whether this is a well-maintained home. Does the invitation to more public child feeding, in fact, intensify the work that was otherwise done in more hidden, galley-style, kitchens?

The core domestic activity of producing daily meals at home is laborious and takes up a lot of women's time, covering up to 70 percent of the meals that children actually consume (Herman et al. 9). Some rightly point out that many men have become much more involved in the production of food in kitchen spaces and that this feminized space has become more democratic. Meah and Jackson suggest, however, that the presence of men in the kitchen is more of a crowding than a democracy, wherein men tend to prepare meals for entertainment, complicating women's ongoing daily obligation to prepare the less exciting everyday meals. Both the popular notion of a "mother" and the practice of daily mothering continue to be centrally organized around the provision of food to her dependents, whether that be the provision of a home-cooked or purchased meal or the provision of breastmilk directly from her body.

Although the home, and especially the kitchen, are essentialized as the right place for child feeding (Dillaway and Paré 440), the notion of the homebound mother as a provider for children is inadequate for the reality of feeding infants and children. Not only is the notion of the kitchen as a feminine or motherly space potentially sexist, but it is also of step with the broad imperative to provision for one's family (Neysmith; Maher, Fraser, and Lindsay). In the debates on mothers' movements between home-unpaid child care and public-paid work in capitalist societies, the notion a stay-at-home mother who earns no income but provides valuable unpaid social reproductive labour is difficult to locate, even in new home designs. Rather, the new ideal mother, if she exists, not only mothers (for free) but also engages in productive labour. Afflerback et al. and Bobel, among many others, discuss the construction of mothers as essential(ized) providers of food. And, I want to add, an essentialized subject is, in part, produced through her spatial location. "If mothers work [eg: feed children] outside the home, this attention (however partial) to another spatial location defines them at once as lesser mothers" (Dillaway and Paré 446). In other words, children might have to be fed anywhere, but the mothers feeding them risk being considered "out of place."

Mothers have been continuously charged with the task of managing public access to kitchens and child-feeding spaces. The open-plan kitchen presents yet another challenge, as it readily displays the interdependent relationship between food work and industry, a relationship that was partially hidden in earlier kitchen styles. Each technological advance has had some impact on what mothers can feed their children, and how much time it takes. Historical accounts of the relationship between motherhood and kitchen work acknowledge numerous outside influences. The impact of technological advances in food conservation such as electric refrigeration (Watkins), the electric or gas stove (Silva) and convenience foods (Inness) and later, the presence of take-out food, baby-feeding gadgets, computers built into fridge doors, and the ever-present electronic toys of all descriptions aimed at children underscore the permeability of kitchen spaces and the extent to which women are responsible for constructing appropriate food experiences for their children.

Moving the production and serving of food to young children to ever more public spaces (even within the home) underscores a reluctant disassociation of domestic space with mothering and exposes this important practice to public scrutiny. *Being seen* not only to provision food but also to mother appropriately is important. Good mothering may require the provision of food to one's children, but it is also thought to require the teaching of manners, avoidance of mess or disturbing others while eating. Thus, preparing food for children is often overly scrutinized or conversely, in the case of new home design, made invisible and devalued as a component of social reproductive labour.

Feeding children and babies is not only hard work but a key activity through which personality, taste, and identity are formed (Dillaway and Paré), making it a flashpoint that other family members, and even random strangers feel entitled to comment on. Though not unpleasurable, these cultural and social goals imbue the preparation of meals with a range of meanings that are reflected in the spatial practices women develop around feeding children, which possibly explains why mothers seek privacy about what, how, how much, and where they feed their children when outside their homes. The obesity "epidemic" is a case in point where mothers are either targeted by the media and researchers for compromising the health of their children or celebrated for embracing the newest most labour-intensive child feeding plan (O'Key and Hugh-Jones). But when children are fed in the back seat of the car, at a bus stop, or in the mall, out of snack cups, off of cafeteria trays, sippy cups, plastic baggies or containers, with ready-packaged vitamin-packed snack bars, fast food, snack cups, thirty second rule (dust it off)—their public foodwork potentially ignites a host of cultural values and broken imperatives that fuel our understanding of where and how to feed children because it is out of place. In other words, the home simply cannot contain the busy lives of mothers and children and so adapting to feeding children in open-plan kitchens, in public, or "on the run" is an important spatial practice that that exists in conversation with economy.

Back in the pages of glossy mock-ups of new home design, the domestic labour to maintain the stainless steel appliances and to clean acres of floor space is invisible, as are children and babies. Anyone engaged in the daily care of small children would ask themselves: who really lives here? Kitchen spaces in North American home design are thus spatial expressions of normatively racialized and classed mothering and child-feeding practices, which suggests that consumers should limit how they engage in these practices. New home designs overtly exclude the diverse range of practices of mothering and child feeding organized around the food provisioning activities undertaken by a range of people. New home designs could be more fully informed by a range of child feeding practices that includes mothers with low incomes who cannot afford extensive spaces in which to parent (Herman et al.); rural-dwelling families who out of necessity may still provide for themselves from the land (Brumbach and Jarvenpa) or rely on groceries whose cost are grossly inflated (Myers, Powell, and Duhaime); recently immigrated families in which mothers are tasked with making new foods palatable to children or seeking out old familiar ones (Dyck and Dossa); mothers who head extended families (Christie), and queer families who may align child feeding around a parent's personal talents and interests rather than gender roles (Gabb). Floyd argues that the way in which mothers are expected to contend with tasks in the kitchen can be improvisatory, rebellious, and even sensual (65-67), challenging the design of this place as a mundane stage for food work. The very act of re-serving a meal or not serving a meal could be seen as a new transgressive power held by female cooks. However, feminist geographers have explored normatively raced and classed diverse organizations of food spaces within the family home in transnational context (Johnson, "Browsing the Modern Kitchen," "Hybrid and Global Kitchens") to demonstrate that the range of women's creativity in the kitchen is nothing new, as mothers have shown themselves to be endlessly adaptable out of necessity when it comes to the spatial organization of their homes even if home designers are not listening.

CONCLUSION

This chapter examines the relationship between practices of mothering and food production through a spatial analysis of Western nuclear family homes that considers relations of power, such as heteronormativity, class, and race. It is well worth considering the extent to which the food work associated with mothering is a spatial practice and, more broadly, how mothers negotiate important spaces, such as the kitchen, as a part of their food work with children and babies. The homogenization of different phases of kitchen design in different times and places has to a certain extent imposed normative child-feeding spatial practices when, in fact, there are diverse possibilities. Back in my kitchen, what this means is that since the streamlining of the "modern" kitchen, the space that I cook in and feed my children has steadily begun to resemble that of many other caregivers across North America. Yet the possibility remains for any parent to reorganize, appropriate, shift, and disturb spaces in order to meet the needs of children as well as to make this activity meaningful and pleasurable.

WORKS CITED

Afflerback, Sara, Shannon K. Carter, Amanda Koontz Anthony,

and Liz Grauerholz. "Infant-Feeding Consumerism in the Age of Intensive Mothering and Risk Society." *Journal of Consumer Culture* 13.3 (2013): 387-405. Print.

Bobel, Chris. *The Paradox Of Natural Mothering*. Philadelphia: emple University Press, 2002. Print.

Brumbach, Hetty Jo, and Robert Jarvenpa. "Woman the Hunter: Ethnoarcheological Lessons from Chipewyan Life-Cycle Dynamics." Eds. Mary-Ellen Kelm and Lorna Townsend. *In the Days of Our Grandmothers: A Reader in Aboriginal Women's History in Canada*. Toronto: University of Toronto Press, 2006. 200-215. Print.

Christie, Maria Elisa. "Kitchenspace: Gendered Territory in Central Mexico" *Gender, Place and Culture* 13.6 (2006): 653-661. Print.

Cieraad, Irene. "'Out of My Kitchen!' Architecture, Gender and Domestic Efficiency." *The Journal of Architecture* 7.3 (2002): 263-279. Print.

Deutsch, Tracey. "Memories of Mothers in the Kitchen." *Radical History Review* 110 (2011): 167-177. Print.

Dillaway, Heather, and Elizabeth Paré. "Locating Mothers: How Cultural Debates about Stay-at-Home Versus Working Mothers Define Women and Home." *Journal of Family Issues* 29.4 (2008): 437-464. Print.

Dyck, Isabel and Parin Dossa. "Place, health and home: Gender and Migration in the Constitution of Healthy Space." *Health & Place* 13.3 (2007): 691–701. Print.

England, Kim. "Mothers, Wives, Workers: The Everyday Lives of Working Mothers." *Who Will Mind the Baby: Geographies of Child Care and Working Mothers*. Ed. K. England. New York: Routledge, 2005. 109-122. Print.

Floyd, Janet. "Coming Out of the Kitchen: Texts, Contexts and Debates." *Cultural Geographies* 11.1 (2004): 61-73. Print.

Gabb, Jacqui. "Imag(in)ing the Queer Lesbian Family." *Mother Outlaws: Theories and Practices of Empowered Mothering*. Ed. Andrea O'Reilley. Toronto: Women's Press, 2004. 123-130. Print.

Hayden, Dolores. *The Grand Domestic Revolution: A History of Feminist Designs for American Homes, Neighborhoods, and Cities*. 2nd Edition. Cambridge, Mass.: MIT Press. 1983. Print.

Inness, Sherrie A. *Secret Ingredients: Race, Gender, and Class at the Dinner Table*. London: Palgrave Macmillan, 2005. Print.

Johnson, Louise C. "Browsing the Modern Kitchen—A Fest of Gender, Place and Culture (Part 1)." *Gender, Place & Culture: A Journal of Feminist Geography* 13.2 (2006): 123-132. Print.

Johnson, Louise C. "Hybrid and Global Kitchens—First and Third World Intersections (Part 2)." *Gender, Place & Culture: A Journal of Feminist* Geography 13.6 (2006): 647-652. Print.

Land, Leslie. "Counterintuitive: How the Marketing of Modernism Hijacked the Kitchen Stove." *From Betty Crocker to Feminist Food Studies: Critical Perpsectives on Women and Food*. Eds. Arlene Voski Avakian and Barbara Haber. Boston: University of Massachusetts Press, 2005. 41-61. Print.

Maher, Jane Maree, Suzanne Fraser, and Jo Lindsay. "Between Provisioning and Consuming?: Children, Mothers and 'Childhood Obesity'." *Health Sociology Review* 19.3 (2010): 304-316. Print.

McMurry, Sally Ann. *Families and Farmhouses in Nineteenth-Century America: Vernacular Design and Social Change*. Oxford: Oxford University Press, 1988. Print.

Meah, Angela, and Peter Jackson. "Crowded Kitchens: The Democratisation of Domesticity?" *Gender, Place & Culture* 20.5 (2013): 578-596. Print.

Monterrosa, Eva C., et al. "Constructing Maternal Knowledge Frameworks. How Mothers Conceptualize Complementary Feeding." *Appetite* 59.2 (2012): 377-384. Print.

Myers, Heather, Stephanie Powell, and Gerard Duhaime. "Setting the Table for Food Security: Policy Impacts in Nunavut." *Canadian Journal of Native Studies* 24.2 (2004): 425-445. Print.

O'Key, Victoria, and Siobhan Hugh-Jones. "'I Don't Need Anybody to Tell Me What I Should Be Doing.' A Discursive Analysis of Maternal Accounts of (Mis)Trust of Healthy Eating Information." *Appetite* 54.3 (2010): 524-532. Print.

Parr, Joy. "Editor's Introduction: Modern Kitchen, Good Home, Strong Nation." *Technology and Culture* 43.4 (2002): 657-667. Print.

Neysmith, Sheila, et al. "Provisioning: Thinking about All of Women's Work." *Canadian Woman Studies/les cahiers de la femme* 23.3 (2004): 192-198. Print.

Silva, Elizabeth B. "The Cook, the Cooker, and the Gendering of the Kitchen." *Sociological Review* 48.4 (2000): 612-629. Print.

Sutton, David. "Cooking Skills, the Senses, and Memory: The Fate of Practical Knowledge." *Food and Culture: A Reader.* Eds. Carole Counihan and Penny Van Esterik. London: Routledge, 2013. 299-319. Print.

Von Bremzen, Anya. *Mastering the Art of Soviet Cooking: A Memoir of Food and Longing*. New York: Broadway Books, 2013. Print.

Watkins, Helen. "Beauty Queen, Bulletin Board and Browser: Rescripting the Refrigerator" *Gender, Place & Culture: A Journal of Feminist Geography* 13. 2 (2006): 143-152. Print.

20. Yamatji Mothers Negotiating Economic and Social Capital

MELANIE DEMBINSKY

MOTHERHOOD HOLDS DIFFERENT MEANINGS and significance for individual women. Among Yamatji, an Australian Aboriginal group consisting of various smaller communities in Western Australia, motherhood, as for many but not all women, is part of women's identities and a means to gain social capital. As mothers, women are often the primary carers of children and responsible for the provision of food, among other things. Yamatji kinship follows similar rules to those outlined by Morgan (Fortes and Morgan), in what he categorized as the "Iroquois kinship system." According to this model, kinship terms are conflated for certain individuals. For example, among Yamatji the term "mother" is used for a biological or adoptive mother as well as for all the mother's sisters, and it is not uncommon for female siblings to breastfeed each other's children. It is equally common for children to spend a considerable amount of time with other family members when their biological mother is unable to take care of them.

Regardless of the presence or absence of fathers in the household compositions, women are generally in charge of the household. Female-headed households are common among Yamatji and a variety of family forms exist (Dembinsky). Single parenthood is as prominent as skipped generation households or cohabitation. Skipped generation households refer to households were grandparents are raising their grandchildren in the absence of the parents. There exists a preference for common-law over de jure marriages. As has been shown by several authors (Blackwood; Safa; Hogarth), common-law marriages are as equally stable and enduring, or unstable, as de jure marriages. Where there are single parents, the children most frequently stay with their mother who will commonly live with her own mother or other female relatives, such as a sister, cousin, or grandmother. It is these women's responsibility to provide healthy food options to their children to ensure their well-being and development and instil healthy eating habits. Many Yamatji survive on minimal budgets,[1] where the question no longer is what should we eat to remain healthy, but what can we afford to eat. Faced with the stark reality of economic and social inequality, Yamatji mothers stand at the intersection of not only conflicting forces but also an internal one. In order to address this conundrum, Yamatji mothers employ several strategies that are examined throughout this chapter in light of the negotiations made by Yamatji women between social and economic capital and the cultural practice of demand sharing.

DEMAND SHARING AND ECONOMIC CAPITAL

Demand sharing is a form of reciprocity, or rather generosity, which is practised among Australian Aboriginal peoples (Peterson). According to the imperative of demand sharing, an individual can insist on generosity through the use of verbal and/or non-verbal direct requests. This culturally specific "forced" generosity contributes to the constitution of social relationships; however, it should be noted that because of the reaffirmation of social bonds through the practice of demand sharing, not every individual can make demands on another. The highest demands are usually made of kin, although for many Yamatji this spans an extensive web of social relations over, sometimes, large geographical distances.

Yamatji food choices are made based on a multitude of factors. Economic resources are one of these additional factors that Yamatji need to negotiate. Saethre states that "there is no meal planning or budgeting from week to week" among his research participants (190). I have not witnessed any meal planning among Yamatji during any of my research trips, conducted over twelve months between 2010 and 2014 but did notice some form of budgeting. For example, basic food items, such as bread and milk, would frequently be purchased to allow for two to three days use. Payments were received on Thursdays, on a fortnightly basis for the majority of women participating in my doctoral and subsequent research visits; on these days, money was in "abundance." When payments have been received, groceries are purchased, mobile phones topped up, gasoline filled into cars, and bills paid. Concessions on spending would be made for petrol, phones, and so on to accommodate for the budget available within a two week period. When money was becoming tight, other close relatives would be approached to either lend a few dollars to tide individuals over until the next payday or to demand sharing would be invoked.

Furthermore, the condition of homes and the availability of kitchen appliances, such as refrigerators and freezers, also affect food purchases and consumption. In many homes, the appliances were working most of the time with considerable consistency; however, when things do break down, it often is difficult to replace appliances on a minimal budget, so they tend to be used with limited function. This affects the preservation of food stuffs, especially during the hot summer months, from about December to the end of May. Food storage is, therefore, negotiated between the availability of supplies and desire to store food. Take-away food provides an easy solution in these circumstances. It allows working mothers to feed their children during their lunch hour in school holidays, as the children, depending on age, can meet their mother at a take-away restaurant without anyone having to worry about purchasing and cooking food.

Take-away food, specifically type and quantity of food consumed, is often high in fat, sugar, and salts, making it a food stuff that does not generally qualify as healthy eating (Freeman; Currie; Pereira et al.; Kwate). It is the mother's responsibility to provide healthy food options to her children to ensure their well-being and development and to instil healthy eating habits.

Considering that most Yamatji families live on a minimal budget, mothers in particular need to negotiate balancing the limited economic resources with their children's and their own needs. These negotiations frequently involve buying cheaper products and food items than those desired, which would potentially hold higher nutritional value. White breads, instant noodle packages, cordial, and other cheap, but filling, food items are the norm. In addition, meat is purchased for stews, roasts, or curries when on sale and shared among numerous family members. When finances are particularly tight, demand sharing is invoked among family members. In some instances, this pertains to older family members being asked for cash advances or directly for particular food items, such as white bread, butter, or tea. Frequently, mothers also purchase and share alcohol and cigarettes, or "play cards" (gambling). Purchasing groceries and paying bills are seen as legitimate uses for welfare payments, but take-away food, alcohol, cigarettes and gambling are not. Neither is their living off governmental benefits payments.

Whereas the women in Hennessy's study adhered to the mantra "any job is a good job" (567), Yamatji women did not view any job as a good job. On the contrary, Yamatji women would frequently question their lower pay and the frequency with which they were offered part-time jobs over full-time employment. As Kawash states, "choices surrounding work and family are morally freighted and tied to deep cultural structures that shape self-understanding and definitions of meaningful life" (575). Although the "work commitment discourse promises that [employment] will bring poor mothers dignity and respect" (Hennessy 567), the family centred discourse promises exactly the same to poor women. Finding employment is dependent on many different factors, some of which are not easily influenced by the individual's actions, such as the availability of jobs. Motherhood is less dependent on uncontrollable variables and, perhaps, provides more stability in realizing this goal.

Kawash and Hennessy's studies "explicitly posit that people's worldviews and actions regarding work and family are not only or even primarily economic, strategic, or reactive but rather are imbued with moral significance and emotional salience" (Blair-Loy qtd. in Henessey 558). It is also predominantly middle-class and upper-class people who shape policies, whereas mothers on welfare or with low income have to live on a daily basis in this structure bound by policies made by upper- and middle-class representatives that do not necessarily reflect their own moral universe. Like many other women, Yamatji "mothers cannot and will not submit to the (white, middle-class, heterosexual) norms of good mothering" (Kawash 979). When Yamatji mothers decide to reduce the amount or quality of foodstuffs purchased to engage in gambling or to consume items, such as alcohol and/or cigarettes, their moral character is questioned, and they are construed as "bad" mothers by many non-Aboriginal women whom I have spoken to from the same communities. Despite living on a minimal budget and spending this limited amount of economic capital on items deemed as inappropriate by non-benefit recipients in Yamatji country, there are particularly desirable food items that Yamatji mothers try to purchase for themselves and/or their children.

These particularly desired foods include fresh fruit and vegetables, cakes, and prime meat cuts. Purchasing these items and redistributing them among Yamatji provided me with an opportunity to establish rapport and become, slowly, part of their social universe. Nectarines, watermelon, and other coveted fruits, such as mangos and peaches, were high on the list of food items that were desired but seldom bought, as they were more expensive than other fruits. Freshly brewed coffee or high-quality teas were also coveted but not often purchased due to economic constraints. Although certain food items were sought among Yamatji, others were perceived to be less desirable. Among these foodstuffs were pickles and gherkins of any kind, and lettuce, which was seen as appropriate as a supplement for sandwiches but not as a meal on its own. Pasta and rice are staples in the diets of Yamatji. Rarely have I seen Yamatji consume raw vegetables as recommended in many health education programs. Instead, certain vegetables, such as carrots and cabbage, are regularly cooked to accompany a meal. The variety of vegetables served is often limited to a small amount, and mothers often buy the same vegetables over and over. This was not necessarily due to costvbut because these were familiar, and their preparation was not complex as might have been the case with other kinds of vegetables. They were also often chosen for their suitability in stews, which is a dish I frequently observed being prepared. Similarly, older Walpiri, an Australian Aboriginal group, explained that they chose certain foods because they were what they have been eating for decades (Saethre).

Eating habits are passed on from one generation to the next. Being fed on a steady diet of white bread, sweets, and cooked vegetables could lead to future generations of Yamatji having a propensity for exactly those foods that they grew up with. During one of my return visits to the area, I had a discussion with several Yamatji teenaged girls about eating raw vegetables and salads, which they said were not particularly desirable. Fresh fruits on the other hand, especially nectarines, peaches and mangoes were taken and eaten the second that I had purchased them, and were often eaten away from family members, relatives, or friends so that they would not need to be shared. When I brought along some fresh, raw vegetables, the enthusiasm was subdued, and most often the vegetables would not be eaten raw but taken home to be cooked. As Saethre maintains, food choices "are not the result of a lack of nutritional awareness, but rather due to income, cost, availability and a desire to avoid excessive reciprocity" (179).

Food choices and purchasing are affected by the cultural practice of demand sharing, as it would be considered particularly rude to deny a demand for food. "The desire to escape giving away substantial portions of purchased food affects spending choices" (Saethre 181). The cultural practice of demand sharing, thus, seems to be somewhat of a paradox, at least to an outside observer. On the one hand, its invocation helps alleviate budgetary constraints in food purchasing power for an individual, while, at the same time, limiting that of another. In order to avoid demand sharing, two dominant strategies are apparent: first, purchasing limited amounts of goods, especially food stuffs, and food items that are not greatly desired; and second, buying take-away food, as it can be consumed immediately, limiting the possibility of demand sharing. Through the cultural practice of demand sharing, social and economic capital are interconnected—economic capital is dispersed through the social capital accumulated.

SOCIAL CAPITAL AND MOTHERHOOD

Children are an intrinsic part of social capital, as they promise future social bonds to be drawn on. Bourdieu defines social capital as the aggregate of the actual or potential resources which are linked to possessions of a durable network of more or less institutionalized relationships of mutual acquaintance and recognition—or in other words, to membership in a group—which provides each of its members with the backing of the collectivity-owned capital (51).

A large family network increases the possibility to draw on social capital established through biological and marriage connections. Having multiple children enhances the possibility to draw on a large social network in times of need, which is often relevant for people with low economic resources. "Middle-class stereotypes dismiss poor, unmarried mothers either as incompetent in their unwillingness or inability to use birth control, or else as malicious schemers using children as a way to gain access to more welfare benefits" (Kawash 979). Although Kawash's findings are drawn from her research in the U.S., the same sentiments are voiced by middle-class women I have encountered against Yamatji women. These assumptions ignore other important aspects, such as the accumulation of social capital through motherhood. "For poor women with few prospects, motherhood is perceived not as an unwanted burden, but as a way to experience joy, value, and achievement" (Kawash 979). One Yamatji woman I know quite well told me about her struggles of finding a job after having completed her apprenticeship at a local organization. She was desperately trying to find something to do that would allow her to be busy and contribute to the family income. After looking for employment for approximately ten months, she told me that she was pregnant again. When I asked her if she wanted to have another child, she stated that she likes to be a mother, that she is good at it, and that she is already looking forward to the newest family addition. According to McLanahan and Percheski (262), women of lower socio-economic standing "believe in their ability to perform the role of mother and receive psychological benefits from taking care of children." Among Yamatji no such distinction appears to be present. Even highly educated Yamatji women drew considerable importance from motherhood, and I have yet to meet an educated Yamatji woman who has not also been a mother. It can be argued, then, that motherhood does not lose importance among Yamatji regardless of educational status.

Edin and Kefalas contend that poor women, living in North America, place a higher importance on motherhood than marriage, the latter often being less attainable in the first place. The "cultural imperative of self-reliance and self-sufficiency was a powerful factor in shaping rural white single mothers' expectations of themselves and others" (Henessey 560). This means that as mothers, women need to be able to financially provide for their children and to provide them with the basic comforts of life. Among Yamatji, self-reliance and self-sufficiency take on different connotations. Self-reliance and self-sufficiency are inclusive of accepting assistance from other family members, especially female ones in a Yamatji context. Accepting assistance from relatives is not seen as a personal failure or as negatively affecting perceptions of self-sufficiency, and is, sometimes, even expected. As social bonds are constantly reaffirmed through sharing of resources, to not include other female relatives Yamatji would send a powerful statement that the social bonds are strained between them.

Contrary to the "bad" mother, the "good" mother places the needs and desires of her children before her own. "Such a gift [food] relates more evidence of care, a demonstration of affection, than does an actual commodity bought, wrapped and presented to an individual by the giver" (Lupton 47). Hence, when mothers do not provide adequate food to their children, this is interpreted as a lack of affection and care, regardless of the circumstances. Often, single mothers are held accountable for their own blight and are seen to be failing in their responsibilities as mothers. Using part of the already limited economic resources to buy cigarettes and alcohol jeopardizes not only the mother's morality in the eyes of the non-Aboriginal public but also the children's and mother's health.

In their role as primary caregivers, mothers are also commonly portrayed as moral guardians of the family (King 23). As such they are held accountable for the well-being and development of their children, of which food is an important component. Aside from biological connections, among the Yamatji, food assumes a central role in maintaining and reaffirming social relationships through commensality—the act of eating together and, most often, the same types of food. As Lupton adequately notes, "sharing ... food is a vital part of kinship and friendship networks in all societies" (37). As such, food is an intrinsic part of Yamatji sociality.

Food can have multiple meanings, from the nutritional to the symbolic. One particular dish Yamatji associate with being

Aboriginal is kangaroo stew. This dish is also often used by non-Aboriginal organizations during public events to show a level of cultural awareness and tolerance. However, in discussions with Yamatji, it transpired that serving kangaroo stew does not show any kind of cultural awareness or sensitivity but rather resembles mere tokenism to them when served outside of their homes. Although kangaroo stew does hold significance in the Yamatji diet, it is not necessarily regarded as an "identity" dish. As Saethre notes, among his participants, certain foods continue to be eaten "almost exclusively, despite a range of alternatives sold" (180) because these are the foodstuffs that they are used to and familiar with. These foods are continuously consumed at home, and the next generation is exposed to them frequently, making foods like white bread and meat items that they will be used to and familiar with. This can perpetuate a cycle of eating habits, whereby the same food items are consumed, regardless of nutritional value, because they are associated with childhood, bringing forth a myriad of emotions when consumed, aside from familiarity. Other foods that are steeped in cultural and symbolic meaning for Yamatji are damper and bush tucker, both of which are associated with feelings of comfort.

Damper is a simple mixture of water, salt and flour, making a bread-like dough, which is then baked. It appears to have gained significant importance when rationing for Australian Aborigines was in place. Bush tucker can refer to any food that can be found in the environment (kangaroo stew sometimes is included in this). Bush tucker, then, can be wild growing fruits, nuts and other plant-based foodstuffs growing in Australia's outback, but can also include protein sources, such as insects, small lizards and birds. In the case of bush tucker, some of the women I spoke to indicated that it also symbolizes a relationship to *country*, thereby gaining an additional meaning of closeness and healing. The association with healing properties of bush tucker is brought about by the use of some bush tucker items as ingredients in the preparation of bush medicine. As demonstrated, "eating practices reproduce as well as construct identity; in addition, both identity and alimentary symbolism, not just taste or availability or cost, significantly affect food choice" (Jones 130).

CONCLUSIONS

Belonging to a marginalized group, Yamatji mothers often find themselves negotiating conflicting demands. As mothers they are frequently seen as moral guardians, and, as such, they are held accountable for the welfare of their children. Food plays a vital role in this, as the links between diet and several chronic diseases have been firmly established. As part of their constrained economic agency, Yamatji mothers negotiate the demands between healthy diet, food preferences, and economic resources through demand and resource sharing, while they maintain their social capital. Social capital is one of the few available avenues for Yamatji women to gain status within their communities and is tightly linked to motherhood, which, in turn, has a strong effect on women's identities. It is, therefore, unlikely that Yamatji women will forgo motherhood to alleviate budgetary constraints. In addition to providing social capital, motherhood allows women to be considered full adults within their communities, which something that they can achieve fairly easily. It is a daily struggle. And if one looks at the precarious state of health for many Australian Aboriginal peoples, it is a struggle that Yamatji mothers appear to be losing.

NOTE

[1]Minimal budget is dependent on family composition and age. A single mother will receive unemployment and childcare benefits. According to the Australian Bureau of Statistics, the gross household income for Aborigines was approximately AU$460 per week, approximately 62 percent of the non-aboriginal rate.

WORKS CITED

Australia. Australian Bureau of Statistics. "Income: Household Income." Government of Australia, 2010. Web 25 April 2015.

Blackwood, Evelyn. "Wedding Bell Blues: Marriage, Missing Men, and Matrifocal Follies." *American Ethnologist: The Journal of the American Ethnological Society* 32.1 (2005): 3-19. Print.

Bourdieu, Pierre. "The Forms of Capital." *Handbook of Theory and Research for the Sociology of Education*. Ed. J. Richardson. New York, Greenwood, 1986. 241-258. Print.

Currie, Janet M. *The Effect of Fast Food Restaurants on Obesity*. Cambridge, Mass: National Bureau of Economic Research, 2009. Print.

Dembinsky, Melanie. "Caring Women: Matrifocality and Its Impact on Yamatji Breast Cancer Experiences and Health Seeking Behaviours." *Durham Journal of Anthropology Special Issue* 19.1 (2014): 45-61 Print.

Edin, Katheryn, and Maria Kefalas. *Promises I Can Keep: Why Poor Women Put Motherhood before Marriage*. Berkeley: University of California Press. 2005. Print.

Fortes, Meyer, and Lionel H. Morgan. *Kinship and the Social Order: The Legacy of Lewis Henry Morgan*. London: Routledge & Paul. 1969. Print.

Freeman, Andrea. "Fast Food: Oppression Through Poor Nutrition." *California Law Review* 95.6 (2007): 2221-2260. Print.

Hennessy, Judith. "Morality and Work-Family Conflict in the Lives of Poor and Low-Income Women." *The Sociological Quarterly* 50.4 (2009): 557-580. Print.

Hogarth, Hyun-Key Kim. *Matrifocality in Korean Society: Hindrance or Help towards Gender Qquality?* The Royal Anthropological Institute. *The University of Sydney*, N.p, 2009. Web. 14 Mar 2012.

Jones, Michael O. "Food Choice, Symbolism, and Identity: Bread and Butter Issues for Folkloristics and Nutrition Studies (American Folklore Society Presidential Address, October 2005)." *Journal of American Folklore* 120 (476) (2007): 129-177. Print.

Kawash, Samira "New Directions in Motherhood Studies." *Signs* 36.4 (2011): 969-1003. Print.

King, Samanth. *Pink Ribbons, Inc.: Breast Cancer and the Politics of Philanthropy*. Minneapolis. University of Minnesota Press, 2006. Print.

Kwate, Naa Oyo A. "Fried Chicken and Fresh Apples: Racial Segregation as a Fundamental Cause of Fast Food Density in Black Neighborhoods." *Health & Place* 14.1 (2008): 32-44. Print.

Lupton, Debra. *Food, the Body, and the Self*. London: Sage Publications. 1996. Print.

McLanahn, Sarah, and Christine Percheski. "Family Structure and the Reproduction of Inequalities." *Annual Review of Sociology* 34 (2008): 257-276. Print.

Pereira, Mark A., Alex I. Kartashov, Cara B. Ebbeling, Linda Van Horn, Martha L. Slattery, David R. Jacobs, and David S. Ludwig. "Fast-Food Habits, Weight Gain, and Insulin Resistance (the CARDIA study): 15-year Prospective Analysis." *Lancet* 365 (9453) (2005): 1-7. Print.

Peterson, Nicolas, "Demand Sharing: Reciprocity and the Pressure for Generosity among Foragers." *American Anthropologist* 95 (1993): 860-874. Print.

Saethre, Eirik, J. "Demand Sharing, Nutrition and Warlpiri Health: The Social and Economic Strategies of Food Choice." *Ethnography and the Production of Anthropological Knowledge. Essays in Honour of Nicolas Peterson.* Eds. Y. Musharbash and M. Barber. Canberra: Australian National University Press, 2011. 175-186. Print.

Safa, Helen. "The Matrifocal Family and Patriarchal Ideology in Cuba and the Caribbean." *Journal of Latin American Anthropology* 10.2 (2005): 314-338. Print.

21.
(Re)Defining Femivorism

Connections between Food, Motherhood, and Spirituality

AUDREY LUNDAHL

FEMIVORES—A BRAND OF CONTEMPORARY WOMEN, mostly mothers—are creating a movement that values food and family above all else. These women believe in the importance of food to care for their families, as they focus on food as life itself: nurturing bodies, minds, and the environment. This movement has great potential for healing the environment, but femivorist thinking is a philosophy of opting out of traditional means of getting contaminant-free food—as in through corporations and government regulations. In turn, middle-class privileged families are those who can afford to opt out.

Peggy Orenstein, a columnist, wrote a *New York Times* column in 2010 exploring this new and more demanding homemaking trend among women. Women whom Orenstein identifies left their demanding jobs and their Friedan-esque feminist promises of self-sufficiency and fulfillment. Instead, femivores have (re)turned to extreme homemaking, sometimes called "homesteading" by more rural participants, as an answer to their fulfillment. These women raise backyard chickens, grow their own vegetables, keep their own bees, and make innumerable foods from scratch in order to provide pure, sustainable food for their families. As such, many scholars and feminists criticize femivorism as a return to gender essentialism as well as to a class-privileged lifestyle choice that leaves those who do not have access to pure, sustainable food in the dust of their (middle-class suburban) backyard gardens. Proponents of this lifestyle, however, venerate their choices as answers to global food, health, family, and environmental crises. The femivore movement has social justice potential and should look for ways to be more inclusive through spiritualized as opposed to class- and gender-based tactics. Femivorism could be more inclusive if it embraced womanist interconnectedness. Perhaps by incorporating spiritually interconnected perspectives inspired by womanist[1] theorizing, the positive ideals behind femivorism can have an impact on a global scale, not just for individual privileged families.

DEFINING FEMIVORISM

Peggy Orenstein coined the term "femivore" in her column, so her description has much authority. The women Orenstein describes, however, have shaped femivorism in varying ways. Since Orenstein's article, several articles in the U.S. have explored this new trend for educated women to embrace homemaking and have called these lifestyle choices femivorism, new domesticity, and radical homemaking. The name "femivorism" is not as important as its dominant characteristic: it mainly consists of women who use do-it-yourself (DIY) ethics to provide healthy food for their families in an environmentally sustainable way.

One goal of femivorism is to revalue motherhood in relation to traditional domestic tasks. Femivorism is best suited for stay-at-home moms because it requires a large time commitment; this revaluing of motherhood places women's socialized gender roles as an important means to achieve environmental health, which legitimizes roles usually assigned to women. Emily Matchar, author of *Homeward Bound: Why Women are Embracing the New Domesticity*, points out that Orenstein's definition of femivorism "helps give social legitimacy to stay-at-home motherhood" (103). Orenstein writes in her column:

> Femivorism is grounded in the very principles of self-sufficiency, autonomy and personal fulfillment that drove women into the work force in the first place. Given how conscious (not to say obsessive) everyone has become about the source of their food—who these days can't wax poetic about compost?—it also confers instant legitimacy. Rather than embodying the limits of one movement, femivores

> expand those of another: feeding their families clean, flavorful food; reducing their carbon footprints; producing sustainably instead of consuming rampantly. What could be more vital, more gratifying, more morally defensible?

Women typically make decisions about what types of food to eat and about how to obtain and cook that food in their households. Since these characteristics are important to femivores, possessing these skills, through socialized female gender roles, must also be significant in order to be a femivore. This seeming contradiction between affirming traditional gender roles yet considering female gender roles as world changing has sparked debates over whether femivores are feminist (or feminist enough or even anti-feminist).

FEMINISM AND FEMIVORISM

Orenstein claims that femivores are a new brand of feminist, although many feminist bloggers disagree: they claim femivorism is just another idealistic identity women will struggle to live up to. But Orenstein's stance on femivorism and feminism is confusing. According to Orenstein, femivores embrace this ideology because it gives them "an unexpected out from the feminist predicament, a way for women to embrace homemaking without becoming Betty Draper." In other words, although these women embrace homemaking in a way that initially appears like an anti-feminist throwback to the 1950s, femivores use their intelligence and creativity to find a sense of purpose in their work in their homes. They are not just passive consumers but active participants in an activist movement. Orenstein's last line is ominous: "if a woman is not careful, it seems, chicken wire can coop her up as surely as any gilded cage." Orenstein is not sure yet if femivorism offers empowerment by escaping excessive consumerism and valuing domesticity or if women now have another pressure to add to their growing list.

Femivorism has garnered more than just conversations and complaints about the troubling name—most agree that it implies femivores eat women; femivorism has, also, sparked much online criticism about its implications. A blogger for the website *Jezebel*, and self-proclaimed femivore, questions the idea that self-sufficiency equals happiness, which femivorism invokes. She writes, "The irony is that while there's no question I'm more resourceful and frugal and self-sufficient in my new life, I actually felt like less of a feminist than ever" (Holmes). She explains that her DIY lifestyle almost cannot function outside of traditional gender roles, so she feels even more dependent on her male partner. Brittany Shoot from *Bitch Magazine* shares a similar concern: "What does bother me is the implication that something we found oppressive seventy-five or even fifty years ago is now suddenly empowering. Context shifts, no doubt, but aren't we sort of screwing up our own progress by going back and forth on these things?" Empowerment and progress are important concerns, but I would suggest definitions of progress are limited by assuming that progress moves linearly. It would be helpful to allow for the possibility that domestic tasks can be empowering and even feminist. I agree with Shoot's later point that "To frame the choice between working a soulless 9-to-5 or building a backyard chicken coop and learning to can tomatoes as the only feminist options is reductive and insulting." But I would add that feminists should not discredit women who do devote their lives to backyard chickens and gardening and consider how their work might have social justice potential. In order to examine such potential, however, it's important to examine the ways that this movement has created an individualistic, privileged lifestyle.

CLASS EXCLUSIONS

Class plays a major role in Orenstein's femivorism, and femivorism has an upper- and middle-class bias. Shoot expresses her discontent with Orenstein's article: "Orenstein says some outright classist crap in roundup of the women who choose to build chicken coops." Shoot's concern addresses implications of added pressure on working women who must become conscious about the source of their food through a strictly middle-class lens. Shoot takes particular offense at Orenstein's mention of everyone being concerned about compost when composting—which requires space, time, and resources—is a mostly middle-class concern. Orenstein's use of the word "legitimacy"—a value word, according to Shoot—also implies a standard. Orenstein's classist lens for viewing femivorism suggests that middle-class people who have the time, money, and resources to embrace a femivorist lifestyle are granted instant legitimacy for their efforts; those who may not have the privilege to "wax poetic" about compost yet are conscious about food and the environment are then not granted legitimacy by Orenstein's explanation, at least not as easily. Class exclusions, I would argue, ultimately stem from the individualist attitude adopted by most femivores. Femivorism sets up boundaries and restrictions by emphasizing a lifestyle only accessible to middle-class families, and Orenstein's view of femivorism places responsibility on individual women and their families as the catalysts for environmental change.

MEET THE FEMIVORES

In presenting her perspective, Orenstein quotes Shannon Hayes, perhaps the quintessential femivore. Hayes has become well known for her blog *Radical Homemakers* and her book *Radical Homemakers*. Hayes's book relies on an argument that seems to be her core belief: "Eating local, organic, sustainably raised, nutrient-dense food [is] possible for every American, not just for wealthy gourmets and self-reliant farmers. But to do it, we need to bring back the homemaker" (12-13). Hayes sees radical homemaking, femivorism, or sustainable farming (which she uses interchangeably) as the answer to economic and environmental woes as well as a solution to social trends that do not honour family and "the simple life." Hayes's blog, started in 2008, explores her life running a sustainable farm, "Sap Bush Hollow," in upstate New York. In reading Hayes's blog, it becomes clear that radical homemaking is just that—radical: I'm daunted by the day-to-day tasks Hayes and her husband, parents, and young children perform in order to reach the level of sustainability that they aim for. Hayes presents her experience as one of still learning about farming, but she grew up on the farm that she now helps run. Socialized into farming since birth, she already has an advantage to running the farm and does not have to acquire a farm. "My inheritance is Sap Bush Hollow Farm," she writes in her blog. It seems simplistic, then, to assume that anyone can accomplish the level of sustainability that Hayes and her family work towards or that everyone reaching sustainability is the ultimate goal. Someone who was not raised on a farm or will not inherit a farm has many more struggles (small business loans, investment, time to learn) reaching this level of sustainability. Furthermore, Hayes's intimidating job of keeping the farm running does not allow her much time to share her knowledge with others. Since Hayes does not offer specific instructions or suggestions in her blog, it reads more like a diary where she shares bits of her personal struggles with her farming practice.

Hayes's lifestyle, almost by necessity, is individualistic and isolated, existing largely outside of political systems. Because Hayes and her family spend so much of their daily lives running their sustainable farm, they lack time to offer support for those without farming abilities. Take, for example, Hayes's concern over her parents' desire to hire an intern. Her aging parents have previously used interns to help with their farm work, and, in turn, they train the interns. During the previous year, however, they decided not to take an intern because training someone who was leaving after a year actually decreased the farm's productivity. Hayes summarizes the problem in her blog:

> This quest to have a "sustainable farm" is never-ending. We look to others, hoping to find models to replicate recipes for success. But there is nothing. Because farm sustainability is a messy equation that gets worked out between the ecosystem, the individual people who are within it, and the gritty economics.

Although Hayes seems to feel a sense of connection to the ecosystem that dictates her farming practices, she does not express a sense of connection to other people in the world, at least not through her blog. Instead, she sees farming as an individual struggle with that ecosystem, and her writing encourages other people to figure out their connections to their ecosystems themselves. Since Hayes and her family's farm struggles are so time consuming, Hayes tells her family, "We shouldn't be focusing on others' educational goals until we'[ve] met our own." With the obviously large task of fully sustaining her farm, it is doubtful if Hayes will ever meet her own goals so that she could help educate someone else, which adds to the individualistic nature of her work.

At its most basic, Orenstein's definition of femivorism describes Jenna Woginrich, a woman who gradually transformed her nine-to-five working life into something resembling a farming life. In her book *Made from Scratch: Discovering the Pleasures of a Handmade Life* Woginrich recounts her first forays into homesteading. She begins with chickens and gardening, adds beekeeping, cooking, training working dogs, and raising rabbits for their angora fibre. Her book is part autobiographical account of adventures in homesteading and part how-to guide. Since *Made from Scratch* was published, Woginrich has expanded her homesteading practice to a full-fledged farm; she no longer works her nine-to-five job and runs her farm instead. Although she is not a mother, Woginrich participates in setting a standard for "healthy" food that affects mothering. She still meets the main criteria of a femivore: a woman who is concerned about nurturing based on new, harder-to-meet standards for nutrition, which rely as much as possible on homegrown foods. Through a closer look at *Made from Scratch*, I started to get an idea about Woginrich's motives for creating a "handmade life."

In her book, Woginrich gushes about the fulfillment that homesteading provides her, but she also talks about the basic enjoyment of eating. In this sense, she does not regard homesteading as a basic necessity. Instead, she expresses food production in terms of wants. Her wants are clear when she discusses keeping chickens. She writes, "All I could think about was what the summer would be like with these [chickens] strutting around the backyard, laying eggs for me every day" (17). Her excitement about these chickens stems from her use of their eggs and, ultimately, her enjoyment of the eggs. In her beekeeping section, Woginrich writes, "If you can get [bees] through [the first winter], you can expect to harvest some gold for yourself at the end of the following summer" (53). Woginrich refers to the honey as "gold," implying that the only purpose of caring for bees is the end result—the highly desired product that they produce. Woginrich explains her purpose for gardening: "It's not just about pride or independence, or even connecting with nature. It's about wanting hash browns on a Saturday morning and being able to run out to the backyard in your bathrobe to grab some potatoes from the garden" (37). Although Woginrich briefly acknowledges the connection with nature homesteading might foster, her main goal is a satiated appetite and the satisfaction of satiating it herself—herself being the most important part.

OPTING OUT

As an answer to society's environmental, social, and moral woes, femivorism has its appeal, yet the opt-out narrative is troubling. Women who might otherwise be active in changing social policy that allows everyone, not just privileged people, access to healthy food eschew these systems to focus on themselves and their families. Matchar quotes a woman concerned with these systems: "As one mother, a lawyer and women's health advocate, quoted in a *New York Times* story, puts it: 'Professional experience showed me that neither corporations nor the government could be counted on to care for my family'" (106). Femivores share this concern. Yet instead of pushing for better policies and corporate regulations, or even going out into the community themselves to help other people, femivores have decided to opt out and to only take care of their own families and to save them from the harm of the contemporary food industry.

Matchar interviewed several women who have embraced a DIY lifestyle. The women who talk about food in Matchar's interviews have a similar reverence for it as Woginrich. For example, one woman Matchar interviewed decided to quit working so that she could take care of her two sons who had severe behavioural and neurological issues. This woman was eventually convinced that food preservatives greatly affected these conditions. Her stay-at-home caring became about cooking "good" food from scratch and avoiding chemicals, preservatives, and dyes. Matchar sums up this woman's perspective, "What's important to her now is 'just focusing on our home, our food, our personal space'" (109). This woman has decided to improve her children's health by controlling their food, yet she is privileged to be able to do so. Someone like her, who could have agency to spread awareness about food and behavioural issues, chose to focus on her own family. This perspective could be symptomatic of an individualist attitude that haunts U.S. culture. Although I think advocating for more environmental and social health is important, to do so, I argue, mothers, especially femivorist mothers, must think of themselves as part of a global community, so they not only feed their own families the best food but also ensure that everyone has access to the best food for themselves and for the environment. Womanism offers a spiritual strategy for shifting such individualistic attitudes.

WOMANIST MOTHERING

Womanism is a social change perspective that values interconnectedness (between everything), "commonweal," and mothering, among other things. Womanist spirituality, which values interconnections for the sake of universal well-being as defined by Layli Maparyan, is already concerned with the environment. Maparyan's womanist environmental concerns and the environmental concerns of femivores are similar, but womanism focuses on interconnectedness on a wide scale rather than on individual eco-systems as with the writings of Hayes and Woginrich. The work femivores do in their homes could extend to a global interconnectedness with a shift in perspectives. As the femivore attitude is privileged, extending the definition of femivorism to working-class women—by emphasizing doing what you can with what you have instead of setting sustainability standards—could allow the philosophy of femivorism to become even more important to a sustainable world culture. Instead of establishing boundaries for mothers in terms of femivorism, womanism focuses on everyday struggles and everyday problem solving of marginalized women of colour. Maparyan writes:

> Womanism is a social change perspective rooted in Black Women's and other women of color's everyday experiences and everyday methods of problem solving in everyday spaces, extended to the problem of ending all forms of oppression for all people, restoring the balance between people and the environment/nature, and reconciling human life with the spiritual dimension. (xx)

This passage indicates that although women of colour and/or working women do not have the ability to practice an extreme form of femivorism, they may still be concerned about the environment in spiritual terms and everyday actions. Womanism takes this concern a step further and emphasizes feeding the community, not just individuals and families. Maparyan quotes Alice Walker to this end: "[Womanist] would have to be a word that affirmed connectedness to the entire community and the world, rather than separation" (Walker qtd. In Maparyan 19).

Womanism focuses on self-care, something familiar to femivores, but self-care is ultimately related to the idea of "commonweal." As defined by Maparyan, "Commonweal is the state of collective well-being; it is the optimization of well-being for all members of a community" (xxv). This focus on commonweal would lead to community-wide solutions to problems such as environmental degradation and poor nutrition. Reaching commonweal requires the health of every member of the community so that they may contribute to the overall health of the community. Maparyan also emphasizes what she means by health: "From a womanist perspective, all people have a right to live in conditions that are not merely physically, emotionally, mentally, spiritually, socially, and environmentally *adequate*, but rather are positively *superlative*" (44, her emphasis). Since femivores focus on eating the most nutritious and whole food, I would say their goals and views for health are similar to Maparyan's. Womanism, however, is interested in ensuring everyone and everything lives superlatively; it shifts the focus beyond individuals limiting their personal impact on the environment and feeding themselves and their family healthy food. This shift in thinking about communities also redefines mothering.

Womanism emphasizes nurturing as a method of social change, which is a basic method for femivores. Maparyan defines nurturance via motherhood when she writes, "Nurturance is the spirit of caretaking, a motherly stewardship concerned with the optimal development of some entity for which one has assumed responsibility" (46). Femivorism critics have implied that, according to a femivore mentality, women are solely responsible for nurturing, including nurturing the environment. Maparyan, however, claims that everything is connected, so everyone is responsible for their role in the global community, which includes the environment (47). Maparyan changes this focus by shifting the definition of mothering. She writes:

> [M]ost if not all of us have the ability to take turns mothering each other along the paths of individual and collective liberation and evolution. The bottom line is this: the very things that an actual biological mother does with her child and children to facilitate well-being and optimal development can be done by people of any sex, gender, or sexual orientation with people biologically related to them or not (or even nonhuman beings). (62-63)

By shifting this definition, Maparyan highlights that it is within everyone's ability and is everyone's responsibility to nurture the people and things around them.

If femivores apply womanist thinking and consider themselves a part of a larger earth community, then they should be concerned not just about feeding themselves and mastering their relationship with their ecosystem to that end. Instead, they should consider other people, near and far, as part of an earth ecosystem. How does keeping chickens affect other people as well as the environment? How can femivores balance potentially negative effects on other members of the community with positive effects on the environment? How can all mothers ensure that everyone receives healthy food that is also good for the environment? Perhaps womanism can add richness to food movements such as femivorism so that their concern becomes more than just opting out and feeding their own families the best food possible. Womanism extends mothering beyond biology or other traditional definitions of family and children by emphasizing interconnections that could help feed and nurture the earth and its many interconnected communities.

NOTE

[1]I understand "womanism" as a social and spiritual movement rooted in Black women's everyday lived experiences but extended to everyone through the work of Layli Maparyan.

WORKS CITED

Hayes, Shannon. "Grassfed Cooking." *The Radical Homemaker*. N.p., n.d. Web. 20 March 2014.

Hayes, Shannon. *Radical Homemakers: Reclaiming Domesticity from a Consumer Culture*. Richmondville: Left to Write, 2010. Print.

Holmes, Anna. "I'm a 'Femivore' And I'm Having a Dilemma." *Jezebel*. N.p, 15 March 2010. Web. 20 March 2014.

Maparyan, Layli. *The Womanist Idea*. New York: Routledge, 2012. Print.

Phillips, Layli, ed. *The Womanist Reader*. New York: Routledge, 2006. Print.

Matchar, Emily. *Homeward Bound: Why Women Are Embracing the New Domesticity*. New York: Simon & Schuster, 2013. Print.

Orenstein, Peggy. "The Femivore's Dilemma." *New York Times*, 13 March 2010. Web. 20 March 2014.

Shoot, Brittany. "The Biotic Woman: What the Hell Is a Femivore?" *Bitch Media*. N.p., 19 March 2010. Web. 20 March 2014.

Woginrich, Jenna. *Made from Scratch: Discovering the Pleasures of a Handmade Life*. North Adams: Storey Pub., 2009. Print.

22.

Becoming Mother, Becoming Matter

The Agential and Affective Capacity of Food in Performances of the Good Mother

EMILIE DIONNE

IT IS COMMON TO SEE IN THE NEWS and popular media scientific, medical, and expert-approved information that advises pregnant persons and mothers on how to eat and feed well their fetus or infant. Concerns and social pressure to emulate the ideal of the "reproductive citizen/good mother" (Lupton, "Configuring Maternal, Preborn, and Infant Embodiment"; Lupton, "'Precious Cargo'"; Lupton, "Foucault and the Medicalisation Critique"; Weir) also rise when scientific findings reveal the detrimental effects that some edible substances can have on bodies. Examples include raw and/or unpasteurized food, such as fish, milk and cheese, and honey, as well as allergic-reaction-inducing food, such as nuts and seeds, gluten and dairy products, and alcohol products.

Reproducing citizens requires first fashioning an optimal ecological-bodily site. A person's desire to fashion such a good body as environment must begin well before conception. The adoption of healthy food habits is needed for this process. In light of this, pregnancy and motherhood are also ethical projects; they require of the person a constant attention to and care for her body as environment and a desire to increase her knowledge about health, food and eating and feeding practices. Such knowledge putatively already exists and is deemed readily and easily accessible. One has but only to reach out for the well-established, accredited network of experts (Lupton, "Configuring Maternal, Preborn, and Infant Embodiment"; Holdsworth and Robinbson; Hays; Mansfield "Environmental Health as Biosecurity").

The ideal of the mother is vital for the reproduction of neoliberal values. For pregnant persons and mothers, this means that they are strongly invited to adhere to a "reproductive" mode of citizenship. Western societies also put great value on self-sovereignty, meaning that the burden of breeding citizens falls primarily (if not solely) on the shoulders of the mother or mother-to-be. Yet combining the ethos of the "responsible self" and the "reproductive citizen/good mother" do not simply complicate the lives of pregnant persons and mothers; these two ethea prove mutually exclusive in practice. By effect, the pregnant person and the mother must emulate unambiguously a fundamentally ambiguous figure.

The social pressure to emulate the ideals of the "good mother" and of the "reproductive citizen" coupled with the fear of inadequacy in meeting social and moral expectations can exacerbate the anxieties linked to experiences of pregnancy and mothering (Beck 133; Lupton, "Configuring Maternal, Preborn and Infant Embodiment" 9). These experiences are often shaped by negative feelings (Coxhead and Rhodes; Holdsworth and Robinson; Keenan and Stapleton; Mansfield "Gendered Biopolitics of Public Health"; McNaughton). In addition, the value placed on self-sovereignty often translates into a withdrawal from public space when faced with feelings of inadequacy in emulating both ethea. Hence, while common to most pregnant persons and mothers, these anxieties are largely lived privately—and secretly.

This chapter addresses this concern by providing a more positive, sustainable, and innovative avenue to value and experience pregnancy and motherhood—to make it *matter* otherwise[1] in attempts to combine two contradictory figures, the ambiguous person that emerges can be deployed in ways that expose the illusiveness of the model of the "responsible self." This ambiguity becomes more visible when considering the relationship that the pregnant person and/or mother has to edible matter. These experiences can shape an ethico-onto-epistemological experiment whereby the pregnant person and mother can experiment with edible matter—and edible matter, experiment with her. Her position is unique for it gives us new insight into matter's dynamism, resiliency, and agency. Matter as agential can enable personhood to matter differently, notably during transient states, such as pregnancy and motherhood; it thus allows pregnant persons and mothers to envision and live their transient states more positively, ethically, and innovatively.

PREGNANCY AND MOTHERHOOD: TRANSIENT STATES OF BODILY AMBIGUITY

Bodily ambiguity fosters social anxiety. Pregnancy and mothering are transient states that configure new bodies, and bodily processes, as if the person were to become a different person to others as well as to herself. These transient states are the source of public concern when a pregnant person publicly displays bodily needs, such as food cravings, mood swings, leakage of fluids, or behaviours resulting from hormonal imbalances.

Eating practices are constitutive parts of one's identity, and, indeed, tastes are one of the first venue through which one emerges as a unique person. Changes in taste are often associated with a change of personality. Such incorporeal changes can arise because of brain damage of which there are manifold causes, be it the result of an illness (e.g., Alzheimer) or an injury suffered during a car accident (Malabou). Relatives and friends often get a sense that the person who displays changes in their tastes and food practices is someone that they do not know. A similar situation arises during the transient states of pregnancy and post-pregnancy (i.e., breastfeeding). A pregnant person may experience food cravings, loss of appetite, and a desire for foods that she previously disliked or for a normative combination of foods (Harper and Rail "Gaining the Right Amount for My Baby"; Harper and Rail "Contesting"; Jette and Rail "Ills From the Womb"; Jette and Rail "Resisting, Reproducing, Resigned?"; Shildrick). In some cases, however, experimentation with food can provoke uneasy feelings, whereby one gets a sense that she has become estranged from her own self.

Such social anxieties arise out of the prevalence given to the figure of the "responsible self." This figure is informed by a mind-body dualism in which matter (i.e., the body) is associated with the abject. Matter is conceived of as ambiguous and leaking when undisciplined but also as raw and malleable (Foucault, *La naissance de la Clinique* 1, 90; Kristeva 15). The body must be disciplined for civilizing purposes and, as such, requires a "self" to instantiate control. The "responsible self" is a "dispositive" of biopower, that is: a discursive narrative deployed to discipline bodies and create the person as self-sovereign and a contributing member of society (Butler; Foucault *Surveiller et Punir;* Foucault *Histoire de la sexualité*).

The self needs a "healthy" body to emerge—the same goes for the fetus (or infant), imagined as a potential self (Barad; Kristeva). Creating a self requires ongoing care, and food intake is an important part of this process (Foucault *Histoire de la sexualité;* Foucault *La naissance de la Clinique*). Although "health" is commonly depicted as a value that finds no opponent, the ideal for what constitutes the healthy body is loaded with many unspoken moral considerations and ethical expectations (Kirkland and Metzl). The dispositif of the "responsible self" requires abiding by a conception of health grounded in the mind-body dualism, which depicts matter as raw and malleable. The body as matter can (and must) be subjected to the control of the mind. This dualism foregrounds the illusive figure of the "responsible self," for a "healthy" state is viewed as achievable as a result of individual choice.

A person must develop a "responsible self" to become a contributing member of society. But to achieve this figure, a person must first display authority over her body, will-power (i.e., a capacity to discipline its needs, cravings, and instincts). Yet the pregnant person, the mother, is deemed temporarily less apt to do so because of the bodily ambiguity that her transient state heightens. She is, thus, strongly advised to attend to such concern privately, to withdraw from public spaces (Bridges; Clarke et al.; Keenan and Stapleton; Lupton, "Configuring Maternal, Preborn and Infant Embodiment" 6; Lupton, "'Precious Cargo'" 338; Lupton, 'The Best Thing for the Baby'" 642; Mansfield "Environmental Health as Biosecurity").

Anxieties toward the body as abject exacerbate the ambiguous position in which pregnant persons and mothers find themselves because their aptitude to generate an optimal ecological site is counteracted by the iterative performative force of the dispositif of the "responsible self" (Butler). Withdrawal from public space often means that one will not have access to the resources that are however essential to live through such transience, to cultivate positively a physically and emotionally healthy person. Hence, although bodily ambiguity is inevitable (and even required) during transience, pregnant persons and mothers often dread ambiguity because of the pervasiveness of the ethos of the "responsible self."

The neoliberal ideal of the mother thus reveals a troubling conundrum. She is expected to work with consistent care, notably in acquiring the resources and knowledge needed to create an optimal ecological site for the fetus. Yet the dispositif of the "responsible self" hinders her aptitude to experience positively her transient state; it disables the feasibility of creating successfully a flourishing site. The range of possible expressions of pregnancy and motherhood is also significantly reduced, in particular ones that could lead to more positive, livable, sustainable, creative, and inspirational experiences. Therefore, adherence to the regime of the "reproductive citizen/good mother" signifies that the pregnant person and the mother steps onto a trajectory largely delineated by feelings of inadequacy and anxiety. How can this process be reversed?

TAKING CONTROL OR SHARING CONTROL: AGENTIAL MATTER AND THE IDEAL OF THE GOOD MOTHER

Recent studies have linked the development and/or exacerbation of particular human moods and affective states to certain lipids (Bennett). These studies show that the material effects of dietary fats are not only quantitative but also qualitative: food affects personhood and, thus, can disrupt the project of responsible selfhood. But the availability of knowledge on the affective capacity of food on human moods and affective states also signifies that a person can use food to (re)instate control and balance. Indeed, diets and consumption practices of certain food have been documented and have shown that food is regularly used as a form of self-medication, to treat atypical depressions, such as seasonal affective disorder or premenstrual disorder (Fernstrom and Wurtman; Moller; Wilson, "Organic Empathy" 394). In light of these studies, pregnant people and mothers may attempt to use food to control bodily processes and moods. But this attempt remains tainted by the illusive model of the "responsible self," a figure that putatively can tame matter, be it bodily processes or edible matter. This model is illusive, however, because the idea of self-sovereign autonomy on which the "responsible self" is grounded conceals how social conditions can and will privilege or hinder one's ability to achieve self-governance (Butler; Foucault *La naissance de la clinique*). By extension, food is regarded as inert rather than affective and agential.

Facing transient states of bodily ambiguity accentuates the desire of control of the "responsible self" because these states make the abject body all too perceptible. Social anxieties often arise when witnessing the relationship that pregnant persons and mothers have with food; they often display a more affective rather than authoritative relation to it, thereby exposing the bodily ambiguity that characterizes all bodies (Butler; Grosz; Kristeva; Shildrick). Pregnant persons and mothers cause concern because "their" body does not comply with the illusion of unity of the deemed "normal" self; in addition to being permeable, open, and unstable, her body is not one (i.e., it is at once not one and more than one) because pregnant persons and mothers play a role in the making of a potential citizen.

Yet her transient state can also matter for its epistemological potential. Such a state can reveal that there is no fixed matter, be it bodies or edible matter, but only mattering processes—bodies composed of matter that is in a process of ongoing materialization.[2] Food intake during transient states of bodily ambiguity allows us to attest to the permeability of "the" body, an ongoing process of mattering, always in the making (Barad; Butler; Grosz; Ristovsky-Slijepcevic et al.; Wilson, "Organic Empathy"). Much like the embryo, the pregnant body never ceases to change, meaning that the pregnant person cannot (nor should she) succeed in maintaining a somewhat relative identity, stability, and coherence with her (prior) self and body because her body (and person) "is nothing other than its continuous modification in time" (Lefebvre 94).

Matter affects what and how a body matters. Yet what remains largely unknown (or unacknowledged) is that matter does not sit still. It has agential capacity (Barad; Bennett: Wilson, "Gut Feminism"). Mainstream discourses about food intake, and pregnancy and motherhood have largely focused on using food to discipline bodily processes (Blum; Bridges; Keenan and Stapleton; Jette and

Rail "Ills from the Womb"; Jette and Rail "Resisting, Reproducing, Resigned?"; Lane; Longhurst, *Bodies*; Longhurst, *Maternities;* Longhurst, "Pregnant Bodies, Public Scrutiny"; Lupton, "'Developing the "Whole Me"'; Lupton, "The Reproductive Citizen"; Mankens *et al*;; McNaughton; Pollitt; Warin *et al.*). Absent from these studies is an attention to how food can be resilient of its own volition. To explore this counter-narrative, recent developments in the fields of feminist science studies and the "new wave" of feminist materialism (Barad; Bennett: Grosz; Wilson, "Organic Empathy"; Wilson, "Gut Feminism") have brought about an ontological shift that, notably, has many ramifications for the viability of the model of the "responsible self."

Examining what matter is up to, feminist science studies reveal that matter is at its the core dynamic and indeterminate, and that it tends toward indeterminacy; "it" is ontologically resilient to processes of determination (e.g., knowledge practices) (Barad). Matter is uncanny, endowed with its own unique desires and tendencies, and these are also always in the process of mattering otherwise. Consequently, although one might try to use the affective capacity of food to meet one's ends, feminist science studies reveal that edible matter may simply not comply. In fact, matter even partakes in processes of materialization and of significance (Barad; Bennett; Grosz; Wilson, "Gut Feminism").

Most bodies' ambiguity-dynamism is so very slight that it is mistaken for stability (Lefebvre). However, the dynamism inherent in matter becomes perceptible in cases of bodily ambiguity. Hence, pregnancy and motherhood are epistemologically well positioned to reveal this aspect of matter. The peculiar and uncanny experiences with food cravings can serve as a cradle for imaginative practices regarding the agency of edible matter. Eating practices during pregnancy and mothering provide insights about how various modes of embodiment (and persons) matter and can matter. Yet the hegemonic status given to the "responsible self" prevents their experience to matter (e.g., epistemologically).

To evade the social anxiety that this model provokes, I suggest using the idea of matter as agential, a way of celebrating pregnancy and mothering as experimental experiences that expose matter's "truth nature," a matter ontologically ambiguous. To do so, I turn to Jane Bennett's concept of the "thing-power." The thing-power is an imaginative tool, an ethics and a politics, whereby inanimate matter is encountered as endowed with vibrancy. Inanimate food is an "actant inside and alongside intention-forming, morality-(dis) obeying, language-using, reflexivity-wielding, and culture-making human beings, and as an inducer-producer of salient, public effects" (Bennett 39).

Food as vibrant matter signifies that edible matter is capable of affecting and provoking humans (and their bodies) in unexpected, unforeseeable, and uncanny ways. Food can and will partake in the processes of materialization that a body and a person are (Barad; Bennett). With the thing-power, I hope to enable pregnant persons and mothers to embrace their peculiar relation to food as generating a bodily assemblage with unique ethico-onto-epistemological capacity.

Food cravings and novel tastes illustrate that all matter (e.g., bodies and food) emerges as something concrete in relational processes. In other words, there is no fixed "self" prior to such encounters but only an ever-slight movement that steps onto new trajectories of possible materialization, by ways of relating. Eating practices are configurations of metabolic activity; they engage human and non-human components whereby "a series of mutual transformations blur the border between inside and outside" (Bennett 49). This means that bodily processes (e.g., processes of metabolization), eating habits, and edible matter form a bodily assemblage—and this assemblage is the soil from which a person can emerge. Each component, human and non-human, "bear some agentic capacity" (Bennett 49) in ways that exceed the sole addition of each component.

To encounter matter as vibrant signifies becoming curious about matter, to follow it, to become corporeally and incorporeally available to what it, itself, is up to and can do. The thing-power therein exposes the inherent flaws and inadequacies of the neoliberal model of the "responsible individual" and reveals that affect is an essential component to understanding how politics and ethics work (Bennett 174). Affect and agency exceed the human, meaning that the model of the neoliberal responsible self is at odds with everyday experiences of personhood and bodily processes. It is deceitful, and it partakes in performative modes of ignorance in regard to what, how, and to whom a person matters or not.

The vibrancy, dynamism, inherent in matter collapses the distinction between body and mind on which the ethos of the "responsible self" rests. Yet matter is neither infinitely malleable nor compliant (Barad; Wilson, "Gut Feminism"). Enactments leave marks, and these marks become part of who or what a person is and can become. With attention to food, this is important because each body bears the traces of their different encounters with other bodies and matter. Take for example how, in conjunction with the rise in the dietary tastes for Japanese cuisine in the past decades in Western societies, pregnant persons have been repetitively urged to avoid raw fish and unpasteurized food. One dietary model, thus, cannot fit all bodily configurations.

CONCLUSION

Pregnancy and motherhood are unique experiential ethico-onto-epistemological practices. Using the tool of the thing-power, these transient states can provide us with novel and inspirational insights about matter and, by extension, about personhood. Following edible matter brings about new bodily configurations from which different projects of personhood, experiences of pregnancy, and motherhood emerge. The worlds of today are in much need of different ways of being, becoming, belonging, and sharing the world so to allow more people to matter positively, creatively, and in sustainable ways. Each pregnancy is unique—and each should be celebrated for such uniqueness as well. The thing-power enables the enabling of pregnant persons and mothers to value their transient becoming, to make it matter as a unique opportunity to generate knowledge about the variation of bodies and persons and about bodies and persons as variations. And it offers us a powerful tool to begin this celebration.

NOTES

[1]I use italics when using the term "matter" to convey two meanings at once. I here draw from Judith Butler's *(Bodies That Matter)* and

Karen Barad's (*Meeting the Universe Halfway*) works. They use "matter" to refer to a topic of interest and to something material. "Matter" is used as a verb to emphasize the processes whereby a "matter" becomes a topic of concern or interest and whereby a "matter" materializes as a context-specific entanglement *of* meaning and *of* matter.

[2]With attention to bodily becoming, *processes of materialization* pertain to the specific configuration that a mode of embodiment takes in context, both in regard to its physicality and to the ascription of meaning to "this" matter (which include the possible ways of relating to it).

WORKS CITED

Barad, Karen. *Meeting the Universe Halfway.* Durham: Duke University Press, 2007. Print.

Beck, Ulrich. *Risk Society: Towards a New Modernity*, London: Sage, 1992. Print.

Bennett, Jane. *Vibrant Matter: A Political Ecology of Things.* Durham: Duke University Press, 2010. Print.

Butler, Judith. *Bodies That Matter: On the Discursive Limits of Sex*. New York: Routledge, 1993. Print.

Blum, Linda M. "Mother-Blame in the Prozac Nation Raising Kids with Invisible Disabilities." *Gender & Society* 21.2 (2007): 202-26. Print.

Bridges, Khiara M. "Pregnancy, Medicaid, State Regulation, and the Production of Unruly Bodies." *Nw. JL & Soc. Pol'y* 3.1 (2008): 62-106. Print.

Clarke, Adele E., et al. "Biomedicalization: Technoscientific Transformations of Health, Illness, and US Biomedicine." *American Sociological Review* 68.2 (2003): 161-194. Print.

Coxhead, Lauren, and Tim Rhodes. "Accounting for Risk and Responsibility Associated With Smoking Among Mothers of Children With Respiratory Illness." *Sociology of Health & Illness* 28.1 (2006): 98-121. Print.

Foucault, Michel. *Histoire De La Sexualité: Le Souci De Soi.* Paris: Gallimard, 1984. Print.

Foucault, Michel. *Surveiller Et Punir.* Paris: Gallimard, 1993. Print.

Foucault, Michel. *Naissance de la Clinique*. Paris: Gallimard, 1963. Print.

Grosz, Elizabeth. *Volatile Bodies: Toward a Corporeal Feminism*. Indianapolis: Indiana University Press. 1994. Print.

Harper, Emma A., and Geneviève Rail. "'Gaining the Right Amount for My Baby': Young Pregnant Women's Discursive Constructions of Health." *Health Sociology Review* 21.1 (2012): 69-81. Print.

Harper, Emma A., and Geneviève Rail. "Contesting "Silhouettes of a Pregnant Belly": Young Pregnant Women's Discursive Constructions of the Body'." *Aporia* 1.3 (2010): 5-14. Print.

Hays, Sharon. *The Cultural Contradictions of Motherhood*. New Haven: Yale University Press, 1996. Print.

Holdsworth, Clare, and Jude E Robinson. "'I've Never Ever Let Anyone Hold the Kids While They've Got Ciggies': Moral Tales of Maternal Smoking Practices." *Sociology of Health & Illness* 30.7 (2008): 1086-100. Print.

Jette, Shannon, and Geneviève Rail. "Ills From the Womb? A Critical Examination of Clinical Guidelines for Obesity in Pregnancy." *Health* 17.4 (2012): 1-15. Print.

Jette, Shannon, and Geneviève Rail. "Resisting, Reproducing, Resigned? Low-Income Pregnant Women's Discursive Constructions and Experiences of Health and Weight Gain." *Nursing Inquiry* 21.3 (2013): 202-211. Print.

Keenan, Julia, and Helen Stapleton. "Bonny Babies? Motherhood and Nurturing in the Age of Obesity." *Health, Risk & Society* 12.4 (2010): 369-83. Print.

Lefebvre, Alexandre. *The Image of Law: Deleuze, Bergson, Spinoza*. Redwood City: Stanford University Press. 2008. Print.

Lupton, Deborah. "Foucault and the Medicalisation Critique." *Foucault, Health and Medicine*, Eds. A. Petersen and R. Bunton. London: Routledge, 1997. 94-110. Print.

Lupton, Deborah. "Risk and the Ontology of Pregnant Embodiment." *Risk and Sociocultural Theory: New Directions and Perspectives*. Ed. D. Lupton. Cambridge: Cambridge University Press, 1999. 59-85. Print.

Lupton, Deborah. "'Developing the "Whole Me"': Citizenship, Neo-Liberalism and the Contemporary Health and Physical Education Curriculum." *Critical Public Health* 9.4 (1999):

287-300. Print.

Lupton, Deborah. "'The Best Thing for the Baby': Mothers' Concepts and Experiences Related to Promoting Their Infants' Health and Development." *Health, Risk & Society* 13.7-8 (2011): 637-651. Print.

Lupton, Deborah. "Configuring Maternal, Preborn, and Infant Embodiment." *Sydney Health & Society Group Working Paper No.* 2. (2012): n.pag. *Social Science Research Network*. Web. 6 March. 2015

Lupton, Deborah. "'Precious Cargo': Foetal Subjects, Risk and Reproductive Citizenship." *Critical Public Health* 22.3 (2012): 329-340. Print.

Lupton, Deborah. "The Reproductive Citizen: Motherhood and Health Education." *Health Education: Critical Perspectives*. Eds. K. Fitzpatrick and R. Tinning, R. London: Routledge, 2014: 48-60. Print.

Longhurst, Robyn. "Pregnant Bodies, Public Scrutiny: 'Giving' Advice to Pregnant Women." *Embodied Geographies: Spaces, Bodies and Rites of Passage*. Ed. Elizabeth Kenworthy Teather. New York: Routledge, 1999. 78-90. Print.

Longhurst, Robyn. *Bodies: Exploring Fluid Boundaries*. Vol. 11. London: Routledge, 2001. Print.

Longhurst, Robyn. *Maternities: Gender, Bodies and Space*. Vol. 7 London: Routledge, 2008. Print.

Mansfield, Becky. "Environmental Health as Biosecurity: "seafood Choices," Risk, and the Pregnant Woman as Threshold." *Annals of the Association of American Geographers* 102 (2012): 969-76. Print.

Mansfield, Becky. "Gendered Biopolitics of Public Health: Regulation and Discipline in Seafood Consumption Advisories." *Environ. Plann. D* 30.4 (2012): 588-602. Print.

McNaughton, Darlene. "From the Womb to the Tomb: Obesity and Maternal Responsibility." *Critical Public Health* 21.2 (2011): 179-90. Print.

Pollitt, Katha. "'Foetal Rights': A New Assault on Feminism." *Sociology of the Body: A Reader*. Eds. Jacqueline Low and Claudia Malacrida. London: Oxford University Press, 2008. 183-88. Print.

Ristovwki-Slijiepcevic, Svetlana, Gwen E Chapman, Brenda L. Beagan. "Engaging with Healthy Eating Discourse(s): Ways of Knowing about Food and Health in Three Ethnocultural Groups in Canada." *Appetite* 50.1 (2008):167-178. Print.

Shildrick, Margrit. *Leaky Bodies and Boundaries: Feminism, Postmodernism and (Bio)ethics.* New York: Routledge, 1997. Print.

Warin, Megan et al. "Mothers as Smoking Guns: Fetal Overnutrition and the Reproduction of Obesity." *Feminism & Psychology* 22.3 (2012): 360-75. Print.

Wilson, Elizabeth A. "Organic Empathy: Feminism, Psychopharmaceuticals, and the Embodiment of Depression." *Material Feminisms*. Eds. Stacy Alaimo, and Susan Hekman. Indianapolis: Indiana University Press, 2008. 373–99. Print.

Wilson, Elizabeth A. "Gut feminism." *Differences: A Journal of Feminist Cultural Studies* 15.3 (2004): 66–94. Print.

About the Contributors

Davod Ahmadi Gheidari is a PhD student at the Department of Sociology at Laval University, Quebec. He earned his Bachelor of Arts from the University of Tehran and his Master of Arts in sociology from Tehran Tarbiat Moallem University. His work focuses on food, nutrition, and health. His current project is a comparative study of Anglophones and Francophones family meals status, with a focus on "the French Paradox" thesis in a Canadian context.

Megan Aston is an associate professor at the School of Nursing at Dalhousie University and holds an honorary appointment at the IWK Health Centre. Her program of research focuses on maternal and child (in particular, newborns) health, both in the community and in the hospital. She uses feminist post-structuralism informed by discourse analysis to examine how nurses and clients negotiate beliefs, values, and practices that have been socially and institutionally constructed through relations of power.

Bernadine Atugabirwe is a co-coordinator for the Gender and Development Programme; a project under Caritas Mbarara, Mbarara Archdiocese. She received her BA in social sciences-sociology from Makerere University, Kampala, Uganda and earned her MA in development studies from Uganda Martyrs University, Nkozi. Her work focuses mainly on team monitoring and support, especially in participatory approaches employed in project planning, monitoring, and evaluation.

Simone Bohn is associate professor of political science at York University, where she is the co-ordinator of Brazilian studies. One of her current research projects (supported by the Social Sciences and Humanities Research Council of Canada) examines the changes in the strategic partnership between the women's social movement and the state after the so-called left wave in Brazil.

Tanya M. Cassidy is a Canadian sociologist who received her doctorate from the University of Chicago. Recently, she won an EU Horizon 2020 Marie Skłodowska Curie Fellowship housed at the University of Central Lancashire (UCLan) in the United Kingdom. She is also an affiliated researcher in the Department of Anthropology at the Maynooth University in Ireland, where she has also lived and work since the 1990s, and where she held her Cochrane Fellowship following her maternity/career break. Tanya continues to be an adjunct professor with the Department of Sociology, Anthropology, and Criminology at the University of Windsor, Ontario, Canada (where she received her initial training).

Laurel Cohn has been a book editor for twenty-five years. She is currently a PhD candidate at the University of Queensland in the School of Communication and Arts, researching the ways in which we, as a culture, communicate the meaning of food to young children through picture books. As a freelance editor, she helps writers develop their work for publication and works with small publishers.

Neri de Kramer, a mother and classically trained chef, is a doctoral candidate in cultural anthropology at the CUNY Graduate Center and an adjunct instructor of anthropology at the University of Delaware. She holds an MA from the University of Amsterdam and is also a graduate from the French Culinary Institute.

Melanie Dembinsky is currently a post-doctoral researcher at Queen Mary University of London as part of an interdisciplinary team evaluating the effectiveness of a commissioned health DVD to raise breast awareness among BME (Black and Minority Ethnic) women in East London. Prior to this, she held a lectureship in social anthropology at the University of Kent, Canterbury, UK, where she completed her PhD. Her doctoral thesis focuses on Yamatji women's breast cancer experiences in Western Australia.

Katherine J. Denker is an associate professor and basic course director at Ball State University. Her work centres on issues of power and voice in both the instructional and interpersonal context, with a further focus on couples' co-constructions of work-life concerns. Her work has appeared in journals including the *Journal of Family Communication*, *Women & Language*, and the recent book *Gender in a Transitional Era: Changes and Challenges*.

Kahurangi Dey (Nga-ti Pu-kenga, Nga-i Te Rangi) is a mother to three vibrant school children. She hopes to show them that they can do amazing things with their lives. Undertaking a PhD in management education at the University of Waikato (New Zealand), she is concerned with issues of integrative, holistic, and relational aspects of humanity and is a grateful recipient of a University of Waikato Doctoral Scholarship.

Emilie Dionne is a part-time professor at the Institute of Feminist and Gender Studies at the University of Ottawa, Ontario. She recently completed a two-year post-doctoral research project at the Department of Feminist Studies at University of California, Santa Cruz. She earned her PhD in social and political thought at York University and her MA in political science at University of Ottawa. Her work focuses on feminist materialist approaches, ecomaterialism, post-humanist ethics, and ecological thinking. She is currently working on a book manuscript entitled *Material Empathy, Affective Ecologies, Corpo-Realities: An Ethics of Material Care*.

Vivian Halloran is associate professor of English and American studies at Indiana University, Bloomington. She earned her PhD in comparative literature from UCLA. She is the author of *Exhibiting Slavery: The Caribbean Postmodern Novel as Museum* (University of Virginia Press, 2009) and *The Immigrant Table: Food, Ethnicity, and Diaspora* (Ohio State University Press, 2016). She has written multiple articles on food studies, covering everything from competitive eating and "Top Chef" to memory work performed by African American cookbooks.

Heather Hewett is associate professor of English and Women's, Gender, and Sexuality Studies at the State University of New York at New Paltz. Her academic work is published or forthcoming in *WSQ*, *MELUS: Multi-Ethnic Literature of the United States*, and *Atlantis: Critical Studies in Gender, Culture and Social Justice*. She has published personal essays in venues such as *The New York Times* Motherlode blog, *Allergic Living* magazine, and *The Good Mother Myth: Redefining Motherhood to Fit Reality* (Seal Press).

Rachel Lamdin Hunter is a registered nurse who has specialized in child, family, and women's health. She now teaches in the Bachelor of Nursing program at Waikato Institute of Technology in Hamilton, New Zealand, and is undertaking a PhD at University of Waikato, where she studies the well-being of women and children in mother-led households. She is mother to three daughters, whose robust critique of the world (including families) inspires her to think and write (and occasionally run away).

Jennifer L. Johnson is associate professor and chair, Department of Women's Studies, Thorneloe University federated with Laurentian University. She holds a PhD in women's studies from York University, Canada. Her research interests include feminist geography, gender, race, and neoliberalism in the global economy. In her undergraduate courses "Feminism and Food: Sites of Meaning and Re-Production" and "Gender, Food and Health" she approaches the production, serving, and consumption of food through a feminist anti-imperialist perspective.

Amber Kinser is a professor and the chair of communication at East Tennessee State University. Her research intersects communication studies with women and gender studies and motherhood studies. She is editor of the anthology *Mothering in the Third Wave*, co-editor of the upcoming anthology *Performing Motherhood*, and author of *Motherhood and Feminism*. She currently is conducting grant-funded research on communication, motherhood, and family meals.

Sara F. L. Kirk is a professor of health promotion in the School of Health and Human Performance, Faculty of Health Professions at Dalhousie University where she also holds a Canada Research Chair. She is a research associate in the Atlantic Health Promotion Research Centre and cross-appointed with the IWK Health Centre. The focus of her program of research is on how to create supportive environments for chronic disease prevention, with a focus on the physical, social, and economic factors that help or hinder the attainment of optimal health status.

Florence Kyomugisha is Professor in the Gender and Women's Studies Department at California State University—Northridge. Kyomugisha has a PhD in urban studies and a graduate certificate in women's studies. Her research focuses on health issues in women and minority populations as well as families in the United States and the African Diaspora. Kyomugisha collaborated on the GAD Mabrara food project in summer 2012.

Simon Langlois (Doctorat en sociologie, Université de Paris-Sorbonne) is Professor in the Department of Sociology at Laval University. He teaches sociology of consumption. He edited a special issue of *L'Année sociologique* (Paris) on "La sociologie du bien-être" (2015). He is the president of the Academy of Social Sciences of the Royal Society of Canada.

Tracey Leigh Dowdeswell is a practising lawyer and a PhD candidate at Osgoode Hall Law School, where she studies the international laws of war and legal history. She is also a "frugal mother" to three young children, and very much enjoys cooking and gardening. She has recently published an article on the history of mothering for Demeter Press in *Mothering Mennonite*.

Audrey Lundahl is a PhD candidate in women's studies at Texas Woman's University. Her dissertation research explores homesteading as a form of spiritual activism. She teaches women's studies at TWU and English courses at North Central Texas College. She also works as editorial assistant for *Films for the Feminist Classroom,* an online, open-access journal.

Catherine Morley's primary interest is meanings of eating with changed health status and implications for nutrition education. An assistant professor in the School of Nutrition and Dietetics at Acadia University and an adjunct professor at Mount St. Vincent University, Catherine has worked as a clinical dietitian, in public health, and as a consultant.

Caroline Nshemereirwe is field extension staff in the Gender and Development Programme of Caritas Mbarara, Mbarara Archdiocese. She earned her BA degree in development studies from Mbarara University of Science and Technology, Uganda, and her MA degree in human resource management from Uganda Management Institute. Her current work focuses on empowering communities for self-sustenance.

Alissa Overend is an assistant professor in the Department of Sociology at MacEwan University. Her research explores the discursive framings of illness, and with the ways in which social institutions (namely government organizations and the media) normalize, regulate, and construct what society deems a "disease." Her work has appeared in *Women's Health and Urban Life*; *Food, Culture and Society*; and *Social Theory and Health*.

Florence Pasche Guignard completed her PhD in the study of religions at the University of Lausanne (Switzerland). In 2012, she joined the Department for the Study of Religion at the University of Toronto to complete her post-doctoral research project, funded by the Swiss National Science Foundation and entitled "Natural Parenting in the Digital Age. At the Confluence of Mothering, Religion, Environmentalism, and Technology." Her research engages issues at the intersection of religion, ritual, gender, embodiment, and material culture, integrating approaches from motherhood studies and media studies.

S. Meaghan Sim is a PhD candidate (interdisciplinary studies) at Dalhousie University. Her dissertation explores breastfeeding practices within the context of food insecurity and excess maternal weight using feminist post-structural theories. Her research interests are in understanding dietary practices within underrepresented populations and issues concerning maternal and child health.

Simona Stano is a postdoctoral research fellow at the University of Turin and a senior researcher at the International Semiotics Institute. She holds a PhD in sciences of language and communication from the University of Turin and a PhD in communication sciences from the University of Lugano. Her research mainly deals with semiotics of culture, food semiotics, and visual, urban, and communication studies. She has contributed to a number of books and renowned journals, and has presented papers at various national and international conferences.

Luciana Veiga is Associate Professor at the Department of Political Science at Universidade Federal do Estado do Rio de Janeiro—UNIRIO (Brazil). She earned her MA and PhD in political science at Instituto Universitário de Pesquisa do Rio de Janeiro—IUPERJ. Her work focuses on political behaviour and public policy analysis. Her current project is about economic voting research focused on recent democracies.

Gale. E. West (PhD, Iowa State University) is a full professor in the Department of Agricultural Economics and Consumer Sciences at Laval University, Quebec City, Quebec, Canada, where she teaches an undergraduate course on food consumption. Her research has focused on food consumption issues, including genetically modified foods, functional foods and, food consumption in long-term care institutions. More recently, she has been studying farm-level adoption of sustainable food production practices, such as pesticide reduction and enhancement of rural water quality.

Deborah Whitehead is Associate Professor in the Department of Religious Studies and a senior faculty research affiliate with the Center for Media, Religion, and Culture at the University of

Colorado Boulder. She is author of *William James, Pragmatism, and American Culture* (Indiana University Press, 2016) and several articles on religion, gender, media, and popular culture. She is currently working on a second book on U.S. evangelicals and new media, forthcoming with Routledge.

Emilie Zaslow is an associate professor in communication studies at Pace University in New York. Her research focuses on gender and media with a particular emphasis on girls and motherhood. She is the author of *Feminism Inc.: Coming of Age in Girl Power Media Culture* (Palgrave, 2009) as well as several scholarly articles, including "Revalorizing Feminine Ways of Knowing: The Challenge to Biomedical Epistemology in an Online Mothers' Health Community" (*Information, Communication, & Society,* 2012).